# Tricks of the Trade

# A Century-Long Journey Through Every Trade Made In New York Rangers' History

## Volume I

### Conn Smythe - Craig Patrick

### (1926-1986)

By Sean McCaffrey

Edited by Diane Eck

Cover and format designed by Rob Staggenborg

Printed in the United States of America

First Edition.

Paperback ISBN - 9798352389577

Hardcover ISBN - 9798352389614

# Tricks of the Trade

## A Century-Long Journey Through Every Trade Made In New York Rangers' History

### DEDICATION

*This book is dedicated to all of the players who ever wore the familiar diagonal letters of R-A-N-G-E-R-S (and New York) on their chests.*

*This book is also dedicated to all of the Rangers' general managers in franchise history - men who had to make many difficult decisions during their time in the big seat.*

# TABLE OF CONTENTS

# Foreword

Frankly, I can't recall exactly when Sean McCaffrey bounced into my life - but I'm not sorry that he did.

Since the hockey journalism fraternity is smaller than any one of the Cocos Islands, I'm surprised that I didn't meet this indefatigable chronicler of Rangers' history -- small and large -- a lot sooner.

But as Detroit's Mud Bruneteau said after scoring in the sixth overtime in the NHL's longest game - *"Better Late Than Never."*

This McCaffrey guy (who I've nicknamed "Young Maven") is very special; mostly because he never sleeps.

Really, I wonder how he manages to stay alive writing so much -- and so well -- about his beloved Blueshirts. Then again, it's none of my business.

My business happens to be reading and writing and talking and arguing about hockey. And since I've managed to avoid doing real work for more than half a century, I know what I'm talking about as a hockey critic.

Hence, I can say without fear of contradiction -- except, perhaps from an Islanders supporter -- that Sean is best at his craft.

He's more than meticulous about his research and never stops improving his phraseology each time he hits the computer. (Two minutes for wrong hitting!)

So, what you're seeing here is another deep look at the Rangers that would impress even an electron microscope.

Whether he's telling you about Hub Macey or Hib Milks or Bill Moe or Elwyn Morris; or Edgar Laprade and Hy Buller, rest assured it's the product of hard work and a rare passion for the New York Rangers.

I know what I'm talking about because I achieved a status that few -- if any -- can claim.

I was vice president of the Rangers Fan Club in the early 1950s, and I was the only one to write NHL President Clarence Campbell, telling him that he was too kind to Bernie Geoffrion, who nearly took Ron Murphy's head off during an otherwise glorious Rangers-Canadiens fight to the finish!

Enjoy!

Stan Fischler aka "The Maven"

Kibbutz El-Rom, Israel

"The Maven and "Young Maven," prior to a Rangers vs. Islanders game from April 13th, 2013

# Author's Note

Thank you for purchasing "Tricks of the Trade – A Century-Long Journey Through Every Trade Made In New York Rangers' History." And that's not a hollow "thank you" - I truly appreciate your purchase - and your thirst for Rangers' history.

What you have in your hands is the biggest (and I hope the best) history book ever written about the New York Rangers. This title also dives into the histories of every other NHL franchise, both from the past and present.

When my first book, "The New York Rangers Rink of Honor and the Rafters of Madison Square Garden," received overwhelming reviews (and the sales of the book were also equally encouraging - I'm sorry for the humble brag - but it plays into what I'm about to say next), I wanted to write another book - a book that not only met the standards and quality of my first book - but shattered these standards and quality.

What I didn't know when I first started this book in August of 2021 was all of the many roads I'd travel. Some of these travels are discussed on the back cover of this book.

My first book was a product of the COVID-19 pandemic, meaning I had a ton of free time on my hands, mainly spent in my house. Since there was only so much "Tiger King" one could watch, I wanted to do something productive with my time - hence "The New York Rangers Rink of Honor and the Rafters of Madison Square Garden."

I didn't know how my book would sell. I just knew I wanted to praise the many Ranger legends that the franchise, for whatever reason, ignored and continues to ignore to this very day.

While I knew I had a readership from my work on BlueCollarBlueShirts.com, I didn't realize the reach and traction the book would receive. However (following an assist from Alex

3

Shibicky Jr.), my book reached the desk of Stan Fischler - "The Maven" - now living in Kibbutz El-Rom, Israel.

(And if you don't know who Mr. Fischler is - for shame! As we now joke about - I'm trying to catch up to the over one hundred books that he's written!)

Without trying to pat myself on the back too much, writing a book somewhat made me "credible." Yes, I was still nothing more than a blogger/fan, but because I was able to put out a decent product - many doors soon opened for me.

While working on this book, and with Fischler centering the line, I've now had my work featured in "The Hockey News" and on NHL.com. I only bring this up because, going into my first book, I really had no qualifications or standards to adhere to. Now I do.

As Fischler brought up during his foreword - I don't sleep much, and I love talking and writing about the Rangers and their history. However, when I was working on this book during the off-days of the Blueshirts' 2021-22 season, something historic happened. Under a new regime, Chris Drury's Rangers pulled off the greatest 180 in all of franchise history, where his team ultimately fell two wins shy of qualifying for the right to play in the 2022 Stanley Cup Final.

Perhaps Fischler anointing me as a Rangers' historian got to my head a bit!

Once the Rangers were eliminated from postseason contention (a six-game Eastern Conference Final series loss to the Tampa Bay Lightning), I personally felt like some sort of a historical accord was needed. After all, as someone who has now written two lengthy books on Rangers' history - I can tell you this first-hand.

The end result? As I was nearing the finish line of this book, my editor Diane Eck and I put together a four-volume set entitled "One Game at a Time - a Season to Remember." Admittedly, the books are mainly a compilation of my writings from the Rangers' 2021-22 season.

While perhaps fans of today might not want to read nearly 2,000 pages on another Rangers' Cup-less season (especially since most of this content is/was available for free on my website) - I'm hoping that there will be someone out there like a Fischler or myself in 25, 50, 100 years time - and then be able to use that four-volume set for reference when writing their own tale on Blueshirts' history.

In other words, after having my first book published (540 pages), I then released a four-volume set of books that almost clocked in at 2,000 pages.

As "One Game at a Time - a Season to Remember" went to the printers, I was putting the finishing touches on this book - the biggest passion project that I have ever completed - and a title that I hope future Ranger historians will enjoy when I'm long dead and buried!

Similar to the four-volume set I recently released, this title is also a volume set, albeit only three books instead of four!

I would have preferred to put everything in between a front cover and a back cover (in my ode to Francis Ford Coppola), but due to page limits/space specifications (paperback and hardcover versions) - I was forced to split this title into volumes. (In addition, I was also told that no one wants to lug around a 1,600-page book!)

If you're familiar with my writing style (as I'm prone to not getting straight to the point - a flaw that I'm aware of!), this was my long way of saying that I didn't realize this book would be thrice the size of my first book! It also took me three times as long to finish this title as compared to my first book.

However, I do think all the hard work and sleepless nights that went into this title were well worth it. I hope that when you finish this book - you will agree.

One more time - thank you for your support in this title.

Let's Go Rangers!

Sean McCaffrey

September 1st, 2022

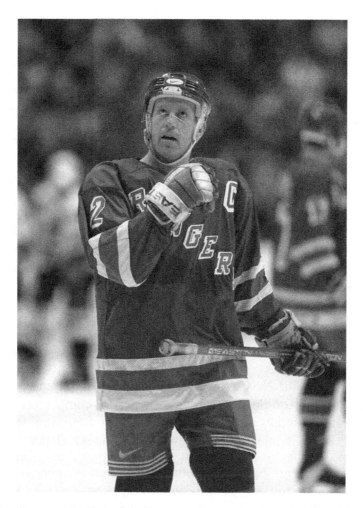

Just wait until you reach the "Sather Era." I have never forgiven Glen Sather for trading Brian Leetch - where akin to the #2 on the back of Leetch's sweater - Sather traded Leetch twice during his tenure as general manager of the New York Rangers.

Photo Credit: Håkan Dahlström of Flickr.com. Thanks to Mr. Dahlström for making this picture available for creative commons purposes!

# Introduction

*"Greetings and salutations, everyone"* is always my opening line whenever writing one of my blogs on my BlueCollarBlueShirts.com website. In that same vein, I would like to greet and thank you for purchasing and reading this book - my second title exclusively dedicated to the New York Rangers and their storied history.

In August of 2021, I published my first book entitled "The New York Rangers Rink of Honor and the Rafters of Madison Square Garden." For a first-time author, the book was a smashing success and received many rave reviews. In fact, many of you may have purchased this book you're reading right now because you enjoyed "The New York Rangers Rink of Honor and the Rafters of Madison Square Garden."

I bring up my maiden voyage as an author in this introduction (after having already done so in my "Author's Note") for two reasons.

One, reading "The New York Rangers Rink of Honor and the Rafters of Madison Square Garden" is a perfect companion piece for this title - "Tricks of the Trade – A Century-Long Journey Through Every Trade Made In New York Rangers' History."

Two, in an effort to not reprint what I've already written, in addition to attempting to lower the page count of this massive title - I will be referencing the "The New York Rangers Rink of Honor and the Rafters of Madison Square Garden" whenever applicable rather than repeating what's already been printed/published.

In my first book, I profiled 102 different men who contributed to the Rangers throughout the franchise's first ninety-five years. Most of these men and their names will also appear in this book, but this book isn't solely about profiling ex-players and/or former general managers. Instead, this book discusses every trade made by the New York Rangers, including what led to each trade and the aftermaths of these transactions.

I opened with the following:

*"On November 26th, 1926, the New York Rangers would make their NHL debut at Madison Square Garden. At the time, this variation of Madison Square Garden was known as 'The House That Tex Built' - a reference to the first owner in New York Rangers' history, George Lewis 'Tex' Rickard."*

After that paragraph, I explained "The New York Rangers Rink of Honor and the Rafters of Madison Square Garden." I also provided a recap of the early days of the New York Rangers and how the franchise came to be. If you read that book, it will help you understand the subject matter discussed in this book.

For example, "The New York Rangers Rink of Honor and the Rafters of Madison Square Garden" discussed all eras of the Rangers' history. In addition, it thoroughly explained the many failures in their numerous quests to win the Stanley Cup.

Whether it was the way draft rights were determined by the league before "The Great Expansion of 1967," World War II and its aftermath, the circus, or another mitigating factor, in any event, the Rangers, historically, found themselves behind the proverbial eight ball.

This book will examine and discuss every trade made in Rangers' history, with the best and worst trades made by the franchise both in depth and at length.

This title will hit many "real" and "sensitive" topics, including substance abuse, arrests, plane crashes, wars, concussions, disease, pandemics, defections, and more. These subjects are brought up because, in some cases - but not all - these events factored into a trade.

To many fans and historians, the worst trade in Rangers' history was made on November 7th, 1975, when the Rangers sent Brad Park, Jean Ratelle, and Joe Zanussi to the Boston Bruins in exchange for Phil Esposito and Carol Vadnais. You may have heard about this trade before!

Despite many people considering this trade to be the worst trade in franchise history, as discussed in "The New York Rangers Rink of Honor and the Rafters of Madison Square Garden," if you take your Rangers fandom and attachment to Park and Ratelle out of the equation, this trade wasn't all that bad, even if this trade is thought of as a loss.

After all, three seasons following this deal, with Phil Esposito now the best player on the team - the Rangers made it to the 1979 Stanley Cup Final. Would the Rangers have reached the Stanley Cup Final (and won it) had this trade never happened? We'll never know.

In my opinion (and to be transparent with you - outside of giving you the facts and details about every trade - all the trade summaries in this book come from my own well-informed and researched opinions), the worst trade in Rangers' history was Phil Esposito-related. Still, it wasn't the Esposito trade itself.

In my opinion, the worst trade in Rangers' history happened on May 26th, 1976, when the Rangers sent the young Rick Middleton to Boston in exchange for an over-the-hill Ken Hodge.

The reasoning for this trade was to reunite Hodge, Esposito's linemate from Boston, back on a line with #77. Unfortunately, this trade failed terribly as Middleton then went on to have a legendary career with the Bruins while the mediocre Hodge wound up playing in only 96 games with the Rangers. In fact, during Hodge's last season with the organization, he spent most of the 1977-78 season with the New Haven Nighthawks, the Rangers' AHL affiliate club of the time.

When you're a franchise approaching the age of one hundred years and have made nearly 700 trades in your existence, when making trades, you're bound to have some swings and misses. No one is perfect and bats 1.000. At the same time, you're bound to hit some balls out of the park too. As they say, a broken clock is right twice a day!

When you take a deep dive into the annals of New York Rangers' history and all the trades the franchise has ever made, to me, hands down, the October 4th, 1991 trade of Bernie Nicholls, Steven Rice, and Louie DeBrusk to the Edmonton Oilers in exchange for Mark Messier and future considerations (Jeff Beukeboom), is the greatest trade the franchise has ever made.

While everyone knows about all the contributions Mark Messier made on behalf of the franchise (including as the face of the 1994 Stanley Cup winning team, which, duh - is Messier's signature moment with the Rangers), the Rangers acquired Jeff Beukeboom, too, a key piece, and part of the Blueshirts' top defensive pairing (with Brian Leetch) during that run.

Of course, analyzing and breaking down trades can be subjective. Yes, some trades have clear-cut winners and losers, but at the same time, some trades can be debated from both sides of the coin.

When it comes to these debates, one pertinent thing to think about is what both teams were looking for at the time.

For example (and in what may be obvious to you), sometimes Stanley Cup-chasing teams will trade off young talent for veterans (where the young talent could have become a household name) in exchange for a chance to win the Stanley Cup.

In these cases, perhaps "mortgaging the future" was the right call, even if the team didn't get the final result desired.

Yes, sometimes the old adage, *"you have to be in it to win it"* applies.

If you need a defining example of this, look no further than to the trades Neil Smith made before the 1994 NHL Trade Deadline, a rare moment in Rangers' history where this philosophy truly panned out for our beloved Blueshirts.

Another factor to keep in the back of your mind when assessing trades is knowing the era in which a trade took place.

Before the Original Six era (1942-1967), the NHL had many teams that frequently opened and closed shop in the early years of the NHL. Sometimes these franchises had to make trades for strictly financial purposes.

Case in point; on December 14th, 1934, the Montreal Maroons traded the best goaltender of the era, Davey Kerr, to the New York Rangers in exchange for straight cash. (Ironically, the Montreal Maroons would win the Stanley Cup in 1935, only to fold three years later.)

In this book, I will chronologically detail every trade ever made by the New York Rangers and the general managers who made them. (And, yes, this task was an overwhelming undertaking that was much more extensive than I had initially envisioned! But, hey, it was worth it!)

As you'll soon see, eras are important when discussing these trades. This is because most of the trades made are a product of the era and/or time they were transacted.

In the Rangers' early years, the franchise often made trades involving players for cash. With no NHL Entry and/or Amateur Draft, there was no such thing as trading draft picks, although, at times, the rights of players (usually minor leaguers) were traded amongst franchises.

It should also be stated that compared to today's 32 NHL franchises, there weren't as many NHL clubs in existence back then. So, minor league hockey was much more prominent than it is today.

In addition, until the inception of the World Hockey Association (1972), there wasn't much NHL interest in European and Russian players. That has most certainly changed over the years, where today, it's commonplace to see European and Russian names at the top of the NHL Draft Class.

What once began as a league full of Canadian players (with a few Americans sprinkled in between), the NHL is now a global league featuring numerous players from a growing list of countries.

The NHL first instituted a player draft system in 1963, which, at the time, was known as the "NHL Amateur Draft." (In 1979, the draft was rebranded as the "NHL Entry Draft.")

The draft, an attempt to somewhat balance the league, would soon provide a new wrinkle into trading - draft picks being used as bargaining chips.

Most of these early draft pick trades were nothing of real significance. After all, swapping a seventh-round pick for an eighth- and ninth-round pick usually won't have much of an effect!

Of course, there are exceptions to every rule, and some of these late draft pick trades did work out well.

Just like anything else, draft pick trades have evolved over the years, including, but not limited to, conditional picks, supplemental picks, and expansion pick protection.

Another thing one must understand is the four dirtiest words in the NHL today, "the hard salary cap."

Following the 2004-05 NHL season lockout (where a greedy battle between millionaires vs. billionaires wiped out both an NHL season and a Stanley Cup tournament), a hard salary cap system was installed for the first time in the NHL that has only gotten worse over the years. (A fact, not an opinion!)

Seven years later, during the partial 2012-13 NHL season lockout (all games in 2012 were canceled, and once coming to terms, the NHL then played an abbreviated 48-game season in 2013 as opposed to the standard 82-game season as was previously scheduled), some of the loopholes in the NHL's hard salary cap system were closed. (Glen Sather was a master of exploiting salary cap loopholes, as we'll get into in this title.)

Unlike previous eras, while the NHL did have a salary cap in place after the players and owners reached an accord in 2005 after ending the 2004-05 season lockout, once the players and owners agreed to a new contract bargaining agreement following the 2012-13 negotiations, a new brand of trading would soon gain prominence; "salary cap dump" trades. No longer could NHL general managers bury bad contracts with their AHL affiliates. (Hello, Wade Redden!)

The NHL (and the way trades were done in the league) changed forever once the players and owners came to terms on a ten-year contract bargaining agreement on January 6th, 2013.

From this point in time, and as it continues today, players' salary-cap hits are just as important as any other stat on the back of a player's trading card.

As we've seen repeatedly since January 6th, 2013, players are no longer traded based solely on ability or where they fit on one's roster. Instead, this evolution (regression?) has led to many players being traded only because of their salary.

Every general manager can only work under the parameters dictated to them in their era, no matter what. So you either roll with the punches and adapt - or look for a new line of work.

Lester Patrick (the first general manager to make a trade on behalf of the Rangers) never had to hear the phrase "salary cap dump" in his time. Conversely, Chris Drury, the current Rangers' general manager, isn't trading players for straight cash money either - a common practice in Patrick's day.

As the Rangers inch closer to the age of one hundred years old, and with the franchise producing nearly 700 trades during that timespan, needless to say, it took a lot of time and research to compile every trade that the Rangers have ever made. I had a lot of help and used many sources when writing this book, especially when it came to getting exact dates for some of these trades.

In order of no importance, the following people, websites, and sources helped me when compiling this book: Stan Fischler, "The New York Times," Wikipedia, HockeyDB.com, Hockey-Reference.com, NHL.com, NHLTradeTracker.com, CapFriendly.com, and the magazine archives of "The Hockey News."

Furthermore (these works will be cited whenever referenced), I used both player and general manager autobiographies and memoirs for assistance.

As we wind down this introduction, in my attempt to give you as much information as possible, it should also be mentioned that when it comes to the early years of Rangers' and NHL history (specifically whenever discussing player-for-cash trades), in many cases, the exact dollar amount exchanged in these trades were never disclosed.

Part of the reason was that NHL general managers never liked to discuss player salaries and cash exchanges, fearing their players would want more money. Jack Adams (Detroit) and Art Ross (Boston) were notorious for this.

Keep in mind that before the institution of the NHL Players' Association union, founded in June 1967, general managers and team owners would trade away players if they ever dared utter the word "union." Just ask Ted Lindsay.

Additionally, before the founding of the NHLPA, previous attempts by the players to unionize were quickly stomped out by NHL owners and their general managers.

While on the topic of the "Original Rangers Era," I should note that the New York sports media weren't hockey savvy. Of the newspapers/sources that were around at the time, only the New York Times (and its archives) continue to exist today.

As you read along, you'll notice that there is more information provided about players and trades as the Rangers grew older. There are several reasons why, such as: you didn't have a very active media to pull quotes from; no game footage available to dissect/comment about; smaller roster sizes; shorter schedules; hockey wasn't a full-time job; and unfortunately, when most of these players passed away, they took their stories to the grave with them.

On the subject of death, I tried to limit such talk unless it was essential to discuss. I didn't want to make this book sound morbid or read like a never-ending obituary.

In addition, as time has passed, there are now more reasons/ways to make trades than ever due to the NHL, as mentioned above, Entry Draft, the hard salary cap, etc. This practice should continue as the league evolves from era to era.

Whether it is the year 1927 or the year 2022, one thing has remained the same throughout NHL history. NHL general managers prefer to be as tight with their purse strings as possible and have always tried to keep player salaries as low as possible.

When it comes specifically to these player-for-cash trades discussed in this book (where the dollar amount is unknown or forgotten due to the passage of time), I have simply listed "cash" as part of the transaction.

Lastly, as we get to the end of this introduction, this book will be broken down into chapters, with each Rangers' general manager getting their own chapter.

I will list every trade ever made by these general managers and give you an overall assessment and history.

As a spoiler, you'll see a lot of this phrase, or an iteration of it, "this trade was a wash."

In other words, more trades have amounted to nothing rather than major splashes or crashes. After all, that should be the case, considering the number of trades the franchise has made over the years.

If you know anything about me, I am a big fan of tradition and believe in the principle of *"if it ain't broke, don't fix it."*

That's why at this time, I will conclude this introduction similar to "The New York Rangers Rink of Honor and the Rafters of Madison Square Garden."

Without further ado, may I present "Tricks of the Trade – A Century-Long Journey Through Every Trade Made In New York Rangers' History." I hope you enjoy reading this book as much as I enjoyed writing it.

And, before you flip the page, I'd be remiss if I didn't say this - "LET'S GO RANGERS!"

While Neil Smith's acquisition of Mark Messier is considered the best trade in Rangers' history, Lester Patrick's trade for Dave Kerr was mightily impressive.

Original Photo Credit: Crown Brand Hockey. The picture of this trading card is from my own personal collection.

Conn Smythe (far right) put together the first Rangers team in all of franchise history. Smythe and his team from an unknown date in October of 1926, during a Rangers' training camp session in Toronto, Ontario.

Photo Credit: The Conn Smythe archives. The Ottawa Journal originally took the picture. This photo is reprinted under Common Creative Usage laws.

## CONN SMYTHE

Tenure as Rangers General Manager: March of 1926* - October 27, 1926*

(The exact date of when Smythe put pen to paper is unknown. In his 1981 autobiography, "If You Can't Beat 'Em in the Alley," released shortly after his death in November 1980, Smythe said he was hired in March 1926. However, other sources have reported that Smythe was first hired in April 1926, while some believe that Smythe officially signed on May 16th, 1926. Smythe also said he was fired in mid-October 1926, but other reports have Smythe fired/Patrick taking over on October 27th, 1926.)

The iconic Conn Smythe, who was inducted into the Hockey Hall of Fame in 1958, began his epic NHL career with the Rangers. As you can see, he didn't last long in New York. Instead, he made his hockey legacy in his hometown of Toronto, Ontario.

Prior to his quick firing from the Rangers, Smythe had played and coached at both the collegiate and amateur levels in Toronto. He was 31 years old and had spent the 1925-26 season coaching the University of Toronto when the "expansion" Rangers hired him.

During Smythe's days as the bench boss at the University of Toronto, his team played road games in the Boston, Massachusetts, area. In Boston, he first got the attention of then Bruins' owner, Charles Adams. When the NHL awarded Tex Rickard (the first owner of the Rangers who also owned the Madison Square Garden corporation at the time) a franchise in 1926, Adams suggested that the new club hire Conn Smythe - and that's what Rickard (and Rickard's hand-picked team-president, Col. John S. Hammond) did.

Smythe, like Adams, thought he was the best candidate for the job in New York, where Smythe would be tasked to become not only the team's first general manager but to serve as the club's first head coach.

For historical purposes, Smythe is the first Rangers' general manager on record - but he would never coach a game for the franchise.

During his memoir/autobiography, "If You Can't Beat 'Em in the Alley," Smythe recalled his hiring:

*"I knew every hockey player in the world right then. I'd been going to Toronto St. Patricks games for years and was familiar with players on the seven teams then in the NHL. I also had a pretty good line on the players in the Western Hockey League.*

*"The real edge I had on other NHL managers was that for years, I'd been coaching amateur hockey, watching men on the way up. Some who were playing senior or semi-pro hockey. I knew these players were good enough for the NHL.*

*"There isn't a man today who could do what I did then.*

*"When Hammond's offer to me arrived I jumped at it. It was the chance to move into big-time hockey that I had been waiting for."*

Smythe, who I covered extensively in "The New York Rangers Rink of Honor and the Rafters of Madison Square Garden," put together the "Original Rangers," - a team that his successor, Lester Patrick, would soon have success with.

Smythe, in his autobiography, also recalled his negotiations with the many eventual Hall of Famers he recruited for the Rangers at the time. Once hired, he built a team consisting of Frank Boucher, Bill Cook, Bun Cook, Taffy Abel, Ching Johnson, Reg Mackey, Murray Murdoch, Billy Boyd, Stan Brown, Paul Thompson, and goaltender Lorne Chabot.

Most of these "Original Rangers" had never played hockey at a professional level. In total, Smythe's team ran Rickard with a price tag of $32,000 (roughly the equivalent of $481,000 in 2022). The core players that Smythe signed would then go on to win the Stanley Cup in 1928 - the last Stanley Cup Rickard saw before his passing on January 6th, 1929.

There were several reasons why Smythe was fired before seeing the team he put together take the ice. One reason was that the more charismatic, accomplished, and well-known Lester Patrick had become available. Another reason was that Smythe wasn't too keen on living in New York, as his family and businesses were in Toronto.

While Smythe was definitely the "hockey man" between Hammond and himself - Hammond was the boss. Smythe didn't want Dye because he thought the player was too individualistic and not a team player. Hammond wanted the big name to put on the marquee.

Smythe talked about his firing in his memoir:

*"By mid-October, and after enough other big wheels in the NHL kept on telling Hammond that he should have picked up Dye when he had the chance (instead of letting him be sold to Chicago), I had the Rangers working out in the Ravina Gardens in west Toronto. I was staying at a hotel near the rink when I got a call to meet Colonel Hammond at the railroad station.*

*"When Hammond got off the train and walked down the platform, Lester Patrick was with him. I got the message. Hammond offered me $7,500 to settle my contract and told me that Patrick would take over from there. I thought he owed me $10,000, the way the contract read, but I was so downcast that I took the $7,500.*

*"To say that I was shattered was putting it mildly - but I didn't stay shattered for long."*

Following this firing, a major "what if" question came to light, the first of many throughout Rangers' history, as in *"what if Smythe wasn't fired by John S. Hammond?"*

While we'll never know what Smythe would have done with the Rangers, it's very likely that he, and his hockey-naive boss, would have bumped heads about something else, especially since, at the time, Smythe (who was sometimes described as a "tyrant" in Toronto) wasn't established like Patrick was.

Simply put - Hammond was more comfortable with Patrick at the helm, and in turn, the team president allowed his new general manager, his second, free reign over the club.

What we do know for sure is that the Maple Leafs and their blue-and-white color scheme (Smythe used the blue-and-white colors to match the colors of his paving/gravel business) would have never come into existence or at the very least, not the incarnation we know today.

Smythe endured after his Rangers' dismissal and soon founded the Maple Leafs and their new arena, the Maple Leaf Gardens. The native of Toronto, who served in both World War I and World War II, would ultimately have his name etched on the Stanley Cup on eight separate occasions - all with the Leafs.

The Conn Smythe Trophy, established in 1965, is awarded to the most valuable player of a Stanley Cup tournament.

Since Smythe built his "expansion" team by signing "free agents," he never made a trade in his brief tenure as General Manager of the New York Rangers.

And that Lester Patrick fellow, now as the second general manager and first head coach on record of franchise history? "The Silver Fox" would go on to have a heck of a run himself.

Lester Patrick, twelve years older than Smythe, had already built a solid reputation in the hockey world, mainly due to his work in the league he co-founded with brother Frank, the Pacific Coast Hockey Association. While most know about Patrick's one game played in net in the 1928 Stanley Cup Final, the longest reigning head coach and general manager in franchise history also played in one game during the Rangers' inaugural season, 1926-27, as a defenseman.

Photo Credit: The Patrick Family archives. This picture also appeared in Eric Whitehead's 1980 " The Patricks: Hockey's Royal Family" and has since been included in the Hockey Hall of Fame. This photo is reprinted under Common Creative Usage law.

## LESTER PATRICK

Tenure as Rangers' General Manager: October 27, 1926 – February 21, 1946

As discussed in depth in "The New York Rangers Rink of Honor and the Rafters of Madison Square Garden" (a banner for Lester Patrick should be hanging from the iconic ceiling in the arena the Rangers call home), is the most successful Rangers' general manager in franchise history.

As of this 2022 writing, Patrick is the general manager on record for 75% of the team's Stanley Cup victories, three in all (1928, 1933, and 1940).

As noted during the introduction of this book, I don't want to repeat what I've previously written. For this book, it should be mentioned that while Patrick was the most successful of all Ranger general managers - he was also a product of his time/era.

During Patrick's era, teams had total control of their players. There wasn't that much "free agency" to worry about. If a player wasn't working out, there were plenty of players to select from the multiple minor league affiliates across North America that each NHL club had direct or indirect control over.

While it's not my intent to take away from what Patrick did (far from it), not only did he inherit a team that Smythe had built - he didn't have to worry about 31 other teams either.

When the Rangers won the Stanley Cup in 1928, the NHL was a ten-team league. Five years later, in 1933 (when the Rangers won their second Stanley Cup), the NHL was now down a team, nine franchises in total (the Pittsburgh Pirates folded). Come 1940, when the Rangers won their third and final Stanley Cup, until 1994, the NHL was now a seven-team league after losing both the Montreal Maroons and Ottawa Senators due to financial reasons.

Despite the small number of teams (compared to today), the Rangers, as the new kid on the block and playing in a city where hockey wasn't as popular as the other major sports (including college football), had major disadvantages.

Between draft rights of the era (teams had automatic rights to players who lived within a one-hundred-mile radius of their home city - with most NHL players being Canadian - this didn't help the team from New York City), being forced to play road games in the playoffs (because of the more profitable circus at MSG in the springtime), and the off-ice distractions that NYC provided (Smythe, once establishing the Leafs, said that being fired by the

Rangers was one of the best things to ever happen to him due to all of the "song and drink" in New York - despite American Prohibition in effect at the time) - Patrick had a lot to contend with.

In twenty years as the general manager of the Rangers, most of Patrick's trades were of the player-for-cash variety, including his best one, Dave Kerr for cash.

In these two decades, Patrick made 68 trades on record (there's a chance that lesser trades may have slipped through the cracks due to the passage of time, ones of the minor-league variety) - or as Phil Esposito would say, *"just another Monday!"*

(And, yes, I'm exaggerating about Esposito, but as you'll soon read - he made 43 trades in his three-year tenure as Rangers' General Manager. This is just another example/comparison about how the "Art of the Deal" grew as the NHL evolved - even if Esposito was an extreme case, a one-of-a-kind executive.)

Once stepping down from the Rangers, Patrick was inducted into the Hockey Hall of Fame in 1947.

Arguably, even if Patrick never came to New York, he most likely would have become a Hall of Famer due to his days as a player (he won two Stanley Cups in 1906 and 1907 with the Montreal Wanderers and then won another in 1925 as the head coach of the Victoria Cougars) and because of his role as the co-owner of the successful Pacific Coast Hockey Association.

In the end, Patrick's time with the Rangers cemented his Hall of Fame legacy.

Patrick, one of hockey's pioneers and innovators, was not only successful in New York (due to his charisma, speaking ability, and nurturing of the media), but he eventually became one of the NHL's most iconic and revered figures.

As a result of Smythe's firing, Lester Patrick is the first Rangers' general manager on record to execute a trade.

At this time, let's get into Patrick's first trade and all trades made by Patrick thereafter.

Leo Bourgeault is the first player that the Rangers ever traded for. Bourgeault, who is featured in my first book, then went on to win the Stanley Cup in 1928 - the first championship in Rangers' history.

Photo Credit: Creative Common Use. Original photographer unknown.

**DATE OF TRADE: January 1st, 1927**

**RANGERS ACQUIRE: Leo Bourgeault**

**TORONTO ST. PATRICKS ACQUIRE: Cash**

As noted in the introduction section of this book, the terms of many of Patrick's cash deals weren't made available to the public, including this one.

However, we know that this first trade in Rangers' history was a good one, as Bourgeault, a defenseman by trade, was a valuable asset.

Bourgeault, a native of Sturgeon Falls, Ontario, and as profiled in "The New York Rangers Rink of Honor and the Rafters of Madison Square Garden," spent parts of five seasons with the Rangers and was a member of the 1928 Stanley Cup championship team.

This trade turned out to be an easy win for both the Rangers and Patrick- a strong start if I say so myself!

**DATE OF TRADE: January 17th, 1927**

**RANGERS ACQUIRE: Cash**

**BOSTON BRUINS ACQUIRE: Hal Winkler**

Hal Winkler, from Gretna, Manitoba, who was known as "Baldy" in his day (due to losing his hair at an early age), was the first goaltender in all of Rangers' history ever to step foot on the ice, as he was the goaltender on record in the Rangers' home opener on November 16th, 1926, a 1-0 shut-out victory over the Montreal Maroons.

However, Winkler wouldn't last with the Rangers for long, as goaltender Lorne Chabot became the team's starting goaltender as the season progressed. In an era where backup goaltenders weren't carried, Winkler soon became expendable, leading Patrick to trade Winkler.

Winkler would remain in the Bruins organization for parts of the next three seasons following this trade. The goalie also has a rare distinction of having his name engraved onto the Stanley Cup nearly thirty years after first winning it. (Winker played mainly in the Bruins' minor league system when the Bruins won the Stanley Cup in 1929. During the 1957-58 season, one year following Winker's passing on May 29th, 1956, the NHL rectified a perceived wrong and etched Winker's name on the Stanley Cup trophy.)

For the Rangers, in a primitive NHL that was only a one-goalie league at the time, this trade was understandable since the Rangers already had a starting goaltender in Lorne Chabot.

In other words, this trade didn't backfire at all for the Rangers. This trade also gave Patrick extra capital to chase other players.

**DATE OF TRADE: October 1, 1927 (Approximate date, exact date unknown)**

**RANGERS ACQUIRE: Harry "Yip" Foster**

**TORONTO ST. PATRICKS ACQUIRE: Eric Pettinger**

This trade wasn't of much significance, as Eric Pettinger, a left-winger from Bradford, England, only played 97 NHL games (none with the Rangers), while Harry "Yip" Foster, a defenseman from Guelph, Ontario, only played 81 NHL games (31 with the Rangers in the 1929-30 season).

Both played most of their hockey careers in minor leagues across America and Canada. So when you look at this one-for-one swap, this trade was a wash.

In addition, this trade was the resolution from a previous transaction when the Rangers first claimed the rights to Foster. Pettinger was the "make-good" player going the other way.

**DATE OF TRADE: October 10th, 1927**

**RANGERS ACQUIRE: Archie Briden and Harry Meeking**

## DETROIT COUGARS ACQUIRE: Stan Brown

Stan Brown, a defenseman and one of the Original Rangers, had an interesting story. Prior to joining the Rangers, Brown played club (minor/recreation) hockey for the 'Toronto Dentals." As the team's name would imply, Brown studied dentistry at the University of Toronto, receiving his Doctor of Dental Medicine degree in 1922. What a great side gig for a hockey player! Especially in an era where errant pucks shook up quite a few unprotected teeth.

Brown, as he did with the Rangers, would play in only 24 games with the Cougars, the predecessor to the Red Wings, before finishing up his hockey career by playing for minor league teams in Windsor, Ontario.

Brown, also known as "The Bus," was 37 years old at the time of his retirement. The doctor, a native of North Bay, Nipissing District, Ontario, returned home for good after a brief stint in the coaching ranks in the "alphabet soup" of the hockey world at the time. Once he returned home, he practiced dentistry on a full-time basis.

Neither Archie Briden nor Harry Meeking would ever play for the Rangers.

Briden, a left-winger from Renfrew, Ontario, was one of Patrick's players from the PCHA. Once reaching the NHL level in 1926 with the Bruins, he was already 28 years old. Now back under Patrick's employ, he was assigned to the Philadelphia Arrows. This team was rebranded as the Philadelphia Ramblers in 1935 when the club officially became a Rangers' farm team.

Meeking, a left-winger from Berlin, Ontario, played in Patrick's PCHA. In 1925, while playing under Patrick (then as the team's owner/general manager/head coach), Meeking, at 31 years old, won the Stanley Cup as a member of the Victoria Cougars - the last non-NHL team ever to win the prestigious chalice.

Once back with Patrick, Meeking, just like Briden, was sent to Philadelphia and would never play for the Rangers.

This trade featured three players past their prime and near the end of their careers. In turn, nothing was truly lost, nor gained, for either team.

If anything, this trade was more about Detroit's General Manager Jack Adams rebuilding his team than anything else.

**DATE OF TRADE: October 14th, 1927**

**RANGERS ACQUIRE: Laurie Scott**

**NEW YORK AMERICANS ACQUIRE: Cash**

Laurie Scott, a center from South River, Ontario, played 23 games for the Rangers during their 1927-28 Stanley Cup championship season. However, since Scott was sent to the Springfield Indians of the CAHL (a Rangers' minor-league affiliate team) prior to the midway mark of the campaign, his name was left off the 1928 Stanley Cup trophy.

Prior to his short stay with the Rangers, Scott had familiarity with the Cook brothers, having played with Bill and Bun with the Saskatoon Sheiks (WHL). Scott, before joining the Rangers, also played with New York's first NHL team, the Americans, during the 1926-27 season.

After being demoted to Springfield, Scott would never play in the NHL again. In turn, this trade, like many in this book, was pretty much a wash.

**DATE OF TRADE: April 16th, 1928**

**RANGERS ACQUIRE: Butch Keeling**

**TORONTO MAPLE LEAFS ACQUIRE: Alex Gray**

This is the first "major" and huge-win trade for the Rangers.

While right-winger Alex Gray, born in Glasgow, Scotland, but grew up in Thunder Bay, Ontario, was a serviceable third-line winger for the 1928 Stanley Cup champion Rangers, he wasn't Butch Keeling either. In fact, after the Rangers traded Gray, he'd play in only

31

seven more NHL games for the rest of his career before finishing out his days in minor league hockey.

In some Rangers' trivia, Gray was the first Ranger to win a Stanley Cup while wearing the number two on his back. We'll talk about the famous number twos of franchise history as we progress - in addition to players who played like number two!

Melville Sydney Keeling, known as "Butch" in his playing days, grew up in Owen Sound, Ontario, and had the distinction of playing for both Smythe and Patrick at the start of their respective NHL front office/head coaching careers.

Keeling played for the Rangers for ten seasons, where he also won the Stanley Cup with the club in 1933. A left-winger, Keeling routinely finished as a top-five scorer for the Rangers in his peak years. During the 1936-37 season, Keeling led all Rangers with 22 goals scored, which was also good for third-best in the entire NHL.

Aside from the 1935-36 season, Keeling and the Rangers qualified for the playoffs in each campaign of Keeling's tenure with the Rangers. The winger also became a major contributor in the days of the original Bread Line (Bill Cook, Frank Boucher, and Bun Cook).

If you're trying to determine who won and who lost a trade here, very easily, Patrick and the Rangers won this trade that was ironically made by Patrick, and the first general manager of both the New York Rangers and the Toronto Maple Leafs, Conn Smythe.

**DATE OF TRADE: September 1st, 1928**

**RANGERS ACQUIRE: Cash**

**BOSTON BRUINS ACQUIRE: Frank Waite**

Frank Waite, a center from Fort Qu'Appelle, Saskatchewan, didn't play much for the Rangers.

Known as "The Deacon," Waite, who played mainly in the minors, returned to the Rangers for the 1930-31 season, skating in seventeen games total - a number that matches his NHL games-played total.

32

In other words, Waite never suited up for the Bruins. In the 1933-34 season, Waite was with the Philadelphia Arrows, the unofficial Rangers' farm team, where he finished his hockey career.

In short, this trade didn't amount to much for either team.

**DATE OF TRADE: October 13th, 1928**

**RANGERS ACQUIRE: John Ross Roach**

**TORONTO MAPLE LEAFS ACQUIRE: Lorne Chabot and $10,000**

This was a major trade of this era, as this was the first time the Rangers traded a starting goalie for another starting goalie.

As the Rangers' starting goaltender of the 1927-28 Stanley Cup championship season, Lorne Chabot, from Montreal, Quebec, suffered an eye injury in Game Two of the 1928 Stanley Cup Final, a famous (or infamous) injury at that - led to Rangers' General Manager and Head Coach Lester Patrick donning the pads for the remainder of the game.

Over time, Patrick's limited work as the Rangers' temporary goalie became an exaggerated tale of much epicness - much to the chagrin of no one.

After winning the Stanley Cup, Patrick thought Chabot was injury prone and would never recover from his injury. This thinking would prove to be erroneous, as after Patrick traded Chabot, he went on to play in nine more NHL seasons, winning the Stanley Cup in 1932 (against the Rangers, which rubbed salt into the wound) and the Vezina Trophy in 1935. In addition, while Chabot isn't in the Hall of Fame today, many historians have advocated (and still do to this day) for his induction.

Chabot had a much better career than the two goalies involved in this trade.

From Port Perry, Ontario, John Ross Roach spent four seasons with the Rangers as the team's starting goaltender. However, despite

33

some solid regular season finishes - Roach could never propel the Rangers to the Stanley Cup.

In the 1932 Stanley Cup Final (Roach's final games with the Rangers), he had the unfortunate distinction of being known as the goaltender of what was eventually dubbed as "The Tennis Series" - a slight to Roach for giving up six goals in all three Stanley Cup Final games (eighteen in total) against the Toronto Maple Leafs - the same Maple Leafs that had Lorne Chabot in their net.

Despite Roach playing reasonably well for most of his time in New York, this trade was a loss for the Rangers.

Even worse, the Rangers also gave the Maple Leafs $10,000 - a large amount of money at the time.

**DATE OF TRADE: December 12th, 1928**

**RANGERS ACQUIRE: Russell Oatman**

**MONTREAL MAROONS ACQUIRE: Cash**

Russell Oatman, from Tillsonburg, Ontario, played 27 games for the Rangers during the 1928-1929 season. Less than a year after acquiring him, the Rangers sent Oatman to the Hamilton Tigers of the International Hockey League (IHL) - one of the many minor leagues in operation during this era.

A left-winger, Oatman's career sadly ended on March 13th, 1930, following a car accident.

Oatman, who suffered a severely broken leg in the crash, then spent time coaching minor league teams before getting a job in the "real world," as he would go on to work in the pharmaceutical industry.

All in all, this trade was another wash.

**DATE OF TRADE: January 21th, 1929**

**RANGERS ACQUIRE: $7,500**

**BOSTON BRUINS ACQUIRE: Myles Lane**

34

The name of Myles Lane probably doesn't ring a bell for most Ranger and hockey fans, but he soon became involved in a famous story of NHL lore.

Lane, a rare American player of this era, was born in Melrose, Massachusetts. Then-Rangers President, Colonel John S. Hammond, knew that the Bruins wanted Lane. In turn, Hammond and Patrick offered Lane to the Bruins in exchange for Eddie Shore and $5,000.

As Stan Saplin, the Rangers' public relations director at the time, would later recount: Charles F. Adams, then-president of the Boston Bruins, sent a telegram to the Rangers' brain trust, stating, *"GET A LIFE PRESERVER - YOU ARE MYLES FROM THE SHORE!"*

Instead of receiving Eddie Shore, the Rangers settled for $7,500 in return for Lane. Lane won the Stanley Cup in 1929 with the Bruins, as the left-handed defenseman won a championship for his home team.

Lane's interesting life continued once retiring as a hockey player in 1934.

Lane also played college football at Dartmouth College of the Ivy League and was elected into the College Football Hall of Fame in 1970. At the time of his induction, he was a practicing lawyer of over 35 years as the 1934 graduate of Boston College Law School had also passed the bar that same year.

By 1974, Lane, then at 71 years of age, became a New York State Supreme Court justice/judge. Having been appointed to the position, Lane served the court for five years before hanging up the robe next to his skates - skates that he had first hung some 45 years prior.

To go back to this trade itself, while this trade worked out for the Bruins, at the same time - the Rangers didn't need Lane either.

However, it all worked out for Lane, a man who had more success behind the judicial bench in New York compared to his days sitting on the Rangers' bench!

**DATE OF TRADE: April 15th, 1929**

**RANGERS ACQUIRE: $15,000**

**CHICAGO BLACKHAWKS ACQUIRE: Clarence "Taffy" Abel**

The trade of Clarence "Taffy" Abel was a shocker at the time, as Abel was not only an Original Ranger - but also part of the top pair of Rangers' defense, where he was teamed up with Ivan "Ching" Johnson. (The two had previously played minor league hockey for the Minneapolis Millers together, where Smythe first recruited them.)

Born in Sault Ste. Marie, Michigan, Abel was the first American-born player to play in the NHL and the first American player to win the Stanley Cup with the Rangers (1928).

In the latter years of Abel's life, before his passing on August 1st, 1964, at the age of 64, Abel revealed that he was of Native American heritage, a fact he didn't reveal during his playing days out of fear of how people would react.

Ironically, while known as an Original Ranger, Abel spent the bulk of his NHL career with the Blackhawks, where he added a second Stanley Cup championship under his belt (1935).

For those who don't know, the Blackhawks were named after a Native American chief who – yep, you guessed it – was named Black Hawk. Frederic McLaughlin, the team's founder, served with Black Hawk during their days in the U.S. 86th Infantry Division.

Abel, who was still "able" to play at the time of the trade (har-har-har), was pretty much traded away for cold-hard cash more than anything else.

While the money received helped the Blueshirts' bottom dollar, Abel was missed, and this trade ruined the chemistry and dynamic that the Rangers' defense had in the Johnson/Abel pairing. It would take the Rangers four years following this trade to win another Stanley Cup.

**DATE OF TRADE: October 8th, 1929**

**RANGERS ACQUIRE: Cash**

**PITTSBURGH PIRATES ACQUIRE: Archie Briden**

This was a nothing trade, as Briden, who we previously discussed, was pretty much a journeyman.

Following this trade, Briden played only 29 games for the soon-to-be-defunct Pittsburgh Pirates, as the Pirates folded after the 1929-30 season due to the Great Depression. (The Pirates would play the 1930-31 season in Philadelphia as the Quakers before officially folding once and for all.)

Briden would eventually finish out his playing days in the IHL. He then retired in 1932.

**DATE OF TRADE: February 6th, 1930**

**RANGERS ACQUIRE: Leo Reise Sr.**

**NEW YORK AMERICANS ACQUIRE: Cash**

Leo Reise Sr., whose son Reise Jr. won two Stanley Cups (1950 and 1952 with the Red Wings), only played fourteen games for the Rangers before finishing out his career in the IHL.

Reise, a defenseman from Pembroke, Ontario, was similar to Bill Chadwick, as he didn't have vision in one of his eyes, but, unlike Chadwick, who lost his eyesight after a hockey injury, Reise had an optical nerve that didn't function.

This was another insignificant trade, as Reise, who played for Madison Square Garden's other tenant, the team they didn't own (the Americans) for parts of four seasons, wound up finishing his days in the NHL with the Rangers following this 1929-30 campaign.

If you haven't already noticed, when it comes to these cash trades, the big trades involving big-name players (such as Taffy Abel, for example) had dollar amounts reported. In comparison, the amount of cash trading hands was not reported for smaller trades involving lesser names.

## DATE OF TRADE: February 17th, 1930

## RANGERS ACQUIRE: Bill Regan

## BOSTON BRUINS ACQUIRE: Harry "Yip" Foster and $15,000

In hindsight, this trade was a failure for the Rangers - not because of what Bill Regan and the previously discussed Harry Foster would do (not much) - because the Rangers gave the Bruins $15,000, or in other words, the amount of money received by the club in the Abel deal.

Defenseman Bill Regan, from Creighton Mine, Ontario, played 52 regular season games with the Rangers, where the rearguard picked up three points in these games.

Regan played for the Americans during the 1932-33 season before retiring in 1934.

Player-for-player-wise, this trade wasn't a loss, but giving away $15,000 was most certainly a loss, especially when Patrick could have held on to Taffy Abel for the same price.

## DATE OF TRADE: December 7th, 1930

## RANGERS ACQUIRE: Cash

## OTTAWA SENATORS ACQUIRE: Leo Bourgeault

Leo Bourgeault, featured in my first book, who was part of the first-ever trade in franchise history, served the Rangers admirably in his day.

At the time of his trade, Bourgeault was no longer in his prime, although following this transaction, he'd later play in parts of five seasons with both the Montreal Canadiens and the original Ottawa Senators of the NHL.

The Rangers weren't badly burnt by this trade (as they had the young defenseman ready to go), outside of the fact that Bourgeault was a hard-working player and was highly appreciated by Ranger fans at the time.

**DATE OF TRADE: August 25th, 1931**

**RANGERS ACQUIRE: Norm "Dutch" Gainor**

**BOSTON BRUINS ACQUIRE: Joe Jerwa**

Norm Gainor, a native of Calgary, Alberta, had most of his success in Boston as part of the "Dynamite Line" with Cooney Weiland and Dit Clapper, one of the first lines in NHL history to have a flashy descriptive nickname attached.

Gainor, a two-time Stanley Cup champion (Boston Bruins in 1929 and Montreal Maroons in 1935), the center, 27 years of age at the time of this deal, only played in one season for the Rangers with varying degrees of success.

Joe Jerwa, born in the days of the Russian Empire in modern-day Warsaw, Poland, was a defenseman and only 24 years old at the time of the trade.

Once again, this was another trade that didn't amount to much, as Jerwa bounced in and out of the NHL, playing for the Rangers, Bruins, and Americans, in between stints with various minor league hockey organizations.

**DATE OF TRADE: September 27th, 1931**

**RANGERS ACQUIRE: Art Somers and Vic Desjardins**

**CHICAGO BLACKHAWKS ACQUIRE: Paul Thompson**

Paul Thompson, a left-winger out of Calgary, Alberta, was an Original Ranger who was also part of the 1928 Stanley Cup championship team.

Once traded to Chicago, the younger brother of Hall of Fame goaltender Cecil "Tiny" Thompson, the now ex-Ranger, won two more Stanley Cups as a Blackhawk (1934 and 1938).

During the 1938-39 season, Thompson traded in his hockey gear for a whistle and a clipboard and served the Blackhawks as their head coach until the end of the World War II era (1945). After his days in Chicago, he later coached several teams, most notably the Vancouver Canucks (PCHL), in western Canada.

Art Somers, a center from Winnipeg, Manitoba, contributed to the Rangers during parts of four seasons with the team, winning the Stanley Cup with the Blueshirts in 1933. Somers then retired from the league following the 1934-35 season, where he got into coaching once done as a player.

Victor Desjardins, known as Vic, was the least successful player of this trio, although the center was inducted into the United States Hockey Hall of Fame in 1974.

The Sault Ste. Marie, Michigan native, played only 48 games for the Rangers during the 1931-32 campaign. Following the conclusion of the season, he finished up his career playing for various minor league teams.

While this trade was even for the most part, if you had to raise the hand of someone and declare them the winner of this trade - you'd have to determine the Blackhawks as the victors of this transaction.

Following this trade, Thompson remained in the NHL longer than either player the Rangers received while also obtaining much more success.

**DATE OF TRADE: October 19th, 1931**

**RANGERS ACQUIRE: Cash**

## DETROIT RED WINGS ACQUIRE: Frank Peters

This was a nothing trade, as after playing 44 games with the Rangers during the 1930-1931 season, Frank Peters, a long-time Philadelphia Arrow and a defenseman born in New York City, never played in the NHL again. At least the Rangers got a few bucks for him!

Peters, also known as "Frosty," has the dubious distinction of having played the second-most number of games (44) in NHL history without logging a point. Only Gord Strade played in more games without recording a point (61) than the "ice-cold" man known as "Frosty."

**DATE OF TRADE: October 27th, 1931**

**RANGERS ACQUIRE: Cash**

## CHICAGO BLACKHAWKS ACQUIRE: Gene Carrigan

In what may become repetitive as you read this book, this was another much-ado-about-nothing trade here.

Gene Carrigan, a center from Edmonton, Alberta, never played for the Blackhawks. Instead, his career was mainly played out at the minor-league level.

Aside from his 33 games played with the Rangers during the 1930-31 season, Carrigan also had short stints with the Detroit Red Wings (4 playoff games played) and the St. Louis Eagles (4 regular season games played).

Carrigan retired from hockey following a 1941-42 season spent with the Fort Worth Rangers of the old American Hockey Association. He also served the club as their head coach that same season.

**DATE OF TRADE: July 2nd, 1932**

**RANGERS ACQUIRE: Babe Siebert**

**MONTREAL MAROONS ACQUIRE: Cash**

This one was a home-run trade for the Rangers, as Babe Siebert, born Charles Albert Siebert in Plattsville, Ontario, soon made an impact upon his arrival to the Big Apple and helped the Rangers win the Stanley Cup in 1933.

Siebert, the second "Babe" of New York (Babe Ruth being the first), was a physical left-winger for the Rangers and who today would be known as a "sandpaper" player - mainly due to his penchant for pugilism. Once leaving New York, Siebert extended his career by converting to the defense position.

This switch would work, as Siebert would be named an NHL All-Star on three separate occasions, including in 1937 when he won the Hart Trophy as a member of the storied Montreal Canadiens.

As discussed in the introduction of this title, this was a trade strictly for financial reasons, as the cash-strapped Maroons had to sell their perennial all-star and 1926 Stanley Cup champion to the Rangers.

While Siebert would have his best years elsewhere, he did what the Rangers needed him to do en route to the Blueshirts' 1933 Stanley Cup victory.

Sadly, Siebert, who was posthumously inducted into the Hockey Hall of Fame in 1964, died at the age of 35 on August 25th, 1939, after drowning while swimming with his two daughters. Even worse for the Siebert family was that his wife, Bernice Siebert, became a paraplegic after giving birth to their second daughter.

Siebert was known as a dedicated family man, where fans saw the star player routinely carry his wife to her seat before every home game.

Following Siebert's tragic passing, the NHL held a benefit game to raise money for his wife and two daughters. The NHL cut the family a check for $15,000.

**DATE OF TRADE: August 22nd, 1932**

**RANGERS ACQUIRE: $10,000**

## BOSTON BRUINS ACQUIRE: Orville "Obs" Heximer

This was a good trade for the Rangers and Patrick, as they unloaded Orville Heximer, a left-winger, for a sizable amount of cash.

Prior to this trade, Heximer, mainly a minor leaguer, had played nineteen games for the Rangers during the 1929-30 season. At the time of this trade, he was playing for the Springfield Indians, a Rangers' farm team from the Canadian-American Hockey League (CAHL).

The native of Niagara Falls, Ontario, played only 48 games with the Bruins, so nothing was lost by the Rangers. Heximer would later play eighteen games for the New York Americans in the 1934-35 season.

The best thing about this trade? A smooth cash influx of $10,000!

## DATE OF TRADE: September 1, 1932

## RANGERS ACQUIRE: Frank Peters

## DETROIT RED WINGS ACQUIRE: Sparky Vail

The Rangers brought "Frosty" Peters back into the mix again, but he would never play for the Rangers in this second go-around.

Melville Vail, known as "Sparky," was a left-winger-turned-defenseman from Meaford, Ontario.

The southpaw, who had previously played in fifty NHL games for the Rangers from 1928 through 1930, never played for Detroit - or in the NHL ever again. Following a 1935-36 season spent with the Pittsburgh Shamrocks (IHL), the thirty-year-old retired.

In summary, this trade had no consequence for either side.

## DATE OF TRADE: October 25th, 1932

## RANGERS ACQUIRE: $11,000

## DETROIT RED WINGS ACQUIRE: John Ross Roach

At the time of this trade, "The Glasgow Gobbler," goaltender Andy Aitkenhead (who was also profiled in my first book), was now firmly in control of the Rangers' net.

Roach, who as talked about earlier, had a disastrous outing in the 1932 Stanley Cup Final and became expendable.

While Roach had some success with the Red Wings, he had already peaked at the time of the trade. Following the 1934-35 season, the man dubbed as both "Little Napoleon" (due to his 5'5", 130-pound stature, coupled with his cantankerous personality) and "The Port Perry Woodpecker" (in honor of his hometown), retired.

Since the Rangers possessed a new starting goaltender in a one-goalie league, this trade is a win, giving the Rangers an extra $11,000 to play with. Better than that, with Aitkenhead now in net, the Rangers won the Stanley Cup in 1933.

**DATE OF TRADE: December 11th, 1932**

**RANGERS ACQUIRE: $5,500**

**DETROIT RED WINGS ACQUIRE: Carl Voss**

Carl Voss, a center from Chelsea, Massachusetts, was originally acquired by the Rangers on October 4, 1932, following a deal with the Buffalo Bisons of the IHL. Once in New York City, Voss scored two goals in ten games.

After playing in 46 games across parts of two seasons with the Red Wings, the career journeyman, Voss bounced around the league. He later played for the Ottawa Senators, the St. Louis Eagles, the New York Americans, the Montreal Maroons, and the Chicago Blackhawks.

Once retiring in 1938, Voss totaled 34 goals in 261 NHL games played.

While the Rangers lost a veteran player, the Rangers didn't miss him either. Patrick took the cash and saw his team win the Stanley Cup in 1933.

44

**DATE OF TRADE: December 18th, 1932**

**RANGERS ACQUIRE: Cash**

**MONTREAL MAROONS ACQUIRE: Russell Blinco**

Since the Rangers won the Stanley Cup in 1933, it's hard to deem this trade as a bad trade for the Rangers, despite Russ Blinco, who spent his days in the organization with the Blueshirts' farm teams, winning the Calder Trophy (1934), and the Stanley Cup with the Maroons (1935).

Blinco, a center from Grand-Mere, Quebec, has his own special place in hockey history, as he was the first player to wear eyeglasses while playing on the ice.

Blinco ultimately retired following the 1938-39 season at the age of 33, so Patrick didn't miss out on much with this transaction, although Blinco did go on to tally 59 goals in his 267-game NHL career.

**DATE OF TRADE: December 22nd, 1932**

**RANGERS ACQUIRE: Cash**

**NEW YORK AMERICANS ACQUIRE: Wilfie Starr**

Wilfrid Starr, known as Wilfie, played only 27 games for the Americans; after his run there, he bounced in and out of the Detroit Red Wings organization before finishing his career at the minor-league level.

Before this trade, Starr had spent his entire time with the Rangers organization with their farm team, the Springfield Indians, a left-winger from Winnipeg, Manitoba.

This was another "no big deal" for Patrick, where - yep, yet again - the team won the Stanley Cup in 1933. (The Rangers only have four Stanley Cups to their name - I have to soak it all in!)

**DATE OF TRADE: December 23rd, 1932**

**RANGERS ACQUIRE: Cash**

**OTTAWA SENATORS ACQUIRE: Norm "Dutch" Gainor**

This was another "blah" trade, as the previously discussed Gainor played in only two games for the Senators. Gainor retired in 1936 after a season spent with the Calgary Tigers of the Northwest Hockey League.

At the risk of sounding redundant, with the Rangers winning the Stanley Cup in 1933, Gainor wasn't missed, nor did this trade backfire.

**DATE OF TRADE: December 27th, 1932**

**RANGERS ACQUIRE: Cash**

**NEW YORK AMERICANS ACQUIRE: Bill Regan (Loan)**

Following this trade, Regan, as discussed earlier, played fifteen games for the Americans before calling an end to his NHL career.

This was another harmless trade executed by Patrick and a trade that only boosted the Rangers' coffers.

**DATE OF TRADE: October 10th, 1933**

**RANGERS ACQUIRE: Jean Pusie**

**MONTREAL CANADIENS ACQUIRE: $3,000**

Jean Pusie played in nineteen games for the Rangers during the 1933-34 season, where the defenseman picked up two points in that time.

Pusie, a native of Montreal, Quebec, is best known for the many hockey sweaters he collected. He played for 21 different teams throughout his twelve-year career; a career spent in both minor league hockey and the NHL. In total, he changed teams on 28 separate occasions.

This trade was insignificant, outside of the fact that the Rangers parted with $3,000 to acquire Pusie. Patrick would then part with Pusie thirteen months later.

**DATE OF TRADE: October 23rd, 1933**

**RANGERS ACQUIRE: Cash**

**DETROIT RED WINGS ACQUIRE: Gord Pettinger**

Gord Pettinger, from Regina, Saskatchewan, won the Stanley Cup with the Rangers in 1933. He went on to win the Stanley Cup three more times: twice with the Red Wings (1936 and 1937) and once with Boston (1939). As a result, Pettinger is one of eleven NHLers to win the Stanley Cup with three different franchises.

The south-paw centerman, who started his NHL career with the Rangers at only twenty years old, had a respectable tenure in the NHL, where he picked up 42 goals and 74 assists in 292 games.

While it's tough to call this trade of Pettinger a loss for the Rangers, it's not like Patrick was a winner here, either, especially since the cash figure, thought to be minor, is unknown.

In some food for thought, once traded, Pettinger's three Stanley Cup victories were two more Stanley Cups than the Rangers won during Pettinger's post-Ranger days (1940).

**DATE OF TRADE: December 18th, 1933**

**RANGERS ACQUIRE: Roy Burmister and Vic Ripley**

**BOSTON BRUINS ACQUIRE: Babe Siebert**

Combined, Roy Burmister and Vic Ripley played 38 NHL regular season games with the Rangers, with Ripley playing in all 38 of them.

Conversely, after a decent stint in Boston, the previously discussed Babe Siebert would go on to win the Hart Trophy (MVP of the league) in 1937 with the Montreal Canadiens.

Roy Burmister, a left-winger from Collingwood, Ontario, played 67 NHL games during his career, all with the Americans, all taking place before the commencement of the 1932-33 season.

Vic Ripley, a center from Elgin, Ontario, picked up 100 points in 248 NHL games played, where the bulk of his success took place in Chicago, before his days on Broadway.

This trade is a loss. After all, how can it not be - especially since Siebert, once changing positions, then went on to win a league MVP award.

**DATE OF TRADE: January 3rd, 1934**

**RANGERS ACQUIRE: Duke Dukowski**

**NEW YORK AMERICANS ACQUIRE: Cash**

Born Wladislaw Laudas Jozef Dukowski, a native of Regina, Saskatchewan, later became known as "Duke" - a much easier name to write out for hockey reporters of Dukowski's era. (It's also easier for yours truly to write!)

Duke, like many of this era, bounced in and out of the NHL, where the defenseman played only 29 regular season games with the Rangers before retiring from the NHL at the end of the 1933-34 season. (Duke ultimately finished his hockey career a season later after four games played for the Syracuse Stars of the IHL.)

Prior to retiring, "The Duke" had his best years with the Blackhawks, where he posted career highs in goals (7), assists (10), and points (17) in the 1929-30 campaign.

The Rangers were trying to defend their 1933 Stanley Cup championship with this trade, so parting with a little cash was fine. No winner and no loser here.

**DATE OF TRADE: February 15th, 1934**

**RANGERS ACQUIRE: Albert Leduc (Loan)**

**OTTAWA SENATORS ACQUIRE: Cash**

Albert Leduc, a rugged right-handed defenseman known as "The Battleship," prior to this trade, had previously won two Stanley Cups in 1930 and 1931 with the Montreal Canadiens.

However, by the time Leduc, a defenseman from Valleyfield, Quebec, joined the Rangers, he was at the end of his career. In turn, Leduc played in only seven games with the Rangers before retiring a season later, now back with the Montreal Canadiens and after only four games played.

Simply stated, this was another nothing trade.

**DATE OF TRADE: April 11th, 1934**

**RANGERS ACQUIRE: Alex Levinsky**

**TORONTO MAPLE LEAFS ACQUIRE: Cash**

A right-handed defenseman, Alex Levinsky, a native of Syracuse, New York, won the Stanley Cup in 1932 with the Leafs.

Historically, Levinsky has the distinction of being the first Ranger of Jewish descent to ever play for the club.

Before Levinsky arrived in the Big Apple, the Rangers had previously tried fudging the backgrounds of their players in their first season of existence to make their players more marketable to New Yorkers.

At this time, let's go to the person who wrote the foreword of this book, "The Maven," Stan Fischler (nobody spins a yarn or tells a story better than him), who is now doubling as a guest contributor:

*"When the legendary Marx Brothers comedy team was drawing laughs on Broadway in 1926, the New York Rangers were about to launch their first NHL season. And, strangely enough, there was a connection.*

*"In their musical "Cocoanuts," Chico Marx, while checking Florida real estate, turns to his brother Groucho and says, "Maybe*

*it's the house next door." To which Groucho replies, "There is no house next door." Chico: "That's OK, boss, we'll build one."*

*"When Johnny Bruno walked out of the theater showing "Cocoanuts," the skit gave him an idea. Bruno happened to be press agent for the just-minted Rangers and he was worried about putting people in seats. The Blueshirts' debut was coming exactly one year after the New York Americans had become Gotham's first big-league hockey club. What's more, the Amerks had already become a hit. Bruno needed something to grab attention away from the star-spangled rivals. But how?*

*"Bruno estimated the combined population of Jews and Italians in New York at more than a million. If the Rangers could tap into that potential fan base, their attendance worries would be over and maybe the Americans would be forgotten.*

*"We need a good Jewish player," Bruno told one of his Madison Square Garden cronies, "and an Italian, too. Then we'll pack the joint!"*

*"There were two problems: the Rangers had neither a Jew nor an Italian on their roster, nor was there any expectation that they would. What would they do? Scratching his head, Bruno recalled Chico Marx's deathless squelch: "That's OK, boss, we'll build one." Except that Bruno would create an Italian and Jewish stickhandler for New York's newest sextet out of thin air.*

*"Scanning the lineup, Bruno zeroed in on forward Oliver Reinikka and goaltender Lorne Chabot, both Canadians, neither of whom was Jewish or Italian. His family roots in Finland, Reinikka grew up in Shuswap, B.C., and the very French-Canadian Chabot came from Montreal, a very Catholic city.*

*"No sweat. Bruno had the names. He settled on "Ollie Rocco" for Reinikka. And then he transformed Chabot into "Chabotsky." Poof! Just like that, you're Jewish!*

50

*"This seemed a doable jape to pull on unknowing New York fans that were just learning about the ice game, but what happened when the Blueshirts took to the road, especially Canada, where fans were well aware of Ollie as Reinikka and Lorne as Chabot?*

*"The way they worked it," said Stan Saplin, who handled Rangers' PR from 1946 through 1950, "was that 'Chabotsky' played only at home in Madison Square Garden. Chabot played only on the road. Ditto: 'Ollie Rocco' played only in the Garden, Oliver Reinikka only on the road. Bruno even gave Ollie a new hometown: Yonkers, New York."*

*"Nutty as the scheme was, the staid, conservative Rangers patriarch of the era, Lester Patrick, not only never put the kibosh on it, he actually saw the phony names in print after every game night at MSG. So, by the way, did Saplin a decade later.*

*"When he moved into the Blueshirts publicist's chair, Saplin began researching what was to be the NHL's first team guide, "The Blue Book," at the New York Public Library. It didn't take long for him to do a double-take.*

*"I discovered that the first Rangers team had a goalie named Hal Winkler, another named Lorne Chabot, and another named Lorne Chabotsky," he said. "I was struck by a perplexing anomaly: Chabotsky and Chabot had the same first name."*

*"Nobody on the Canadian or American side of the border seemed to mind and through the 1926-27 season the Rocco-Chabotsky ploy rolled along unpenalized.*

*"And that is the way they were listed in Garden programs and referred to in New York newspapers," Saplin said. "In Canadian rinks, where both were known, they had to remain Chabot and Reinikka. But eventually, Chabotsky and Rocco were farmed out, never to be heard from again."*

Eight years following the Rangers' attempt at deception, they finally had a Jewish-American on their roster. However, Levinsky wasn't marketed with the same fanfare as "Chabotsky" once was.

In total, Levinsky only played 21 games for the Rangers before moving on to Chicago, where he won another Stanley Cup in 1938.

All in all, this was another trade to help the Rangers bolster their defensive core, but it didn't account for much - but hey, at least Fischler provided an entertaining story for this trade recap!

**DATE OF TRADE: October 1st, 1934**

**RANGERS ACQUIRE: Cash**

**DETROIT RED WINGS ACQUIRE: Ossie Asmundson**

Born with the first name of Oscar, but known as Ossie, Asmundson was a member of the 1933 Stanley Cup champion New York Rangers.

Asmundson, from Red Deer, Alberta, had spent the 1932-33 and 1933-34 seasons with the Rangers prior to this trade.

Like many players of the era, Asmundson, after three games played with the Red Wings, would bounce in and out of both the NHL and minor-league levels of hockey, where he then had stints with the St. Louis Eagles, New York Americans, and Montreal Canadiens.

A right-winger by trade, the Rangers and Patrick didn't miss Asmundson and pocketed the cash here.

**DATE OF TRADE: November 1st, 1934**

**RANGERS ACQUIRE: Percy Jackson**

**BOSTON BRUINS ACQUIRE: Jean Pusie**

This was another nothing trade. In fact, after one game played with the Rangers, they immediately traded Jackson back to Boston. Let's get into that trade.

**DATE OF TRADE: November 18th, 1934**

**RANGERS ACQUIRE: CASH**

**BOSTON BRUINS ACQUIRE: Percy Jackson**

Percy Jackson, a goaltender from Canmore, Alberta, returned to Boston in this trade made seventeen days following the Bruins first trading him to the Rangers, where he played in only one more NHL game while as a member of the black and gold.

As it was at the time, with no backup goaltender positions available and only a few finite NHL goaltender jobs, Jackson was forced to play most of his career at minor-league levels.

A victim of his era, Jackson continued his career by playing ten more years for various minor league hockey teams. Jackson ultimately wrapped up his career following the 1943-44 season, where he last played for the Vancouver Maple Leafs of the Northwest International Hockey League (NIHL).

Again, a trade of no significance.

**DATE OF TRADE: November 29th, 1934**

**RANGERS ACQUIRE: Cash**

**ST. LOUIS EAGLES ACQUIRE: Vic Ripley**

Vic Ripley, as previously discussed, was acquired by the Rangers less than a year before this trade, the center played only 31 games for the Eagles before finishing his career at the minor-league level. In turn, this trade had no impact on either franchise

**DATE OF TRADE: December 14th, 1934**

**RANGERS ACQUIRE: Dave Kerr**

**MONTREAL MAROONS ACQUIRE: Cash**

DING! DING! DING!

Like a slot machine paying out at a casino, this was not only the best trade that Lester Patrick ever made but also one of the best in all franchise history. (I consider this trade the second-best deal of the Rangers' 95 seasons of existence.)

With then Rangers' goaltender Andy Aitkenhead having psychological problems at the time, Patrick bought Dave Kerr's contract from the financially cash-strapped and desperate Maroons. As a result, the Rangers found their new franchise goaltender, and Kerr became one of the greatest Rangers goaltenders of all time - if not *the* best.

After all, to this very day, Kerr, who was born in hockey-happy Toronto, Ontario, is the only Rangers' goalie to win both the Vezina and Stanley Cup for the organization. Even better, he did it in the same season! (1939-40.)

I profiled Dave Kerr, extensively at that, in "The New York Rangers Rink of Honor and the Rafters of Madison Square Garden," where I don't have anything new to add outside of the fact that one could argue that this was the best trade made in all of franchise history. (As mentioned, I'd go with the Messier trade of October 1991, but if there's a trade that could challenge that one for best of all time, it's this one.)

As discussed in my previous book, despite Patrick acquiring Kerr in this trade, Patrick also ended Kerr's tenure with the Rangers.

Despite Kerr being the greatest goalie in the NHL at the time, following the 1940-41 season, Patrick didn't want to give Kerr a raise. Kerr, who knew he could make more money at home with his "real-life" job (remember, hockey wasn't a full-time job), called Patrick out on his bluff and soon returned home to Ontario.

Much to the chagrin of the then Rangers head coach and a future general manager himself, Frank Boucher, Kerr was more than happy to run his chain of hotels than play hockey for a perceived paltry sum.

It was in Belleville, Ontario, where Kerr lived out his remaining days and was known as a friend to all who encountered him.

Had Patrick given Kerr a few extra bucks, it's most likely that Kerr would be in the Hall of Fame today, as it's the brevity of Kerr's career that currently has him omitted.

---

**DATE OF TRADE: December 23rd, 1934**

**RANGERS ACQUIRE: Harold Starr**

**MONTREAL MAROONS ACQUIRE: Cash**

From Dave Kerr we go to Harold Starr, who played on the Rangers' blue line in 45 regular season games over parts of two seasons.

In his second season with the club, Starr, a native of Ottawa, Ontario, then played for the Cleveland Falcons of the IHL before retiring in 1936.

In summary, this was another wash of a trade.

**DATE OF TRADE: January 15th, 1935**

**RANGERS ACQUIRE: Cash**

**CHICAGO BLACKHAWKS ACQUIRE: Alex Levinsky**

Levinsky, as mentioned previously, went on to win a Stanley Cup with the Blackhawks in 1938.

Known as "Mine Boy," Levinsky didn't have any roots in the field of mining. Instead, Levinsky earned this nickname because his father, who would attend many of his son's games, would routinely shout out *"that's mine boy!"*

**DATE OF TRADE: October 26th, 1935**

**RANGERS ACQUIRE: Sammy McManus**

**MONTREAL MAROONS ACQUIRE: $10,000**

Sammy McManus, as his surname would suggest, was of Irish descent, as the left-winger was born in Belfast, Ireland.

A member of the Maroons' 1935 Stanley Cup championship team, McManus never played for the Rangers.

Following this trade, he was sent to one of the Rangers' affiliate teams of the time - the Philadelphia Ramblers - a considerable price to pay, especially since it cost Patrick a costly ten grand to acquire him.

After leaving the Rangers, McManus played only one NHL game afterward: one outing with the Boston Bruins.

This trade has to be considered a failure due to the cash the Rangers dished out to acquire him. It also makes you wonder why Patrick traded Taffy Abel only to spend a considerable amount of money for McManus.

**DATE OF TRADE: October 30th, 1935**

**RANGERS ACQUIRE: Eddie Wares**

**MONTREAL MAROONS ACQUIRE: George Brown**

Eddie Wares, a right-winger from Calgary, Alberta, only played two games for the Rangers. Following the pair of games in New York, Wares moved on to Detroit, where he won the Stanley Cup in the World War II-plagued 1942-43 season.

Conversely, George Brown, a center from Winnipeg, Manitoba, who'd later go on to play 79 games with the Montreal Canadiens, never played for the Maroons.

Patrick won this trade - but also failed to retain his prize - a prize that most certainly would have benefitted his club during wartime.

At the time of this deal, Wares was only twenty years old. Following his two goals in two games with the Rangers, Wares, who retired in 1952, finished his NHL career with 60 goals and 102 assists in 321 NHL games played.

Brown, who totaled six goals and 22 assists in 79 NHL games played, was out of the league by 1939. Oops.

**DATE OF TRADE: December 28th, 1935**

**RANGERS ACQUIRE: Cash**

**BOSTON BRUINS ACQUIRE: Ray Getliffe**

Ray Getliffe, a left-winger from Galt, Ontario, never played for the Rangers. However, Getliffe, once traded, then went on to have a strong career where he won the Stanley Cup in 1939 with the Bruins and one more time in 1944, now with the Canadiens.

Born on April 3rd, 1914, before his passing on June 15th, 2008, when he was 94 years old, Getliffe was the oldest member of the NHL alumni.

While this trade didn't exactly blow up in the Rangers' face, this trade wasn't a win either.

Getliffe remained in the NHL for many years after this trade, where he ultimately retired following the 1944-1945 season. Like Wares, the Rangers could have used him during the wartime seasons.

**DATE OF TRADE: January 15th, 1936**

**RANGERS ACQUIRE: Art Coulter**

**CHICAGO BLACKHAWKS ACQUIRE: Earl Seibert**

In a trade featuring two members of "The New York Rangers Rink of Honor," this was a unique win-win trade where both players involved not only won the Stanley Cup with their original team, but both players went on to win the Stanley Cup in their new home.

Furthermore, these two men were inducted into the Hockey Hall of Fame. (Seibert in 1963 and Coulter in 1974.)

In this defenseman-for-defenseman swap, Earl Seibert, from Kitchener, Ontario, had won the Stanley Cup with the Rangers in

1933. A year later, in 1934, Art Coulter, a native of Winnipeg, Manitoba, won the Stanley Cup in Chicago.

There was no loser in this trade, but without question, Coulter's impact on the Rangers was much more significant than Seibert's impact on the Blackhawks.

In fact, Coulter was named as the second captain in Rangers' franchise history following the retirement of original Ranger Bill Cook, and with Cook's blessing. Better than that, Coulter was the team's captain for the 1939-40 Rangers' Stanley Cup championship season.

While Seibert went on to play longer (Seibert's last NHL season was the 1945-46 campaign; Coulter was forced into retirement due to World War II, when he served for the United States Coast Guard), it was Coulter who attained more success among these two defensemen.

However, Coulter's name and legacy got lost in the mix a bit due to Coulter despising what the NHL product had turned into after his retirement, opinions that he had no problems sharing with the hockey public.

Despite many offers to return to Madison Square Garden following his forced retirement, Coulter rebuffed all of them and would disparage anything Rangers- and hockey-related during his numerous post-playing interviews.

Following this trade, while Coulter became famously known as the captain of the 1940 Stanley Cup champions, Seibert was most infamously known as the player who accidentally injured the next player that the Rangers traded for - the iconic Howie Morenz.

**DATE OF TRADE: January 26th, 1936**

**RANGERS ACQUIRE: Howie Morenz**

**CHICAGO BLACKHAWKS ACQUIRE: Glen Brydson**

In a way, Howie Morenz is one of the first "big name" players that the Rangers vigorously sought out, a "big name" player that was already a Hall of Famer by the time the Rangers acquired him; a practice that has continued throughout Rangers' history, even to this day.

By the time Lester Patrick had traded for Morenz, Morenz, the center from Mitchell, Ontario, had already won three Stanley Cups (1924, 1930, and 1931), in addition to winning the Hart Trophy (League MVP) three times too (1928, 1930, and 1932).

During the summer of 1934, the Montreal Canadiens changed ownership. Not helping matters was that then-Canadiens' General Manager Léo Dandurand thought that Morenz had peaked and was at the end of his career. As a result, Dandurand shipped Morenz off to Chicago.

Despite a solid first season in Chicago, Morenz never felt comfortable there. Lester Patrick jumped at the opportunity to add a player of Morenz's caliber and didn't bat an eye when trading the right-winger Glen Brydson in exchange for him.

While Brydson, a native of Swansea, Ontario, was no slouch himself (as he'd eventually go on to play in parts of eight different NHL seasons) - he wasn't Morenz either.

This was a good trade for the Rangers, despite Morenz playing in only nineteen games with the franchise. More on Morenz after we talk about Sammy McManus once more.

**DATE OF TRADE: September 1st, 1936 (Approximate date, exact date unknown)**

**RANGERS ACQUIRE: Cash**

**MONTREAL MAROONS ACQUIRE: Sammy McManus**

This was a salvage trade, as McManus, who Patrick had paid $10,000 for the year prior, received less cash in return. You win some and you lose some, and this was a loss. Back to Morenz!

**DATE OF TRADE: September 1st, 1936**

**RANGERS ACQUIRE: Cash**

**MONTREAL CANADIENS ACQUIRE: Howie Morenz**

In the NHL and any sport in general, general managers always try to maintain positive working relationships with their peers. This trade was a clear-cut example of maintaining good business relationships, as Lester Patrick did the returning Cecil Hart a favor here.

The Canadiens, coming off a bad 1935-36 season with both new ownership and general manager issues alike, asked Cecil Hart, who previously coached the team to several Stanley Cups, to return to the franchise. Not only would Hart coach the team, but he would also be the team's general manager.

Hart wanted to return to hockey and said he'd accept this job offer under one condition: the Canadiens had to bring back Howie Morenz. In turn, Lester Patrick did Hart a solid here and sent Morenz back home.

While it's unfair to play the "what if" game when discussing life-and-death issues, one can play the "what if" game from a hockey perspective as a result of this trade. However, before doing that, you have to know what happened to Morenz once returning to Montreal.

On January 28, 1937, Earl Seibert and Howie Morenz, ironically, both played for the Rangers during the 1935-36 season (just not at the same time, as Seibert was gone by the time Morenz was acquired), took part in a Blackhawks vs. Canadiens game played in Montreal.

During the game, Seibert was chasing Morenz around the ice. Morenz's skate accidentally got stuck in the wooden siding by the boards, and Seibert, coming in at full force and unable to stop, crashed violently into Morenz. This hit, which was purely accidental and part of the risk of playing the game, fractured Morenz's left leg in four places.

Just weeks later, on March 8th, 1937, Morenz tragically passed away from a coronary embolism due to blood clotting in his fractured leg. This incident would haunt Seibert for years, even though it was known to be a freak accident and nothing intentional. (Today, in 2022, Morenz's injury would not have been fatal.)

When trying to keep this "what if" question strictly to hockey while also not trying to downplay what happened to Morenz, what if Patrick didn't do the Canadiens a solid here?

I bring this up because, during the 1936-37 season, the Rangers made it to the fifth and final game of the 1937 Stanley Cup Final. Despite having only one home game at Madison Square Garden because of the circus, the Rangers raced out to a 2-1 series lead. But unfortunately, the Rangers could never close out the Red Wings. (The first game was held at MSG, with the remainder of the series in Detroit.)

In the fourth game of the series, the Wings eked by the Rangers 1-0. In the fifth and deciding game of the series, the Wings blanked the Rangers again, this time by a final score of 3-0. Had Howie Morenz not been traded away, Morenz may have swung this series in the Rangers' favor.

As a general manager, sometimes you make sacrifices for the greater good, where in this case, keeping a mutually beneficial relationship with Montreal was in Patrick's best interest. So that is what this trade was for the Rangers.

**DATE OF TRADE: September 10th, 1936**

**RANGERS ACQUIRE: Cash**

**BOSTON BRUINS ACQUIRE: Fred "Bun" Cook**

Similar to Howie Morenz in Montreal and his departure to Chicago, at the time of this trade, Fred "Bun" Cook, from Kingston, Ontario, was a Rangers' legend at the tail end of his career.

However, where Morenz still had plenty left in the tank prior to his tragic passing, admittedly, Bun Cook was at the end of the line.

In fact, Cook would play only one season in Boston before moving on to the coaching ranks. (Cook, historically and statistically, is one of the most successful coaches in all AHL history and in an era when the AHL was a much more prominent league than it is today.)

Bun Cook, who is heavily profiled in "The New York Rangers Rink of Honor and the Rafters of Madison Square Garden" (I believe that Cook's #6 should be hanging from the ceiling of MSG), was part of the greatest line in Rangers' history: The Bread Line.

Bun Cook, the left-winger of the Bread Line, was an Original Ranger and part of two Stanley Cup champion teams (1928 and 1933). However, a new era of Ranger hockey was emerging. After all, following the trade of Bun Cook, Bill Cook retired following the 1936-37 season, and Frank Boucher would retire a season after that upon the conclusion of the 1937-38 season.

(Rangers' Coach Boucher would come out of retirement for the World War II-ravaged 1943-44 season, where he played in fifteen games that season.)

While it was tough for the Rangers and their fans to say goodbye to Bun Cook, this trade didn't backfire either.

**DATE OF TRADE: October 7th, 1937**

**RANGERS ACQUIRE: Cash**

**NEW YORK AMERICANS ACQUIRE: Charlie Mason**

This deal was a loan trade, where the Rangers had the right to recall Charlie Mason following the 1937-38 season. And that's what they did when Patrick recalled the right-winger from Seaforth, Ontario.

However, once recalled, Patrick assigned Mason to the Philadelphia Ramblers.

This trade wasn't much of anything, as Mason didn't even play for the Americans. As you'll soon see, the Rangers would actually trade Mason again just over a year later.

**DATE OF TRADE: January 17th, 1938**

**RANGERS ACQUIRE: $12,500 and John Sherf (loan)**

**DETROIT RED WINGS ACQUIRE: Eddie Wares**

There are two ways to look at this trade.

As mentioned earlier, Wares went on to have a good career once leaving New York. On the other hand, considering the fact that the Rangers would go on to win the Stanley Cup in 1940, and how World War II not only affected the world, but hockey, too, this trade wasn't that bad only because Patrick received $12,500 in return for Wares (the equivalent of $243,000 today). Not too shabby.

John Sherf, a left-winger from Calumet, Michigan, never played for the Rangers. In fact, Sherf only played nineteen NHL games (all with Detroit) in his career.

Despite his limited time spent in the NHL, John Sherf has his own special place in hockey history. Sherf was part of the Detroit Red Wings team that beat the Rangers in the 1937 Stanley Cup Final. As a result, Sherf became the second U.S.-born citizen to have his name etched onto the Stanley Cup. Taffy Abel (1928) was the first. However, Sherf is the first American-born forward to have won the most prestigious prize in hockey.

This trade padded the Rangers' coffers and didn't provide any value from a talent perspective.

**DATE OF TRADE: October 21st, 1938**

**RANGERS ACQUIRE: Cash**

**DETROIT RED WINGS ACQUIRE: Charlie Mason**

Charlie Mason, known simply as Chuck, was a right-winger traded twice by the Rangers. After being loaned to the Americans the year prior, the Rangers found a suitor for Mason in the Red Wings.

Following the trade, Mason played six games for the Red Wings before finishing up his career in Chicago after wearing the Blackhawks' sweater for thirteen games.

This trade wasn't a loss for Patrick. Instead, this was another transaction that put funds into the Rangers' bank account.

**DATE OF TRADE: November 15th, 1938**

**RANGERS ACQUIRE: $4,000**

**TORONTO MAPLE LEAFS ACQUIRE: Norm Mann**

Similar to the Mason trade, this was another deal that gave the Rangers' a cash influx.

Born Norman Mann, the right-winger's nickname of "Norm" combined with his surname of "Mann," when pronounced, wound up being his first name of "Norman." And there's your fun fact about Mr. Mann!

Mann, who was born in the non-traditional hockey town of Bradford, England, grew up in the traditional hockey town of New Market, Ontario. The English-Canadian never played for the Rangers; instead, he played for the Rangers' farm teams.

Mann, throughout the course of his NHL career, played in 31 NHL games over parts of two separate seasons for the Leafs. Mainly a minor-league player, Mann retired from hockey in 1949.

**DATE OF TRADE: January 16th, 1939**

**RANGERS ACQUIRE: Alex Levinsky and $5,000**

**CHICAGO BLACKHAWKS ACQUIRE: Joe Cooper**

Levinsky, previously with the Rangers, was re-acquired by the franchise in this trade. However, Levinsky wouldn't skate for the Rangers during this go-around, as he was assigned to the Philadelphia Ramblers, one of the Rangers' farm teams.

Joe Cooper, a right-handed defenseman from Winnipeg, Manitoba, had played in three seasons with the Rangers before this trade.

Now in Chicago, Cooper continued his NHL career, remaining with the Blackhawks until November 1946. (Of note: there was a brief time where Cooper was a Bruin on paper, but he never played for the organization.) Ironically, nearly nine years after this trade was made, the Rangers would trade back for Cooper in a trade we'll soon discuss.

This trade was a loss for the Rangers, but not a loss of much significance either, especially when you factor in the $5,000 the Rangers received in return, a $5,000 that meant a lot in a non-salary cap league.

**DATE OF TRADE: May 17th, 1939**

**RANGERS ACQUIRE: Cash**

**DETROIT RED WINGS ACQUIRE: Cecil Dillon**

Just like Fred "Bun" Cook before him, Dillon was also an integral part of Rangers' history and was the team's star in the 1933 Stanley Cup Final, a Stanley Cup victory for the Rangers.

And again, just like Cook, Dillon, a right-winger from Toledo, Ohio, was also prominently featured in "The New York Rangers Rink of Honor and the Rafters of Madison Square Garden."

Had the Conn Smythe Trophy (MVP of the Stanley Cup Playoffs) existed in Dillon's era (the trophy didn't come into existence until 1965), Dillon would've won it, as he was easily the best player of the 1933 Stanley Cup Playoffs.

While Cook was an "Original Ranger," Dillon was part of the second wave of Rangers - if not the face of them.

As the "Original Rangers" got older, Dillon topped the legendary Hall of Fame Bread Line in scoring during the 1935–36, 1936–37, and 1937–38 seasons. However, in an era where not many players played well into their thirties, Patrick thought Dillon had aged himself out, as his star forward was now 31 years old. Unfortunately, Patrick would soon be proven correct.

After one season with the Red Wings, Dillon retired from the NHL - just like Cook did with Boston before him.

Unfortunately for Dillon, he was traded prior to the 1939-40 Rangers' Stanley Cup championship season. Since the Rangers won the 1940 Stanley Cup Final, it's hard to call this trade a loss, although the loss of Dillon was a blow to Ranger fans of this era.

**DATE OF TRADE: May 17th, 1939**

**RANGERS ACQUIRE: Cash**

**CHICAGO BLACKHAWKS ACQUIRE: George Allen**

This trade can be perceived as either a win or a loss, but only if you consider the Rangers winning the Stanley Cup in 1940 as your sole reason for this trade being a win. Otherwise, this trade was a loss.

Allen, a left-winger from Bayfield, New Brunswick, has his place as a special footnote of Rangers' history.

When Lynn Patrick suffered an injury in the 1938-39 season, Allen was called up to the roster. In Allen's first game with the Rangers, he scored two goals and picked up an assist for a grand total of three points; this was a Rangers' record at the time for most points scored in a debut. It wouldn't be until 2003 that someone matched Allen's record when Dominic Moore tied Allen with three points in his first game played.

Despite scoring twelve points in nineteen games, Patrick shipped Allen to Chicago for cash. In Chicago, Allen became an NHL regular, playing in 272 games for the Blackhawks before finishing his career in Montreal.

In addition, Allen played in two separate Stanley Cup Finals in his career (1944 and 1947) but, unfortunately for him, never won the top prize.

---

**DATE OF TRADE: May 17th, 1939**

**RANGERS ACQUIRE: Cash**

**CHICAGO BLACKHAWKS ACQUIRE: Bill Carse**

Bill Carse, from Edmonton, Alberta, was similar to George Allen, as he, too, was a left-winger who received limited action with the Rangers and spent most of his career with the Blackhawks.

While Allen had more success in the NHL than Carse, Carse did play three seasons with the Blackhawks before moving on to the Vancouver Canucks of the Pacific Coast Hockey League.

Since Carse didn't have the success nor the tenure that Allen did, this cash trade helped the Rangers and didn't hurt them.

**DATE OF TRADE: April 26th, 1940**

**RANGERS ACQUIRE: Claude Bourque**

**MONTREAL CANADIENS ACQUIRE: Bert Gardiner and Cash**

This wasn't a great trade for the Rangers in this goalie-for-goalie swap, as Claude Bourque, from Oxford, Nova Scotia, never played for the Rangers. Once acquired, Bourque was sent to the AHL and never played in the NHL again.

Bert Gardiner, from Saskatoon, Saskatchewan, would have more success than Bourque, as after only one regular season game played with the Rangers (Gardiner also played six games for the Blueshirts in the 1939 Stanley Cup Playoffs), he then went on to play in 143 more regular season games with the Montreal Canadiens, Chicago Blackhawks, and Boston Bruins.

This trade is even worse when you look at what happened afterward.

While it's understandable why Lester Patrick would move on from Gardiner, since the NHL was a one-goalie-per-team league at the time, and since the Rangers had one of the best in the world in Dave Kerr, following the 1940-41 season, Patrick got cheap in negotiations with Kerr. In response, Kerr retired, which left the Rangers without a true number one goaltender, something that would haunt the franchise throughout the World War II era and beyond. It wasn't until the arrival of Chuck Rayner that the Rangers' misfortune and misery in net were over.

It's debatable to predict what would've happened had Gardiner remained with the franchise following Kerr's retirement, but what isn't debatable was how bad the Rangers' goaltending was in the immediate seasons following this trade.

In what should be noted, this was Patrick's final trade before one of the darkest times in both world and hockey history - World War II. Patrick's next trade wouldn't take place until thirty-one months later, his first trade of the "Original Six" era. (The Brooklyn Americans folded, a whole story, and perhaps in the form of a book, for another time.)

**DATE OF TRADE: November 4th, 1942**

**RANGERS ACQUIRE: Felix "Gus" Mancuso**

**MONTREAL CANADIENS ACQUIRE: Cash**

Wartime wasn't pretty for the Rangers, and neither was this trade.

Gus Mancuso, a right-winger from Niagara Falls, Ontario, didn't have the talent to break into the deep ranks of the Montreal Canadiens. However, Mancuso didn't amount to much with the

Rangers either as he played in only 21 games for the club during the 1942-43 season, a sixth-place finish for the franchise (and dead last).

If you've read "The New York Rangers Rink of Honor and the Rafters of Madison Square Garden" or are familiar with hockey history (and world history in general), Mancuso played during wartime, an era that absolutely decimated the Rangers. In fact, this season marked the first of four-consecutive sixth and last-place finishes for the franchise.

**DATE OF TRADE: November 27th, 1942**

**RANGERS ACQUIRE: Red Garrett and Hank Goldup**

**TORONTO MAPLE LEAFS ACQUIRE: Babe Pratt**

This was a horrendous and downright awful trade by Lester Patrick, even if you can somewhat understand his reasoning for making this brutal transaction.

Born Walter Peter Pratt in Stony Mountain, Manitoba, Babe Pratt was a unique, dominant player of his era. At 6'3", 215 pounds, the southpaw defenseman was an offensive powerhouse during a period long before the days of Doug Harvey, Bobby Orr, and the score-happy NHL defensemen of today.

Pratt began his NHL career with the Rangers during the 1935-36 season and was an essential piece of the 1940 Stanley Cup championship team. However, as his nickname would suggest (he was anointed this nickname as a tribute to the fun-loving Babe Ruth), Pratt was a big player - both on and off the ice.

If a "Page Six" or a "TMZ" existed in Pratt's era, the Rangers' star would have likely been regularly featured in those pages. Had he played in an era where everyone had a video recorder (cell phone) in their pocket - forget it.

Pratt was known to enjoy the finer things in life and vices, too, including chasing women and boozing. Pratt also enjoyed gambling, where similar to the allegations bestowed upon Evander Kane in 2021, Pratt was busted for gambling on hockey games in 1946. (Pratt admitted to betting on hockey games but also said he never bet on his own team. Following his admission, Pratt was suspended by the league, only to later be reinstated under the condition that he'd never bet on hockey games again.)

Between Kerr retiring, World War II, and everything else, giving up on Pratt due solely to his affinity for the nightlife was a major mistake.

Pratt continued to excel in Toronto, as the eventual Hall of Famer (Class of 1966) won a Hart Trophy in 1944 and the Stanley Cup in 1945.

On the Rangers' side of things, defenseman Dudley Garrett, from Toronto, Ontario, who was known as Red, played only 23 games for the Blueshirts before leaving the team to serve in the Canadian Navy during World War II.

Garrett was only twenty years old at the time of his death.

On November 24th, 1944, Garrett was killed while serving on the HMCS Shawinigan on a convoy mission off the coast of the Channel-Port aux Basques, Newfoundland, in the Battle of the St. Lawrence.

Without trying to sound cruel or to make light of Garrett's ultimate sacrifice to his country, while no one knows what Garrett would have done on the ice had this not happened, at the same time, Babe Pratt excelled and had a Hall of Fame career.

In remembrance of Garrett, the AHL created the Dudley "Red" Garrett Memorial Award in 1948, the equivalent of the NHL's Calder Trophy, as the award honors the best rookie of the season.

Hank Goldup, like Garrett, also had his career cut short by World War II, but fortunately for him - the native of Kingston, Ontario, was able to survive the war.

A left-winger, Goldup played 36 games for the Rangers during the 1942-43 season. After serving in the Canadian Army, Goldup rejoined the Rangers for the 1944-45 season and remained with the team throughout the 1945-46 season.

It should be mentioned that, unlike Goldup and Garrett, Pratt, who was older than Goldup and Garrett, didn't serve his country in World War II. So, in turn, Pratt's NHL career was not interrupted.

While no one can question anyone for serving their country, Patrick did misfire here in every way possible. After all, even if World War II didn't happen, this trade was about Pratt's nightlife more than anything else.

**DATE OF TRADE: November 1st, 1943 (Approximate date, exact date unknown)**

**RANGERS ACQUIRE: Ab Demarco Sr.**

**BOSTON BRUINS ACQUIRE: Cash**

Ab Demarco Sr., whose son Ab Demarco Jr. also played for the Rangers during the early 1970s (Demarco Jr. was even a part of the 1971-72 New York Rangers, the team that made it to Game Six of the 1972 Stanley Cup Final - a series loss to the Bruins), played some form of professional hockey for over 25 seasons. It was with the Rangers where Demarco Sr. finished his NHL career.

Demarco Sr., from North Bay, Ontario, was a centerman by trade and played during the absolute worst era of Rangers hockey.

Demarco Sr. was part of the club from the 1943-44 through 1946-47 seasons, where the team finished dead-last all four seasons. While Demarco Sr. himself played well, the team stunk.

Since Demarco Sr. played well, and since it didn't cost Patrick much to acquire him, this trade was a win for the Rangers - a rare victory in a Dark Age of both world and franchise history.

**DATE OF TRADE: November 1st, 1943 (Approximate date, exact date unknown)**

**RANGERS ACQUIRE: Chuck Scherza**

**BOSTON BRUINS ACQUIRE: Cash**

Like Demarco Sr., Charles "Chuck" Scherza was a centerman who also played in a down period of franchise history. However, unlike Demarco, Scherza, from Brandon, Manitoba, played in only 46 games with the Rangers.

Instead of Broadway, it was with the Providence Reds (AHL) where Scherza spent most of his career, playing for the Reds in ten-consecutive seasons following his Rangers/NHL career.

It's tough to evaluate trades from this period because the team was so bad due to World War II. There were also wartime restrictions, where some Canadian players weren't even allowed out of Canada.

In one example, Phil Watson (who we'll later discuss in this book), a member of the 1940 Stanley Cup champions, wasn't allowed out of Canada during the 1943-44 season. In turn, Patrick loaned Watson to the Canadiens (Watson then won the second Stanley Cup of his career), and then Watson returned to New York for the 1944-45 season.

In other words, with most of his trades from this time (with the Pratt deal being a noticeable exception), Patrick dealt from a position of weakness.

At the end of the day, Patrick spent some cash on Scherza and got a few games out of his new player. So this trade is pretty much even, all things considered.

**DATE OF TRADE: November 1st, 1943 (Approximate date, exact date unknown)**

**RANGERS ACQUIRE: Ossie Aubuchon**

**BOSTON BRUINS ACQUIRE: Cash**

This was another "let's see what sticks" type of trade, as Oscar "Ossie" Aubuchon, a left-winger from Saint-Hyacinthe, Quebec, played 38 games for the Rangers in the 1943-44 season.

Aubuchon picked up 16 goals and 12 assists in his "Lone Ranger" season before finishing his career at the AHL level - where most of these wartime Rangers went after World War II.

**DATE OF TRADE: November 1st, 1943 (Approximate date, exact date unknown)**

**RANGERS ACQUIRE: Bucko McDonald**

**TORONTO MAPLE LEAFS ACQUIRE: Cash**

Wilfred Kennedy McDonald, who was known as "Bucko" ever since the days of his youth (his nickname paid homage to both his Irish ancestry and his ability to fight), had an interesting and diverse life. However, his years with the Rangers were the low point of his professional career.

Prior to joining the Rangers, "Bucko" had three Stanley Cups to his name, having won two with the Detroit Red Wings (1936 and 1937) and having won another with the Toronto Maple Leafs (1942). This is where the success stopped for McDonald.

A left-handed defenseman from Fergus, Ontario, McDonald played during the 1943-44 and 1944-1945 wartime seasons with the Rangers, as you know by now, the team finished in last place in both campaigns.

After finishing up with the Rangers, McDonald played some minor-league hockey. It was once retiring from hockey where McDonald's life took an interesting turn as he then entered the Canadian political realm.

As a politician, McDonald served in the Canadian Parliament for a dozen years. After leaving office, McDonald got back into hockey, where he even went on to coach a young Bobby Orr in Parry Sound, Ontario.

This trade was an okay trade for Patrick - but again, "Bucko" was just part of a horrendous time in Ranger history.

**DATE OF TRADE: January 12th, 1944**

**RANGERS ACQUIRE: Kilby MacDonald**

**MONTREAL CANADIENS ACQUIRE: Nestor Lubeck, Hubert Macey, and Spence Tatchell**

James MacDonald, known as "Kilby," was a left-winger from Ottawa, Ontario, who started his professional career with the Rangers after being promoted from their farm system.

MacDonald's timing was perfect.

MacDonald earned his first call-up during the 1939-40 season, where not only did his 15 goals and 13 assists earn him the Calder Trophy (Rookie of the Year) - but he also won the Stanley Cup. Talk about making a debut! But, unfortunately, the good times wouldn't last.

By the 1941-42 season, MacDonald was sent back to the AHL. Come the 1942-43 season, MacDonald joined the Canadian Army. At the time of this trade, MacDonald was property of the Montreal Canadiens, and Patrick wanted to take another chance on his former Calder and Stanley Cup winner.

Of the three players sent to Montreal, only Hubert Macey, a left-winger from Big River, Saskatchewan, played at the NHL level for any decent amount of time, where he skated in twelve games for the Habitants during the 1946-47 season. Conversely, MacDonald played sixty games for the Rangers in parts of the 1943-44 and 1944-45 seasons.

Nestor Lubeck, a left-winger from Chortowetz, Poland, never reached the AHL level, much less the NHL level. He retired in 1949.

Spence Tatchell, a defenseman from Lloydminster, Saskatchewan, is one of many players to have a "one-and-done" NHL career,
74

where he received his lone game of NHL action with the Rangers during the 1942-43 season. Tatchell's career was immediately cut short following this trade, as he, too, joined the war effort.

This trade has to be considered a win for Patrick here, as minor as this win may be, especially since two of the three players who went to Montreal never played for the Canadiens.

---

**DATE OF TRADE: February 22nd, 1944**

**RANGERS ACQUIRE: Aldo Palazzari**

**BOSTON BRUINS ACQUIRE: $3,000**

This trade is unfair to assess, as during a Rangers' practice in 1944, Aldo Palazzari, an alum of the University of Illinois, was forced to retire after suffering an eye injury.

A right-winger, Palazzari, from Eveleth, Minnesota, played only twelve games for the Rangers before retiring. Prior to that, he played only twenty-four games for the Bruins.

**DATE OF TRADE: November 27th, 1944**

**RANGERS ACQUIRE: Guy Labrie**

**BOSTON BRUINS ACQUIRE: $12,000**

In Lester Patrick's final trade as General Manager of the New York Rangers, Patrick received southpaw defenseman Guy Labrie from the Bruins for an eye-popping, staggering $12,000.

Labrie, from St. Charles, Quebec, had previously played fifteen games for the Bruins during the 1943-44 season. He then played only 27 games for the Rangers during the 1944-45 season.

Following the final NHL wartime season, Labrie spent the rest of his career at the minor-league level. He retired in 1954, having last played for the Riviere-du-Loup Raiders of the inferior Lower St. Lawrence Hockey League (SLSHL).

Considering the amount of money involved in this deal, while also keeping in mind what the Rangers were at the time - this trade was a disaster that rivaled the hydrogen bomb.

Up next, a transition we saw a lot of in this era (and in the years to come) - a head coach adding the role of general manager to his title.

During the last ten years, I don't think anyone has written more words about both Lester Patrick and Frank Boucher than myself. Arguably, I may have written more words about Boucher than anyone - including the scribes from Boucher's era! This is my way of saying that Boucher received top billing in "The New York Rangers Rink of Honor and the Rafters of Madison Square Garden!"

Photo Credit: Schaefer Brewing Company. Original photographer unknown. This picture has been deemed licensable by Creative Common Usage laws.

### FRANK BOUCHER

Tenure as Rangers' General Manager: February 21, 1946 – April 22, 1955

What's left to say about Frank Boucher that I haven't already written?

Like many of his time (something we see today), Boucher played his entire career for one team, and once he retired, he became the team's head coach.

Once his predecessor got older, Boucher stepped into the dual role of head coach and general manager. And just like Patrick before him - Boucher would later give up his head coaching gig to focus solely on his general manager duties.

While it was Conn Smythe who first signed Boucher (following the Cook brothers, Bill and Bun, who told the general manager to do so), it was under Lester Patrick where Boucher flourished.

As noted in my first book, Patrick and Boucher went on to have a 34-year friendship and association. However, once Boucher became general manager, the two soon had a falling out that would only be patched up by their wives before Patrick's passing on June 1st, 1960.

(To compare the Boucher/Patrick falling out to modern times, Patrick, after stepping down, assumed the role Glen Sather has today with the team. Patrick was extremely hands-on, and by the end, Rangers' ownership and management sided with their new general manager, stating that they hired Boucher to run the team in the best way he saw fit.)

Prior to his days in the Rangers' front office, Boucher spent twelve years centering the team, with his glory days featuring the Cook brothers as his flanks. As a player, Boucher won two Stanley Cups and seven Lady Byng trophies. Once he retired following the 1937-38 season, Patrick offered him a job to coach the New York Rovers, the Rangers' Eastern Hockey League (EHL) affiliate.

In his first and only season behind the Rovers' bench, the 1938-39 campaign, Boucher and company won the Hamilton B. Wills Trophy - the EHL's equivalent to the Stanley Cup.

Following Boucher's success with the Rovers, Patrick, who was now approaching the age of 56, decided to step down as head coach of the Rangers while maintaining his position as the team's general manager. In turn, Patrick named Boucher as the second coach in franchise history.

Just as he did with the Rovers in his first year behind their bench, in Boucher's rookie year as an NHL bench boss, he won the top prize of the league, as he and his Rangers won the 1940 Stanley Cup.

This much was evident: Boucher, a hockey man through and through (he introduced many innovations and changes to the league), was going to be successful at any hockey job at any level.

However, the Class of 1958 Hockey Hall of Famer would never win a Stanley Cup as general manager of the Rangers.

There were a few reasons why the Rangers weren't successful under Boucher once Patrick, who was then approaching the age of 63, retired.

As discussed in my first book and in the introduction of this one, this era didn't favor the Rangers. Making matters worse was World War II.

Before the war, and in anticipation of it, Patrick sold off many of the Rangers' farm teams and players. Patrick thought that wartime would put hockey in a state of pause.

While lesser leagues would shut down, and the NHL would lose the New York/Brooklyn Americans, too, the NHL, in a much-weakened state after losing so many players who were either drafted or conscripted into the war (or, in some cases, chose to serve their countries), saw the Rangers take the brunt of it.

The beginning of a long, dark age for the Rangers followed the 1940-41 season.

As previously discussed, rather than giving star goalie Dave Kerr a few extra bucks, Patrick nickel-and-dimed the 1940 Vezina Trophy winner to the point where Kerr had had enough. Kerr retired knowing he could make more money back home than by playing professional hockey. Again - this situation was a product of the era.

The Rangers lost many talented players, including most of their core stars from the 1940 team, due to the war. Between no longer having Kerr and all of their top players, it got so bad that during the 1943-44 season, Boucher, now at the age of 42, came out of retirement and became the Rangers' player/head coach for the season.

When Patrick anointed Boucher as his successor, the Rangers were in the middle of their fourth-straight losing season - four consecutive finishes as the worst team in the league (sixth place).

Once taking over from Patrick, Boucher had to start from scratch. His returning players from the war were no longer the same. The farm system was skeletal. And while the Rangers were always at a disadvantage when it came to players' rights, a new wrinkle had emerged during Boucher's tenure; players Boucher traded for either threatened or opted to retire rather than leave their Canadian homes for New York.

If that wasn't enough, even during the best season of Boucher's run as general manager, the 1949-50 season, there was that damn circus once again.

Once reaching the 1950 Stanley Cup Final, not one game was played at Madison Square Garden. This was brutal, especially in an era where not all rinks were the same, which meant "home ice" advantage was even bigger than it is today. The end result? A double overtime Game Seven loss to the Detroit Red Wings.

Boucher would likely have become the first full-time player, head coach, and general manager in Rangers' history to win the Stanley Cup at every level if the Rangers had home games at MSG. (Patrick also won Stanley Cups as a player, head coach, and general manager but only played in one Stanley Cup Final game in relief of injured goaltender Lorne Chabot.)

The 1950 Stanley Cup Final will always be the one that got away for Boucher and company. It would take many years for the Rangers to find their way back to the top of the league, twenty-two years in all following the 1950 loss, to return to the Stanley Cup Final.

Let's now explore the trades that Boucher made.

Back row: Coach Lynn Patrick, Duncan Fisher, Tony Leswick, Trainer Frank Paice, Edgar Laprade, Frank Eddolls, Bing Juckes, Manager Frank Boucher.
Middle row: Fred Shero, Ed Slowinski, Gus Kyle, Bud Poile, Nick Mickoski, Allan Stanley, Pentti Lund, Wally Stanowski.
Front row: Pat Egan, Alex Kaleta, Chuck Rayner, Buddy O'Connor, Don Raleigh.

The 1949-50 New York Rangers. Both Frankie Eddolls and Buddy O'Connor were acquired in the best trade Frank Boucher ever made.

Photo Credit: NHL archives. Photo reprinted under Creative Common Usage Laws. Original photographer unknown.

---

## DATE OF TRADE: June 19th, 1946 (Trade voided after Hollett retired)

## RANGERS ACQUIRE: Bill "Flash" Hollett

## DETROIT RED WINGS ACQUIRE: Hank Goldup and Ab Demarco Sr.

For Frank Boucher, who won two Stanley Cups as a player with the Rangers (1928 and 1933), and one more Stanley Cup as the club's head coach (1940), his first trade was voided. What a start!

Following the 1945-46 season, Boucher had his eye on defenseman Frank William "Flash" Hollett. However, Hollett, born in North

81

Sydney, Nova Scotia, but grew up in Toronto, Ontario, had other plans.

A two-time Stanley Cup champion in Boston (1939 and 1941), Hollet, now approaching the age of 32, was traded to Detroit on January 10th, 1944, where he remained for parts of three seasons - and the rest of his NHL career.

Following a contract dispute with then-Detroit Red Wings' General Manager Jack Adams, who desired to unload a player that he found mercurial, he sent Hollett to the Rangers. However, Hollett didn't want to leave Detroit because he lived a stone's throw away in Ontario.

Simply put, Hollett didn't want to make the move to the east coast. It also didn't help that his wife was also pleading with him to retire instead. And that's what Hollett did - as rather than reporting to the Rangers, he retired and finished out his playing days in the Ontario Hockey Association.

The previously discussed Ab Demarco Sr. and Hank Goldup, now knowing they were on Boucher's shortlist, made the best of it, as Demarco Sr. played for the Rangers in the season that followed, while Goldup remained with the organization, albeit where he played at the AHL level.

**DATE OF TRADE: August 1st, 1946 (Approximate date, exact date unknown)**

**RANGERS ACQUIRE: Cash**

**MONTREAL CANADIENS ACQUIRE: Hubert Macey**

A wartime Ranger, this wasn't much of a deal, as the left-winger Hubert Macey had only played eighteen games with the Blueshirts before this trade. Macey played in twelve more NHL regular season contests with the Canadiens. He also played in seven more NHL contests in the 1947 Stanley Cup Playoffs, where the Leafs knocked off the Habs four games to two.

82

Following the 1947 Stanley Cup Final, Macey bounced around various minor leagues, never to play in the NHL again. In other words, this trade was a wash for the general manager, the former #7 of the New York Rangers.

**DATE OF TRADE: September 17th, 1946**

**RANGERS ACQUIRE: Jack Church**

**BOSTON BRUINS ACQUIRE: $5,000**

This was another trade that amounted to nothing, as Jack Church, a defenseman from Kamsack, Saskatchewan, would never suit up for the Rangers. Instead, he spent two seasons in the AHL, where he played for both the New Haven Ramblers and the Providence Reds.

Church, who previously played for the Leafs, Americans, and Bruins, retired after the 1947-48 season.

**DATE OF TRADE: November 1st, 1946**

**RANGERS ACQUIRE: Joe Cooper**

**CHICAGO BLACKHAWKS ACQUIRE: Cash**

Joe Cooper, as discussed earlier, originally began his NHL career with the Rangers during the 1935-36 season (where he then played two more seasons in New York), returned to the Blueshirts ten years later.

He was also a player that Boucher was familiar with, as the two were once teammates.

A defenseman of 414 NHL games, Cooper played 59 of them in the final campaign of his NHL career, which was this 1946-47 season.

Following the Rangers' fifth-place finish in a league of six teams, Cooper played one more season at the AHL level before retiring.

This was basically a "transition" trade, as the Rangers adapted to post-World War II life.

**DATE OF TRADE: August 19th, 1947**

**RANGERS ACQUIRE: Frank Eddolls and Buddy O'Connor**

**MONTREAL CANADIENS ACQUIRE: Joe Bell, Hal Laycoe, and George Robertson**

Hands-down, this is the best trade Frank Boucher ever made.

Over time, both Frank Eddolls and Buddy O'Connor went on to become team captain of the club. And as you'd imagine - Eddolls and O'Connor are also heavily featured in "The New York Rangers Rink of Honor and the Rafters of Madison Square Garden."

Eddolls, a defenseman from Lachine, Quebec, was involved in several controversial trades throughout his career. (And as described in depth in my first book, Eddolls, through no fault of his own, created splits, wedges, and hostility between Conn Smythe & Frank Selke and Lester Patrick & Frank Boucher.) But, more important than that, Eddolls was also known as a defenseman who could shut down the legendary "Rocket" Maurice Richard.

Herbert "Buddy" O'Connor, from Montreal, Quebec, was a prolific center, and he won both the Hart and Lady Byng Trophies in his first season with the Rangers.

This duo helped change the culture in New York, too, as before their arrivals, the Rangers were in the middle of a five-season playoff drought.

The Rangers reached the 1948 Stanley Cup semifinal in their first year together on Broadway. Two years later, the Rangers made it to the Stanley Cup Final, losing an agonizing Game Seven to the Detroit Red Wings.

Despite the loss, along with goaltender Chuck Rayner and forward Edgar Laprade, the Rangers became relevant again.

Both Eddolls and O'Connor would end their NHL careers with the Rangers. O'Connor, who finished his NHL days following the 1950-51 season, was inducted into the Hockey Hall of Fame in 1988. Eddolls' NHL days concluded following the 1951-52 season.

84

Sadly, retirement wouldn't last long, as on August 13, 1961, at the age of 40, Eddolls passed away after suffering a heart attack.

The three players who went to Montreal, (Joe Bell, Hal Laycoe, and George Robertson) didn't burn the Rangers at all.

Bell, a left-winger from Portage la Prairie, Manitoba, would never play in the NHL again. Following his 62 games (all with the Rangers), Bell played the next ten years of his career for various minor league hockey clubs. He retired in 1956.

Laycoe, a defenseman from Sutherland, Saskatchewan, had more success than Bell, where he played 455 games following this trade (531 total) with the Montreal Canadiens and the Boston Bruins.

Following his retirement in 1956, Laycoe had a lengthy coaching career at both the WHL and NHL levels, where he also became the first bench boss of the NHL Vancouver Canucks.

Robertson, a left-winger from Winnipeg, Manitoba, played in thirty games for the Montreal Canadiens in the 1948-49 season, where following that season, he finished his career in the minors.

Of the five players included in this trade, Robertson lived the longest. He passed away on January 9th, 2021, at the age of 93 as a result of COVID-19.

Without question, this was the best trade that Boucher ever made, which also speaks somewhat to many of the Ranger down years on his watch.

It also didn't help that some of his deals (including his attempt to acquire a teenaged Gordie Howe) and trades were voided because of where the Rangers played (southernmost NHL city of the league) and how bad they were.

**DATE OF TRADE: October 22nd, 1947 (Trade voided when Conacher refused to report)**

**RANGERS ACQUIRE: Roy Conacher**

**DETROIT RED WINGS ACQUIRE: Edward Slowinski and a player to be named later**

Similar to his first trade, Boucher had another trade voided on this date, as Roy Conacher, a left-winger from Toronto, Ontario, and a star of two Stanley Cup winning teams with the Boston Bruins (1939 and 1941), didn't want to play in New York.

Like many NHLers at the time, Conacher had his career cut short by World War II when he left the Bruins to serve for the Royal Canadian Air Force. Once the war was over, then-Bruins' head-honcho Art Ross thought Conacher's skills had diminished, and as a result, he sent his former superstar to Detroit.

Conacher, a Class of 1998 Hall of Famer, had a tremendous season in his first year with the Wings; following it, Ross admitted that he had fouled up big-time. Ross would later say of his trade of Conacher "the biggest mistake I ever made as a general manager."

Prior to the start of the 1947-48 season, notorious penny pincher Jack Adams, Ross' counterpart in Detroit, squabbled over $900 with Conacher. Rather than paying the man, Adams sent Conacher to New York, where Conacher promptly announced his retirement.

Once announcing his retirement, this trade was voided. However, retirement wouldn't last long.

Conacher would come out of his "retirement" after Bill Tobin, the Chicago Blackhawks' owner at the time, spent $25,000 to get Conacher out of Detroit. Conacher won the Art Ross Trophy as a Blackhawk in the 1948-49 season. He was also the club's top scorer in his five seasons in Chicago.

At the time, Edward Slowinski, a right-winger from Winnipeg, Manitoba, was a month shy of his 25 birthday. Ultimately, Slowinski remained with the Rangers, where he spent his entire NHL career with the Blueshirts.

In total, Slowinski played 291 games for the franchise. Better than that, Slowinski led all skaters in assists in the 1950 Stanley Cup Playoffs.

Following Slowinski's time with the Rangers, he spent five more years playing at the AHL level, where he last played for the Providence Reds during the 1957-58 season.

The biggest "what if" question here is the obvious one: what if Conacher was part of the 1949-50 Stanley Cup Finalist New York Rangers? We'll never know.

**DATE OF TRADE: February 6th, 1948**

**RANGERS ACQUIRE: Billy Taylor Sr. and a Player to be named later (Pentti Lund)**

**BOSTON BRUINS ACQUIRE: Grant Warwick**

Grant Warwick, who won the Calder Trophy with the Rangers during the 1941-42 season, spent most of his Rangers' career on some pretty bad teams.

Following this mid-season trade, Warwick, a right-winger from Regina, Saskatchewan, spent two more seasons at the NHL level, playing for Boston and Montreal.

Warwick, who finished his NHL career with 289 points in 395 games played, continued to play hockey at the minor-league level before retiring in 1957.

Billy Taylor Sr., a center from Winnipeg, Manitoba, was 28 years old at the time of this deal and was also thought to have a promising future. Instead, Taylor only played in two games for the Rangers. His career wasn't cut short due to the war or injuries - he was expelled by NHL Commissioner Clarence Campbell for gambling on hockey.

Somewhat similar to the more famous and well-known 1919 "Chicago Black Sox" scandal, Taylor's accomplice and Bruins' teammate, Don Gallinger, was caught on a wiretap with an infamous criminal and known gambler out of Detroit, James Tamer.

The NHL quickly came down on Taylor and Gallinger, especially when it became known that they had been betting on their team at the time, the Boston Bruins, to lose.

The two players, accused of dogging it before the news broke that they were betting on their team to lose, later rationalized these bets by saying, "we're going to lose anyway."

And just like the Black Sox of 1919, due to poor NHL wages at the time, these players could earn more money by gambling on their sport than by playing it.

Following Taylor's 1948 expulsion, it would take 22 years for the expulsion to be lifted and for him to be reinstated. He'd later find work with the Pittsburgh Penguins as a scout, but for the Rangers, this trade blew up in their faces through no fault of their own.

In essence, prior to completing this trade for the "player to be named later," the Rangers gave up Grant Warwick for nothing in return. For Taylor, a career was lost.

On February 17th, 1948, Taylor's gambling came to light - eleven days following this trade. A few weeks later, on April 6th, 1948, the Rangers acquired a power forward in the form of right-winger Pentti Lund to complete the trade.

Lund, who was born in Karijoki, Finland, moved to Thunder Bay, Ontario, at the age of six. He eventually became Boucher's saving grace in this deal.

During his full five seasons in the NHL (before joining the Rangers, he played in three playoff games with the Bruins), Lund had the best years of his career in New York, winning the Calder Trophy in 1949 and then was part of the 1950 Stanley Cup Finalist Rangers.

After scoring thirty points in his rookie year, he scored eleven points in twelve games played in the 1950 Stanley Cup Playoffs.

He was later traded back to Beantown in 1951, a trade we'll discuss soon.

This trade isn't fair to assess, as no one could have predicted what Taylor was involved in.

**DATE OF TRADE: April 26th, 1948**

**RANGERS ACQUIRE: Elwin "Moe" Morris, Orval "Slim" Lavell, and Wally Stanowski**

**TORONTO MAPLE LEAFS ACQUIRE: Cal Gardner, Bill Juzda, Rene Trudell, and Frank Mathers**

Elwin Morris, who won the Stanley Cup in 1945 with the Maple Leafs, was a right-handed defenseman from Toronto, Ontario, who played in only eighteen games with the Rangers during the 1948-49 campaign. In the 1949-50 season, he was assigned to the Providence Reds (AHL), finishing his professional career in 1953.

Orval Lavell, a defenseman from Saskatoon, Saskatchewan, never reached the NHL level. Once acquired by Patrick, "Slim" was assigned to the AHL, where he remained throughout the 1952-53 season. Following his AHL days, he played for three years in Canadian senior leagues before retiring in 1956.

Two years older than Morris, Wally Stanowski won four Stanley Cups with the Leafs (1942, 1945, 1947, and 1948) and was a left-handed defenseman born in Winnipeg, Manitoba. As you can see, Boucher and the Rangers were trying to fortify their blue line with this trade.

Just like in Toronto, Stanowski had more success than Morris did with the Rangers, playing three seasons in total with New York, where he also was hampered by injuries during these years. By 1951, he was assigned to the AHL. A year later, in 1952, he retired.

Cal Gardner, a left-handed center from Transcona, Manitoba, had a great run once leaving the Rangers, winning two Stanley Cups (1949 and 1951 with the Leafs) before finishing his career with both

Chicago and Boston. In all, Gardner played nine more NHL seasons following his run on Broadway. He retired in 1961 after a season spent with the Cleveland Barons (AHL).

Bill Juzda, a rearguard from Winnipeg, Manitoba, also won the Stanley Cup in 1949 and 1951 with Toronto. His time in the NHL came to an end following the completion of the 1951-52 season.

Rene Trudell, like Gardner, was born in Transcona, Manitoba. The two broke in with the Rangers together following their days with the Rangers' EHL affiliate, the New York Rovers.

The right-winger played in three post-war seasons with the Rangers where he totaled 52 points in 129 games played. He would never play in the NHL again after being dealt north of the border, and after one season spent in the AHL, he retired in 1949.

Frank Mathers, a defenseman from Winnipeg, Manitoba, who Toronto boss Conn Smythe had high hopes for, had grand aspirations about continuing his education. In total, Mathers played professional hockey for fourteen seasons between the AHL and NHL, where during that time, he played only 23 games with the Leafs - the extent of his NHL career.

Upon retirement, Mathers had planned on pursuing a career in dentistry. But instead, Mathers spent parts of four different decades (the '50s, '60s, '70s, and '80s) as the head coach of the AHL Hershey Bears. His successful and fruitful duration in Hershey ultimately led Mathers to the NHL Hall of Fame, where he was inducted into the hallowed halls in 1992 as a "builder."

With Gardner and Juzda winning two Stanley Cups in Toronto, as opposed to Morris not lasting long with the Rangers, and Stankowski not having the same success with the Blueshirts as he did with the blue leaf, Conn Smythe's blue-and-white franchise won this trade.

---

**DATE OF TRADE:** October 7th, 1948

**RANGERS ACQUIRE:** Emile "The Cat" Francis and Alex Kaleta

**CHICAGO BLACKHAWKS ACQUIRE:** "Sugar" Jim Henry

Needless to say, at the time of this trade, Frank Boucher had no clue he'd be trading for a future general manager. Sixteen years following this trade, that's exactly what happened, as Emile "The Cat" would spearhead the franchise from October 1964 through January 1976.

Ironically, Frank Boucher had his most significant success with the Rangers as a player, even though he did win a Stanley Cup as the team's head coach in 1940. Boucher's worst tenure with the organization was as general manager, which, as discussed in this book and in "The New York Rangers Rink of Honor and Rafters of Madison Square Garden," wasn't always entirely on him. (Plus, as general manager, Boucher reached one Stanley Cup Final (1950), like Francis would go on to do as the team's GM in 1972.)

In the case of Francis, unlike Boucher, most of his success with the Rangers didn't come as a player - it came as a general manager.

In an era where there were no regular backup goalies, and with Chuck Rayner firmly in place as the team's starting goaltender, Francis, born in North Battleford, Saskatchewan, played 22 games for the Rangers and ultimately finished his NHL career after the 1951-52 season. "The Cat" played in eight more seasons at both the AHL and WHL levels.

Once retired as a player in 1960, Francis accepted a coaching job with the OHA Guelph Royals, a Rangers' farm team. From there, the rest was history. Who knows if Francis would have become one of the most successful coaches and general managers in franchise history without this trade?

While Francis left a bigger legacy with the Rangers, it was Alex Kaleta, from Canmore, Alberta, who meant more to the franchise as a player. The left-winger spent three seasons with the club and was part of the 1950 Stanley Cup Finalist team.

Kaleta is most famously known for his days in Chicago, as he is officially credited by the Hockey Hall of Fame for "inventing" the hat trick.

As the story goes, during the 1945-46 season, Kaleta entered a Toronto hat shop looking for an item to cover his head. Not having enough dough to purchase a hat, store owner Sam Taft made an agreement with Kaleta - score three goals against the Leafs and the hat is yours. Kaleta scored four goals in the game (January 26th, 1946) and the rest is history.

"Sugar" Jim Henry, a close pal of Chuck Rayner (the two ran several businesses together, including a goaltending camp), was a victim of his own time with the Rangers. With no backup goaltender position at the time, Henry, born in Winnipeg, Manitoba, only played when Rayner was injured or unavailable to play.

Originally a goaltender that Boucher scouted and was high on before Rayner's arrival to the Rangers (1945), Henry was the team's starter during the 1941-42 season, his rookie year. World War II then cut into Henry's career, where he joined Canada's war effort in Ottawa.

Once shipped to Chicago, where he served as the team's starting netminder, Henry finished out his career in Boston, tending goal for four seasons.

When you look at every factor in this trade, it changed the course of Rangers' history. Who knows what would've happened had Francis hooked up with another franchise? (At one point, as we'll soon get into, it looked like Francis' front-office career was going to begin in Chicago.)

When it comes to just the players themselves, Francis and Henry canceled each other out. With Boucher also adding Kaleta to this transaction - this trade is easily a win.

**DATE OF TRADE: June 1st, 1949 (Approximate date, exact date unknown)**

**RANGERS ACQUIRE: Bill McDonagh**

**DETROIT RED WINGS ACQUIRE: Cash**

Fun Fact: Did you know that the Rangers previously had a player with the McDonagh surname long before the days of Captain Ryan McDonagh? Neither did I, that is until I started putting this book together!

Not a Fun Fact: The reason why yours truly, and probably you, the reader, weren't aware of Bill McDonagh (no relation) was because the first McDonagh in Rangers' blue only played four NHL games his entire career, with all four of these games taking place in the 1949-50 season.

McDonagh, a left-winger, born in Rouyn-Noranda, Quebec, outside of his four games with the Rangers, spent the bulk of that 1949-50 campaign in the AHL with the New Haven Ramblers.

Following that season, McDonagh played for the inferior minor leagues of his era, such as the USHL, QSHL, NBSHL, CIAU, and the OHA Senior League. He retired in 1958.

Long story short, not much of a trade here.

**DATE OF TRADE: August 16th, 1949**

**RANGERS ACQUIRE: Norman "Bud" Poile**

**DETROIT RED WINGS ACQUIRE: Cash**

Bud Poile, the father of current long-time Nashville Predators General Manager David Poile, had a cup of coffee with the Rangers - as you'll soon see below.

A right-winger from Fort William, Ontario, Poile spent most of his 311-game NHL career with the Leafs.

The 1947 Stanley Cup champion (Toronto) also spent time with the Blackhawks before being shipped out of Detroit to New York. More on Poile following our next trade.

**DATE OF TRADE: October 7th, 1949**

**RANGERS ACQUIRE: Pat Egan**

**BOSTON BRUINS ACQUIRE: Bill Moe, Lorne Ferguson, and Future Considerations**

Pat Egan, from Blackie, Alberta, had a long career in hockey as both a player and head coach. The defenseman finished his NHL days with the Rangers, where he was part of the 1950 Stanley Cup Finalist team. Once the 1950-51 season was complete, Egan played the last nine years of his career at the AHL and WHL levels before getting into coaching.

Rearguard Bill Moe, from Minneapolis, Minnesota, spent five seasons with the Rangers. His NHL career started at the end of the war (1944) and continued until the time of this trade. Once dealt, he never played in the NHL again. He last played for the Troy Uncle Sam Trojans (no sponsorships back then!) of the EHL in the 1952-53 season.

Lorne Ferguson, a nineteen-year-old left-wing prospect at the time, enjoyed a lengthy career in the NHL, where the native of Palmerston, Ontario, played 422 games for the Boston Bruins, Detroit Red Wings, and lastly, the Chicago Blackhawks. Once wrapping up his NHL career in 1959, Ferguson played minor-league hockey until 1962, when he retired.

The "future considerations" of this trade wound up being cash, but there is no record of the amount Boucher paid.

Since Boucher was trying to bolster his team for what would eventually turn into a Stanley Cup Final run, there's no clear-cut winner of this trade.

Simply stated, the Rangers went for a veteran at the expense of youth. (Ferguson only played three games for the Bruins during the 1949-50 season before becoming a full-timer a season later.)

**DATE OF TRADE: December 22nd, 1949**

**RANGERS ACQUIRE: Cash**

**BOSTON BRUINS ACQUIRE: Bud Poile**

Not happy with the trade he made just four months earlier, Boucher shipped Poile to Boston, as the right-winger joined his fifth Original Six team. This also would be Poile's last NHL franchise, as he never played for the Montreal Canadiens. Had he done so, he would have joined Victor Lynn as the answer to a trivia question - a Lynn who was the only player from the Original Six era to play for all six franchises.

Poile played only 38 games for the Bruins, where following his playing days, he got into coaching and in the front office. He later became the first general manager of both the Flyers and the Canucks.

While this has nothing to do with the trade itself, with six decades of hockey experience, Poile was inducted into the Hockey Hall of Fame in 1990 as a builder. When it comes to this particular trade, it was another wash.

**DATE OF TRADE: September 19th, 1950 (Separate trades)**

**RANGERS ACQUIRE: Cash**

**CHICAGO BLACKHAWKS ACQUIRE: Steve Hrymnak and Jean-Paul Lamirande**

Steve Hrymnak, a defenseman from Port Arthur, Ontario, played eighteen games for the Blackhawks, never to play in the NHL again, sans two playoff call-up games with the Red Wings in 1953. Most of his career was played in the minor leagues, where he skated in 333 AHL contests and 307 WHL contests. Following a 1957-58 season with the New Westminster Royals, he retired as a professional.

Jean-Paul Lamirande, a defenseman from Shawinigan Falls, Quebec, spent four years with the Rangers' organization, bouncing between the Rangers and the New Haven Ramblers (AHL). In total, Lamirande played 49 games as a Blueshirt. Following this trade, he'd never play in the NHL again but would continue his career until 1961 by playing in the minors, mainly in hockey leagues in his home province.

These two moves bolstered the coffers, nothing more, nothing less.

**DATE OF TRADE: November 16th, 1950**

**RANGERS ACQUIRE: Edward Harrison and Zellio Toppazzini**

**BOSTON BRUINS ACQUIRE: Dunc Fisher and Future Considerations (Alex Kaleta on loan)**

Before this trade, Ed Harrison, a center from Mimico, Ontario, played 190 NHL games with the Bruins. He played in four more NHL games with the Rangers, where following that short stint, he'd finish his 194-game NHL career by jumping around various minor leagues before retiring in 1954.

Zellio Toppazzini, a right-winger from Copper Cliff, Ontario, had more success than Harrison - even if the bulk of "Topper's" success came at the AHL level. Even so, Topper played 71 games with the Rangers during the two seasons that followed this trade.

Before his retirement in 1964, "Topper" racked up 723 AHL games under his belt to go along with his 123 NHL games.

To this day, Topper is known mainly for his work with the Providence Reds, which earned him an induction into the then newly founded AHL Hall of Fame in 2012. Topper is also known for being the great-uncle of Justin Williams, with his great-nephew winning three Stanley Cups (2006, 2012, 2014) throughout his twenty-year career that spanned from 2000-2020.

Dunc Fisher, a right-winger from Regina, Saskatchewan, was part of the 1950 Stanley Cup Finalist Rangers. (He scored three goals and picked up three assists in the 1950 playoffs during his twelve games played.) Following the playoffs, he played only eight games for the Rangers in the 1950-51 campaign before being shipped out to Boston.

Fisher's time in Boston was hit or miss, where, like many, he accomplished his most significant feats at the AHL level with the Hershey Bears.

After five seasons in Hershey, Fisher returned to the NHL, albeit for only eight games with the Red Wings before returning to the Bears, where he retired following the 1959-60 season. Once completing his hockey career, he got into the field of aquatics, serving his home city of Regina as their aquatics manager.

Alex Kaleta, on loan, never played for the Bruins. Instead, he played five games for the Hershey Bears before moving on to Saskatoon, where he finished his playing days.

Like many trades on this list, this was another "no harm, no foul" type of deal.

**DATE OF TRADE: May 16th, 1951**

**RANGERS ACQUIRE: Edward Reigle and Stephen Kraftcheck**

**BOSTON BRUINS ACQUIRE: Cash**

A left-handed defenseman out of Winnipeg, Manitoba, Ed Reigle never suited up for the Rangers. Following the trade, he spent the next four seasons of his career playing for the Cleveland Barons (AHL), where his career ended in 1955.

Stephen Kraftcheck, from Tintern, Ontario, was also a defenseman. Kraftcheck had more success than Reigle, who spent the 1951-52 and 1952-53 seasons with the Rangers. Following these seasons, Kraftcheck spent the next eleven seasons of his career at the AHL level, sans an eight-game stint with the Toronto Maple Leafs during the 1958-59 season.

In his post-NHL days, Kraftcheck played in the AHL for the Barons, the Rochester Americans, and the Providence Reds, who he retired with following the 1963-64 season.

Without knowing the exact number of dollars involved in this trade, again, another trade of minimal value here.

**DATE OF TRADE: June 8th, 1951**

**RANGERS ACQUIRE: Gaye Stewart**

**DETROIT RED WINGS ACQUIRE: Tony Leswick**

Gaye Stewart, a perennial NHL All-Star, won the Calder Trophy in 1943 and the Stanley Cup in 1942 and 1947 - all with the Toronto Maple Leafs. Toronto later traded Stewart for Hall of Famer Max Bentley.

The right-winger from Fort William, Ontario, had a solid 1951-52 season with the Rangers, scoring 15 goals and racking up 25 assists. He was traded to Montreal in the following season, in a trade that we'll discuss soon.

"Tough" Tony Leswick, who started his career with the Rangers during the 1945-46 season, was a left-winger from Humboldt, Saskatchewan. He soon became the apple of Detroit's eye based on how he was able to play against Gordie Howe.

Now in Detroit, Leswick would win three Stanley Cups (1952, 1954, and 1955). He also scored the game-winning goal in Game Seven of the 1954 Stanley Cup Final (against the Montreal Canadiens).

While both Stewart and Leswick were born in 1923 - it was Stewart who peaked first. He retired from hockey in 1954. Conversely, Leswick, who also became an All-Star in his years with the Rangers, following this trade, he continued to have great individual and team success. Leswick finally called it a career after the 1959-60 season with the Vancouver Canucks, then of the WHL.

In summary, this trade was a loss for Boucher and the Rangers.

"FUN FACT" time! Leswick's nephew also played in New York, albeit for the New York Mets. His nephew? 1986 World Series Champion, Lenny "Nails" Dykstra.

As you can tell by the "Tough" and "Nails" nicknames - the bloodline produced hard-nosed athletes.

**DATE OF TRADE: September 20th, 1951**

**RANGERS ACQUIRE: Paul Ronty and Cash**

**BOSTON BRUINS ACQUIRE: Walter "Gus" Kyle and Pentti Lund**

Gus Kyle, a six-foot tall, left-handed defenseman from Dysart, Saskatchewan, was part of the 1950 New York Ranger Stanley Cup Finalist team. Following this trade, Kyle played in Boston for the 1951-52 season before finishing his professional career at the WHL level, where he played for four seasons with the Calgary Stampeders. He retired in 1956.

Upon retirement, Kyle spent nearly twenty years with the St. Louis Blues organization as their broadcaster.

Pentti Lund, a Finnish right-winger, and as discussed earlier, spent two more seasons with the Bruins - the team in which he began his NHL career.

As the first Finnish player to score a goal in the NHL (for the Rangers in 1948), Lund was later inducted into the Finnish Hockey Hall of Fame in 1992.

While Paul Ronty, a center from Toronto, Ontario, was never able to eclipse his years with Boston, he was able to record a 54-point season in the 1952-53 campaign - his second of four seasons with the Blueshirts.

A veteran of 312 points in 488 NHL games, Ronty was put on waivers by the Rangers on February 18th, 1955. A day later, the Canadiens claimed him. Ronty played the final five games of his career in Montreal.

Due to his nationality, Lund is perhaps the most famous player of the three players involved. Still, even so, the Rangers got slightly the better of this trade, as Ronty provided the most production and lasted the longest.

**DATE OF TRADE: December 28th, 1951**

**RANGERS ACQUIRE: Clare Martin**

**CHICAGO BLACKHAWKS ACQUIRE: Cash**

Clare Martin, on the victor's side of the 1950 Stanley Cup Final, was nearing the end of his career at the time of this trade - even if he was just two months shy of turning thirty years old.

The defenseman from Waterloo, Ontario, played only fourteen games for the Rangers - the final fourteen games of his 237-game NHL career.

In other words, this trade was much ado about nothing, despite this being a Christmastime transaction.

**DATE OF TRADE: August 18th, 1952**

**RANGERS ACQUIRE: Leo Reise Jr.**

**DETROIT RED WINGS ACQUIRE: John Morrison, Reginald Sinclair, and Cash**

Leo Reise Jr., and his father Leo Reise Sr., became the first-ever father-son duo to make it to the NHL.

Father Reise began his career with the Hamilton Tigers (later the New York Americans) during the 1920-21 season and, as discussed earlier, finished his NHL career with the Rangers after the 1929-30 season.

Son Reise began his career in 1945, giving the family this honorous distinction.

While the elder Reise had a solid career himself, the younger Reise won the hardware, as Leo Reise Jr. won the Stanley Cup in both 1950 and 1952. And just like his father, Reise Jr. also retired from the NHL with the Rangers.

A defenseman from Stoney Creek, Ontario, Reise Jr. had a solid campaign in the 1952-53 season, with four goals and nineteen assists. However, a season later, he had the worst season of his career from an offensive standpoint, with a career low of eight points in seventy games played.

Going to Detroit was the Scottish defenseman John Morrison, who never laced the skates for the spoked wheel, nor reached any prominent minor-league level.

Reggie Sinclair, then 27 years old, was a center from Lachine, Quebec. He picked up eleven goals and twelve assists in his first (and last) season with the Wings. However, Sinclair immediately retired following the season and stayed at his off-season job with Pepsi. He then became a full-time employee of the cola outfit. By 1965, he was Vice-President of Pepsi International.

Had Sinclair continued to play, who knows? However, we can only deal with facts, and the Rangers easily won this trade, even for as minor as this victory was.

**DATE OF TRADE: December 8th, 1952**

**RANGERS ACQUIRE: Cash**

**MONTREAL CANADIENS ACQUIRE: Gaye Stewart**

After losing the Leswick/Stewart trade eighteen months prior, the Rangers/Boucher sold Stewart for greenbacks. Stewart played in only five games for the Habitants, finishing out his career at the AHL level for the Buffalo Bisons.

While the cash figure is unknown, this was pretty much a "cut your losses" type of deal.

**DATE OF TRADE: January 9th, 1953**

**RANGERS ACQUIRE: Pete Babando**

**CHICAGO BLACKHAWKS ACQUIRE: Cash**

Pete Babando, a left-winger from Braeburn, Pennsylvania, has a place in Rangers' history - as a heartbreaking opponent.

Babando scored the double overtime game-winning goal in Game Seven of the 1950 Stanley Cup Final for the Detroit Red Wings. If the Rangers had the home games they were supposed to have during that series or had a shot from Don "Bones" Raleigh not rung off the crossbar - Babando would not have become the villain of Rangers' history.

Boucher sought out a veteran with playoff experience mid-season, but Babando wasn't the right fit.

Babando played only thirty games for the Rangers in 1953. These would be the final thirty games of his NHL career. Overall, throughout the course of his career, Babando played in 351 NHL contests.

Following the 1952-53 campaign, Babando spent thirteen seasons at the minor-league level, with lengthy stints with the Buffalo Bisons (AHL) and the Clinton Comets (EHL).

Babando, who lived to the age of 94 at the time of his passing on February 19th, 2020, was perhaps born ten years too early.

The one-time Ranger killer retired at the age of 42 following the 1966-67 season. In the following season, the 1967-68 campaign, the

NHL doubled in size as a result of "The Great Expansion" - a topic that we will further discuss in this title.

Thanks for nothing, Pete!

This trade was a financial loss, especially since the Rangers finished dead-last in the league during Babando's lone half-season with the club.

**DATE OF TRADE: June 30th, 1953**

**RANGERS ACQUIRE: Doug Bentley**

**CHICAGO BLACKHAWKS ACQUIRE: Cash**

After three seasons without sniffing the playoffs, Frank Boucher went to the veteran well once again, acquiring both Bentley brothers (Doug and Max) - where the two brothers were eventually enshrined into the Hall of Fame after their time in New York. (Doug in 1964, and Max in 1966.) Unfortunately, the duo wasn't inducted into the Hall of Fame for their days with the Rangers.

Older brother Doug, a left-winger from Delisle, Saskatchewan, was approaching the age of 37 at the time of this deal and on the verge of retirement. Boucher successfully lured Bentley out of retirement since the Rangers offered the brothers a chance to play together one more time.

Unlike brother Max, Doug never won a Stanley Cup in his epic career, despite multiple All-Star nominations and scoring accolades. So while it was highly unlikely that the Rangers would win the Stanley Cup in 1954 (spoiler: they didn't even make the playoffs), one last skate with brother Max, a centerman, was enticing enough for Doug to continue his career.

At the time of this deal, Bentley was already adapting to a player-coach role for his hometown Saskatoon Quakers of the WHL. However, Bentley accepted this trade, where he played only twenty games for the Rangers - the worst NHL season of his Hall of Fame career.

For Boucher, he was trying to find anything that could work, where, at this point, he was also trying to put players on the ice who could draw a sold-out house. So while the Rangers, as a team, didn't have success - the box office did.

Following the season, Bentley returned to western Canada, returning to his new role - head coach.

**DATE OF TRADE: August 8th, 1953**

**RANGERS ACQUIRE: Ivan Irwin**

**MONTREAL CANADIENS ACQUIRE: Pete Babando and Ed Slowinski**

Ivan Irwin, a left-handed defenseman from Chicago, Illinois, had only played in four games with the stacked Montreal Canadiens in the 1952-53 season. He'd play in 151 more games in parts of four seasons with the Rangers, where he also spent time with the Providence Reds. (Irwin would later coach the Reds for one season, 1965-66.)

Irwin, who didn't exactly play in the best era of Rangers' history, played his final NHL game with the Rangers in the 1957-58 season. He rounded out his career by playing two seasons with the Buffalo Bisons (AHL) before retiring in 1960.

The two players we discussed, Pete Babando, and Ed Slowinski, would never play in the NHL again after this trade.

This trade was a win for the Rangers, like several wins during the Boucher era - this was a small victory.

**DATE OF TRADE: August 11th, 1953**

**RANGERS ACQUIRE: Max Bentley**

**TORONTO MAPLE LEAFS ACQUIRE: Cash**

This was the second half of Boucher's deal to reunite the Bentley brothers. And like brother Doug, Max only played one season for the Rangers.

104

By the time the younger Bentley arrived in New York, he was already a three-time Stanley Cup champion, winning all three of his championships with Toronto (1948, 1949, and 1951).

Prior to joining the Leafs, the two brothers had played together in Chicago, which made this opportunity to play together one more time attractive. (Max Bentley also won the Hart Trophy in 1946 while in Chicago.)

Four years younger than his older brother, Max had a respectable 1953-54 season, potting fourteen goals and eighteen assists. However, these numbers were the second-worst of Bentley's career. (His worst offensive season was the year before, while in Toronto.)

Once Doug returned to Saskatoon, Max decided he wouldn't return to the Rangers either. The Maple Leafs claimed the rights to Max, but he decided he was through with the NHL and joined his brother in Saskatoon with the Quakers (WHL), where he'd play for three more seasons before retiring.

Just like Doug Bentley, the acquisition of Max Bentley was more about putting butts in the seats than anything else - part of the job description for NHL general managers in any era.

**DATE OF TRADE: June 8th, 1954 (Trade voided when Hy Buller refused to report to Montreal and retired)**

**RANGERS ACQUIRE: Dick Gamble and Ed Dorohoy**

**MONTREAL CANADIENS ACQUIRE: Hy Buller**

Known as the "Blueline Blaster" for his hitting ability, Hy Buller was also one of two Jewish players in the NHL in his era, which for many, included many games at the AHL level. His days in the AHL would later change the trajectory of his life.

Buller's Jewish ancestry attracted Boucher and the Rangers' marketing team. As mentioned earlier, the Rangers were looking to promote ethnicities to the diverse New York population from day one.

Buller did help draw Jewish fans into Madison Square Garden, who, once there, would hang Star of David banners while the media promoted his faith to their respective audiences.

Beginning his NHL career in Detroit, where he played in only nine games for the Wings, the defenseman from Montreal, Quebec, would find more success in New York, playing in 179 games for the Rangers. However, he'd never play again following this trade to Montreal.

As the story goes, Buller didn't want to uproot his family or take a pay cut to play in Montreal, which was ironic since Buller was from Montreal.

Rather than playing hockey, Buller became a salesman in Cleveland, Ohio. (Buller spent four seasons with the AHL Cleveland Barons prior to his days on Broadway and enjoyed the city.)

Once Buller retired, and after Boucher had two trades voided on him after players he acquired refused to report to New York - this trade was also voided.

Buller retired at the age of 28 years old. He passed away at the age of 42 in 1968 after a bout with cancer and was buried in his adopted city of Cleveland.

For what it's worth, Ed Dorohoy, a center from Medicine Hat, Alberta, following his sixteen games played in the NHL with the Montreal Canadiens for the 1948-49 season, never played in the NHL again. Instead, he played fifteen seasons at the minor-league level, most of his time in the WHL. He retired in 1964 and got into coaching.

The man with the name that sounded like that of an adult film star, Dick Gamble, a left-winger from Moncton, New Brunswick, spent most of his career as an AHLer. However, he did win the Stanley Cup in 1953 with the Habs.

With this trade being nixed, and with neither of these three players were game breakers - nothing was lost or gained here.

## DATE OF TRADE: July 20th, 1954

## RANGERS ACQUIRE: Danny Lewicki

## TORONTO MAPLE LEAFS ACQUIRE: Cash

By the time Danny Lewicki turned twenty years old, the left-winger from Fort William, Ontario, had won the Allan Cup, the Memorial Cup, and the Stanley Cup, winning the biggest prize in hockey with the Toronto Maple Leafs in 1951.

Lewicki had career years on Broadway, where in three of his four seasons, the Rangers qualified for the Stanley Cup Playoffs (1956-1958) - a rare feat for the World War II and postwar eras!

As the legend goes, despite Toronto boss Conn Smythe keenly aware of Lewicki's talent, Smythe was also known for his hard-headed quirks. One of those quirks was that he didn't want players to get married, despite Smythe himself being a married man.

In Smythe's 1981 autobiography, *"If You Can't Beat 'Em in the Alley,"* without using Lewicki's name, the former chief of the Leafs admitted as much, and he also expressed that he regretted this decision.

Lewicki was a solid Ranger, where in his best season, the 1954-55 campaign, he posted career highs of 29 goals and 53 points. A season later, he recorded a career high in assists, with 27 in all.

Following the 1957-58 season, the NHL held an intra-league draft, where the Rangers were forced to expose Lewicki. The Montreal Canadiens claimed Lewicki with the sole purpose of weakening Boucher's roster. After claiming Lewicki, the Habs dealt him off to the Chicago Blackhawks, where Lewicki finished his NHL career in 1959.

Despite how his tenure with the Blueshirts ended, this trade was a major win for Boucher and the Rangers.

**DATE OF TRADE: October 25th, 1954**

**RANGERS ACQUIRE: Cash**

**MONTREAL CANADIENS ACQUIRE: Jean-Paul Lamirande**

Jean-Paul Lamirande, as mentioned earlier, played one game for the Canadiens in the 1954-55 season. I think that tells you all you need to know!

Give the Rangers a check mark in the win column for this trade.

**DATE OF TRADE: November 23rd, 1954**

**RANGERS ACQUIRE: Pete Conacher and Bill Gadsby**

**CHICAGO BLACKHAWKS ACQUIRE: Rich Lamoureux, Nick Mickoski, and Allan Stanley**

In Boucher's final trade, he made a blockbuster of a transaction.

Pete Conacher, son of Hall of Famer Charlie Conacher, spent parts of two seasons with the Rangers.

Born Charles William Conacher Junior, the center from Toronto, Ontario, became known simply as "Pete." Pete then played two seasons for the Rangers following this trade, picking up a career high eleven assists in the 1955-56 season.

Sans five games played with the Toronto Maple Leafs in the 1957-58 season, following his days with the Rangers, Conacher spent the next eleven seasons of his career at the AHL level, splitting time with the Buffalo Bisons and Hershey Bears. He retired in 1966.

Bill Gadsby, a twenty-season NHL veteran, was inducted into the Hall of Fame in 1970. However, despite his two decades of service with the Chicago Blackhawks, Rangers, and Detroit Red Wings - he'd never win the Stanley Cup.

With the Rangers, the defenseman from Calgary, Alberta, had the best seasons of his career - seven seasons in total. In two seasons on

108

Broadway (1955-56 and 1958-59), Gadsby eclipsed the 50-point mark with two seasons of 51 points a piece.

When Gadsby retired as an active player in 1966 (he later got into coaching), he was the all-time leader among NHL defensemen in points with 568 in all.

(This number was soon shattered by many different factors, as with each passing era, there is more of an emphasis on offensive defensemen. Also of note: Ray Bourque is now the all-time leader with 1,579 points. As of this 2022 writing, Gadsby is now 51st overall, where his ranking will continue to drop as the years go by.)

On the other end of things, Rich Lamoureux, a left-winger from Calgary, Alberta, would never make it to the NHL. However, he had a lengthy fifteen-year career in the WHL playing for the Phoenix Roadrunners in the 1969-70 season.

Nick Mickoski, a right-winger from Winnipeg, Manitoba, had a solid career, amassing 703 games in the NHL. Following this trade, he played in parts of four seasons with the Blackhawks and had brief stints in both Detroit and Boston towards the end of his NHL career. (Once finishing with the Bruins following the 1959-60 season, he'd then play in five more seasons in the WHL, mainly for the San Francisco Seals.)

The biggest name going to Chicago, and much like Gadsby himself, was another Hall of Famer, Allan Stanley, who received this honor in 1970.

And similar to Gadsby, Stanley, a defenseman from Timmins, Ontario, also spent seven seasons with the Rangers - although his time with the Rangers began at the start of his NHL career. (Stanley was also part of the 1950 Stanley Cup Finalist team.)

Despite playing well in Chicago for two seasons, Stanley was sent off to Boston, where he'd also have two more good seasons. Up next for Stanley were the best and prime years of his career, as from

1958-1968, he became the key cog of the Toronto Maple Leafs' blue line.

Having never won the Stanley Cup prior to arriving in Toronto, Stanley (it was his namesake, after all!) went on to win four championships (1962, 1963, 1964, and 1967).

And yes, as a 1967 Toronto Maple Leafs' member, Allan is part of the last Leafs squad to win the Stanley Cup. The more you know!

Both Stanley and Gadsby were Hall of Fame defensemen, but at the time - the Rangers never had enough firepower to win the top prize of hockey.

It's tough to determine who won this trade, but since the Blackhawks made the mistake of not only giving Gadsby up but by moving on from Stanley - I'd give Boucher one last win on his record.

Up next is the third general manager of franchise history - Muzz Patrick.

Frederick Murray Patrick, better known as "Muzz," followed the footsteps of his father, Lester Patrick and Frank Boucher, as he played, coached, and managed the Rangers. And yep - he's profiled in my first book! (I know these reminders get old, I apologize!)

Photo Credit: Patrick Family archives. The original photographer is unknown. This picture has been deemed licensable by Creative Common Usage laws and has also been featured in the Hall of Fame's archives.

## MUZZ PATRICK

Tenure as Rangers General Manager: April 22, 1955 – October 30, 1964

At one point, it felt like Lester's son, Muzz's older brother, Lynn Patrick, was destined to become the third general manager in Rangers' history. Instead, Lynn was only the third head coach in franchise history.

When Frank Boucher decided to step away from the Rangers' bench and focus on his general manager role midway through the 1948-49 season, perhaps in a case of "paying it forward," Boucher hired his former teammate and a player he coached in the 1940 Stanley Cup Final, Lynn Patrick.

In his first full season as head coach of the Rangers, Lynn Patrick brought the team to the 1950 Stanley Cup Final. Things were looking good. However, following the deep playoff run, Lynn was up for a new contract. Boucher offered Lester's son $9,000. Boston offered Lynn $3,000 more, a sum of $12,000. When Boucher wouldn't match the Bruins' offer, Lynn, a Class of 1980 Hockey Hall of Famer, moved on, and never worked for the Rangers again.

When Lynn shipped up to Boston, Boucher, now in need of a head coach, did what men in his position at the time did - went to their friends, former teammates, and/or players they had previously coached. However, Boucher's buddies and fellow Hall of Fame men, Neil Colville (Class of 1967) and Bill Cook (Class of 1952), didn't pan out. Colville had health issues while Cook had on-ice problems, the team wasn't any good, and he found it hard to coach a roster he didn't build.

Following the departures of Colville and Cook, Boucher returned to the Rangers' bench for a short while. Then, after forty games coached in the 1954-55 season, Boucher replaced himself with Muzz Patrick. Like Lynn, Muzz played under Boucher for the 1940 Stanley Cup champions.

While it was somewhat expected that Muzz would eventually succeed Boucher (providing there were no issues), as Boucher once succeeded Lester, no one knew how soon that day would come.

Prior to his forced resignation, Boucher had told the Rangers' owner, General John Kilpatrick, that maybe it was time to leave. Kilpatrick rebuked Boucher's offer, but following another poor finish (fifth place at the end of the 1954-55 season), Kilpatrick gracefully suggested that now was the time for Boucher and the Rangers to end their 29-year relationship. In other words, instead of firing Boucher, Kilpatrick allowed Boucher to resign with his head held high. Once accepting Boucher's resignation, Kilpatrick hired his head coach to manage the team.

Muzz was like many players of his generation - he had the prime years of his playing career robbed by World War II. The former
112

boxer and NHL defenseman spent four years serving the U.S. military, reaching the rank of captain.

Muzz tried to make a comeback after the war, but the 1945-46 season was his last as a player. When Boucher first hired him as a coach, Muzz had spent the past six years coaching various teams in various leagues.

As general manager, Patrick himself (as he would go behind the bench whenever transitioning between coaches) made six head coaching changes in his nine-year tenure. None of this worked, as the Rangers qualified for the playoffs only four times, where once in the postseason, his team was heartily trampled over in the first round on each occasion.

While Muzz was always well-liked and respected, of the longer-tenured general managers in Rangers' history - had the least amount of success. Of course, his era didn't do him any favors, either, much like his predecessors, but at least his father and Boucher reached a Stanley Cup Final.

One of the biggest knocks on Muzz was that he allowed one of his best friends and another fellow 1940 Cup champ, Phil Watson, to stay behind the Rangers' bench for four seasons.

For as admired and respected as Muzz was, Watson was the complete opposite - especially in his relations with his players and the media. That said, Watson reached the playoffs three times under Muzz, or in other words - 75% of all Ranger postseason appearances.

While Muzz knocked out a lot of his competition throughout his boxing and hockey days, his track record as general manager had more losses than wins. Nevertheless, he was the man behind two mega trades that led Gump Worsley and Andy Bathgate to Stanley Cup championships elsewhere.

One of Patrick's biggest trades, his acquisition of Red Kelly, was voided, shot down when Kelly made it clear that he'd retire before joining a poor team like the Rangers. It was just another blow in a timespan full of them. It would take a new voice to turn the Rangers around, the roar of a "Cat."

Hall of Famers such as Andy Bathgate, Gump Worsley, and Doug Harvey (pictured) were legendary players Muzz Patrick included in his trades.

Photo Credit: The July 1962 issue of the now long defunct and French-Canadian based "Sport Revue" magazine. This photo is reprinted under Creative Common Usage laws.

## DATE OF TRADE: August 18th, 1955

## RANGERS ACQUIRE: Dave Creighton and Bronco Horvath

## DETROIT RED WINGS ACQUIRE: Billy Dea, Adolph "Aggie" Kukulowicz, and Cash

In Muzz Patrick's first trade, which took place prior to the commencement of the 1955-56 season, the new general manager picked up two players who would help the Rangers qualify for the playoffs.

Dave Creighton, a center from Port Arthur, Ontario, played three seasons with the Rangers, where he had the best years of his career with the Blueshirts. Creighton's best season took place in the 1957-58 campaign, finishing with 17 goals and 35 assists, good for a career high of 52 points.

In addition, after five seasons with no playoffs, Creighton was a piece of three-consecutive Ranger postseason runs.

Over his twenty-year career, Creighton played in 800 AHL games and 616 NHL games. He retired in 1969 and briefly got into coaching.

Bronco Horvath (his real name, as "Bronco" wasn't a nickname) was another center, but he didn't have as much success with the Rangers as Creighton did. Horvath, of Hungarian descent, was born in Port Colborne, Ontario, and later returned to the club for the 1962-63 season. However, he lasted parts of only two seasons with the Rangers in his first run.

Horvath found his most success later on in his career with the Bruins. In Boston, he was part of the "Uke" line with Ukrainian-Canadians Johnny Bucyk and Vic Stasiuk, with Horvath competing for the Hart and Art Ross Trophy in the 1959-60 season.

Going the other way was Billy Dea, a center from Calgary, Alberta, who had previously played fourteen games for the Rangers during the 1953-54 season. Dea wouldn't last long in Detroit, as he played in only parts of two seasons there before moving on to Chicago. Following a short stint with the Blackhawks, Dea spent nearly the next decade of his life at the AHL level playing for Buffalo Bisons.

Dea would get one more chance at the NHL following "The Great Expansion of 1967." At the time, he was 34 years old and still "young" enough to play at a high level. Once the league doubled in size, Dea bounced around the Blackhawk, Red Wing, and Penguin organizations before retiring in 1972. Throughout his nineteen seasons as a player, he also played in the AHL and WHL. He later got into coaching, working in Detroit for nine years.

Aggie Kukulowicz is the most interesting name of the lot - but not for what he did on the ice. In fact, the 1953-1954 season was Kukulowicz's last season with the Rangers, when he played in only one game. That one game would be his last in the NHL, as overall, he finished his NHL career with four games played.

116

The man who dropped his first name because of World War II was a center born in Winnipeg, Manitoba, and later became an international figure.

Kukulowicz would never break through in Detroit, so instead, he spent nearly a dozen years playing at the WHL and IHL levels. He also played in senior ice hockey leagues.

Kukulowicz's life story was fascinating because he spoke multiple languages, including Russian and Polish. The multi-linguist took his mastery of language and used that to extend his days in the hockey world, serving both the IIHF and Alan Eagleson as an interpreter. He also served as an interpreter for the Prime Minister of Canada, which is why Kukulowicz was known as the "Henry Kissinger of Hockey!"

As far as the trade itself, Patrick earned a win in his first transaction. While Horvath would have better years elsewhere, Creighton's seasons with the Rangers give the 1940 Stanley Cup winner the nod.

**DATE OF TRADE: August 29th, 1955**

**RANGERS ACQUIRE: Tom McCarthy**

**TORONTO MAPLE LEAFS ACQUIRE: $2,000**

Tom McCarthy, a left-winger from Toronto, Ontario, never played for the Rangers. Instead, he was sent to the Providence Reds (AHL).

McCarthy would later play in sixty NHL games with the Red Wings and Bruins. In essence, this was a $2,000 gamble that didn't pay off - but this didn't hurt the Rangers either.

**DATE OF TRADE: June 19th, 1956**

**RANGERS ACQUIRE: George "Red" Sullivan**

**CHICAGO BLACKHAWKS ACQUIRE: Wally Hergesheimer**

Muzz Patrick didn't know at the time that Red Sullivan would soon become his head coach, which first began during the 1962-63 season. Something else Patrick didn't know? Sullivan's tenure as head coach helped lead to Patrick's eventual dismissal in New York.

Ironically, Emile "The Cat" Francis would succeed both of these men at both the head coach and general manager positions.

By the time Sullivan, from Peterborough, Ontario, joined the Rangers for the 1956-57 season, he was already an NHL veteran, having spent time in both Boston and Chicago. Sullivan would spend the final five years of his career with the Rangers, where after his first season in New York - he'd spend the rest of his career as team captain.

The southpaw centerman saw the Rangers experience many lean years. After a first-round exit in the 1958 Stanley Cup Playoffs (a six-game series loss to the Bruins), Sullivan, as both a player and a coach, wouldn't see the playoffs again.

Wally Hergesheimer, a right-winger, began his NHL career with the Rangers starting in the 1951-52 season. Following a down season in Chicago, Hergesheimer spent the following season in the AHL for the Buffalo Bisons.

Patrick would bring back the native of Winnipeg, Manitoba, into the fold for the 1958-59 season, but the comeback was short-lived. After 22 return games in the Big Apple, Hergesheimer finished his career at the AHL and WHL levels.

This trade was another easy win for Patrick, and depending on what you think about his later trades - perhaps the biggest victory of his tenure too.

**DATE OF TRADE: November 4th, 1956**

**RANGERS ACQUIRE: Cash**

**MONTREAL CANADIENS ACQUIRE: Bronco Horvath**

Following this trade, Bronco Horvath played in only one game for the Habs during the 1956-57 campaign, while also playing in 56 games for the Rochester Americans (AHL).

As mentioned earlier, Horvath found his groove in Boston, with his linemates playing a big part.

When it comes to this trade specifically, the extra money in the Rangers' bank account was a win - although Horvath would later come back to burn the Rangers as a Bruin.

**DATE OF TRADE: January 22nd, 1957**

**RANGERS ACQUIRE: Norm Defelice, Future Considerations (Floyd Smith), and Jack Bionda (Loan)**

**BOSTON BRUINS ACQUIRE: Don Simmons**

This was a rare goalie trade, as Don Simmons took his pads to Beantown. At the time, the Bruins needed a goaltender after Terry Sawchuk temporarily retired from hockey. (Sawchuk had mental health issues in the days when the phrase "mental health" wasn't a thing.)

Simmons, from Port Colborne, Ontario, would have some decent seasons in Boston, but he'd later find his most success in Toronto, where he won three consecutive Stanley Cups (1962, 1963, and 1964).

On the Rangers end of things, Norm Defelice, another goaltender, played in ten games with the Bruins before coming to New York. Defelice, born in Schumacher, Ontario, would never play in the NHL again after this trade. Instead, he spent the bulk of his next thirteen seasons playing in the Eastern Hockey League.

Floyd Smith, from Perth, Ontario, was a sparingly used right-winger while in Boston. He wouldn't crack into the Rangers' lineup until the 1960-61 season, where he played in only 29 games. He picked up fourteen points that season.

Despite not having much success in Boston or New York, Smith would later go on to play in 616 NHL games, where he also played for the Red Wings, Maple Leafs, and Sabres.

It was in Buffalo - while as a Sabre - where he made connections. Following Smith's retirement at the end of the 1971-72 season, he would soon become the team's head coach, leading the franchise to the 1975 Stanley Cup Final. (A six-game series loss to "The Broadstreet Bullies," aka the Philadelphia Flyers.)

Jack Bionda, a defenseman from Huntsville, Ontario, now on loan to the Rangers, never played for the team.

Outside of thirteen games played with the Maple Leafs, Bionda spent his entire NHL career (93 games) with the Bruins. However, hockey was secondary for the rearguard. Instead, it was the sport of lacrosse where Bionda shone most, as he was considered (and still is to this day) one of the greatest Canadian lacrosse players of all time.

While Smith and Simmonds went on to have solid careers, it's tough to decide if this trade was a win or a loss - especially considering that most NHL teams were still under the one-goalie system. This trade didn't give either team a significant edge.

**DATE OF TRADE: June 1st, 1957 (Approximate date, exact date unknown)**

**RANGERS ACQUIRE: Hank Ciesla**

**CHICAGO BLACKHAWKS ACQUIRE: Ron Murphy**

Hank Ciesla, a left-handed centerman from Saint Catharines, Ontario, spent the 1957-58 and 1958-59 seasons with the Rangers, where he amassed 28 points in total. Following his second season in New York, Ciesla spent the final six seasons of his career at the AHL level.

Beginning with the 1952-53 season, Ron Murphy, a left-winger from Hamilton, Ontario, spent parts of five seasons with the

120

Rangers. Following this trade, Murphy spent twelve more seasons in the NHL, playing with the Blackhawks, Red Wings, and Bruins.

In comparison, Murphy played in 889 NHL games, finishing with 479 career points. Ciesla played in 269 NHL games, finishing his career with 77 points.

Needless to say, this trade was a loss on Patrick's ledger.

**DATE OF TRADE: June 4th, 1957**

**RANGERS ACQUIRE: $15,000**

**TORONTO MAPLE LEAFS ACQUIRE: Pete Conacher**

Pete Conacher, who at this time was fully supplanted in the AHL as a member of the Buffalo Bisons, would only play in five games with the Leafs during the 1957-58 season. Aside from these five games, Conacher spent the years of 1955-1966 as an AHLer, where he also played for Hershey Bears.

A cool $15,000 for a player who would play in only five more NHL games is an easy win for Mr. Patrick.

**DATE OF TRADE: December 21st, 1958**

**RANGERS ACQUIRE: $7,500, Future Considerations, and Ray Cyr (Loan)**

**CHICAGO BLACKHAWKS ACQUIRE: Phil Maloney**

A southpaw center, Phil Maloney, from Ottawa, Ontario, never played with the Rangers. Instead, he played for the Vancouver Canucks (WHL), who at the time were a Rangers' farm team.

Once in Chicago, Maloney spent parts of two seasons there, playing in 45 games and picking up fourteen points. At the start of the 1959-60 season, Maloney played mainly for the Buffalo Bisons of the AHL before returning to Vancouver for nine more seasons.

Three seasons following his retirement, at the start of the 1973-74 season, Maloney became the head coach of the Vancouver Canucks - now of the NHL.

Like Maloney, Ray Cyr, another left-handed center, mostly plied his wares at both the AHL and WHL levels. Unlike Maloney, Cyr, from Campbellton, New Brunswick, never played an NHL game.

While Maloney played sporadically for the Blackhawks, this was basically a minor league player for another minor league player swap. This was another "no harm, no foul" trade in Rangers' history.

**DATE OF TRADE: October 3rd, 1959**

**RANGERS ACQUIRE: Noel Price**

**TORONTO MAPLE LEAFS ACQUIRE: Hank Ciesla, Bill Kennedy, and Future Considerations**

Born in Brockville, Ontario, Noel Price had a long NHL career that spanned two decades and 499 games. Along the way, Price, a six-foot-tall defenseman, won the Stanley Cup in 1966 with the Montreal Canadiens. In addition, Price was also an inaugural member of the Atlanta Flames, as NHL expansion (and the formation of the World Hockey Association) extended his days at the top level of hockey.

However, with the Rangers, Price played in only seven games across parts of two seasons, where he didn't pick up a point in any of them. (Price finished his career with 128 points.)

As mentioned, Ciesla wasn't long for the NHL. Neither was Bill Kennedy, a center from Toronto, Ontario, who never made it past the OHA level.

This trade was a small victory since Price continued to play in the NHL following this deal. Of course, the Rangers quickly cut bait on Price, but when it comes to this specific trade, Patrick gets his hand raised.

122

**DATE OF TRADE: February 5th, 1960 (Trade voided after Kelly and McNeil refused to report to the New York Rangers)**

**RANGERS ACQUIRE: Red Kelly and Billy McNeil**

**DETROIT RED WINGS ACQUIRE: Bill Gadsby and Eddie Shack**

One of the smartest things that Red Kelly ever did, and just like Former First Lady Nancy Reagan - he *"just said no"* to the Rangers.

At the time of the trade, Kelly was already a perennial All-Star and a four-time Stanley Cup champion. Like many before him, once having a falling out with Detroit boss Jack Adams (after the Wings' head honcho lied about a previous Kelly ankle injury) and after being dealt to New York - Kelly said he would rather retire than play for the Rangers.

Really, who could blame Kelly for his decision here? The Rangers were awful - especially during the past twenty years at this point, sans the miracle Stanley Cup Finalist run of 1950 - which took place ten years before this trade.

In addition, Kelly had other financial streams coming in, as he owned a bowling alley in his hometown of Simcoe, Ontario, and also spent time as a tools salesman in the offseason. In other words, he didn't need to be playing hockey in New York, a city that may as well have been in China.

After refusing to show up in New York, the trade was voided. Punch Imlach, the bench boss of the Leafs, then reached out, and the rest was history. Not only did Kelly convert from a defenseman to a forward, but he'd also win four more Stanley Cups, eight in all, and was inducted into the Hall of Fame in 1969.

During the latter years of his life, both the Toronto Maple Leafs and the Detroit Red Wings retired his #4 jersey, with his Red Wings honor taking place in February of 2019 - less than three months before Kelly passed away at the age of 91.

What could have been for the Rangers.

Of the other players involved, Billy McNeil, a center from Edmonton, Alberta, remained with the Wings, where he'd later play mainly at the minor-league level. (McNeil also refused to report to the Rangers in the wake of his wife's recent death, as he had a young daughter to raise.)

The Rangers moved power forward Eddie Shack, of Sudbury, Ontario, in the season that followed this voided deal - another mistake that will soon be covered. Ditto Bill Gadsby.

All in all, while this trade never took place, Patrick pooped the bed here. He let it be known that he wanted to move on from both Eddie Shack and Bill Gadsby, two players who, once being traded, would continue to have healthy NHL careers. Red Kelly was the big fish the Rangers couldn't reel in. Another "what if" question for a franchise full of them.

**DATE OF TRADE: February 20th, 1960**

**RANGERS ACQUIRE: Al Rollins**

**CHICAGO BLACKHAWKS ACQUIRE: Cash, Future Considerations, and Ray Mikulan (Loan)**

In 1951, goaltender Al Rollins, then with the Maple Leafs, won both the Vezina Trophy and the Stanley Cup. Three years later, he'd win the Hart Trophy, too, although as a member of the Blackhawks. However, by the time Rollins got to the Rangers, they already had a great starting goalie in Lorne "Gump" Worsley.

In turn, Rollins, from Vanguard, Saskatchewan, would only play in ten games for the Rangers at the end of the 1959-60 season, where he went 3-4-3; these would be the final ten games of his career.

Ray Mikulan, a fellow goalie born in Winnipeg, Manitoba, never cracked into the NHL in his ten-year career. Instead, he played at the minor-league level, splitting time between the WHL, EHL, and IHL.

The Rangers had to make this trade because Worsley had severed a tendon in his pinkie finger, thus ending his season. Rollins was just a stop-gap solution, a band-aid for a temporary problem on a team that finished in last place following the last game played of the 1959-60 season.

In other words, no winner or loser here - of course - except for the Rangers themselves and their last-place finish.

**DATE OF TRADE: August 1st, 1960 (Approximate date, exact date unknown)**

**RANGERS ACQUIRE: Barry Cullen**

**DETROIT RED WINGS ACQUIRE: Pete Conacher**

Barry Cullen (first name Charles), was a right-winger from Ottawa, Ontario, and who played in 219 career NHL games with the Leafs and Red Wings prior to this deal. However, following this trade, he'd never play in the NHL again. Instead, he spent four more seasons at the AHL level with the Buffalo Bisons.

As mentioned earlier, Pete Conacher (who, ironically, had the first name of Charles, too) remained at the AHL level, where he also finished out his career.

This trade was the textbook definition of "Even-Steven."

**DATE OF TRADE: November 7th, 1960**

**RANGERS ACQUIRE: Pat Hannigan and Johnny Wilson**

**TORONTO MAPLE LEAFS ACQUIRE: Eddie Shack**

Yikes. Talk about a bad trade.

After the voided Red Kelly trade, Patrick still looked to move on from left-winger Eddie Shack. In turn, Shack would go on to play for fifteen more seasons. Shack would also go on to win four

125

Stanley Cups with the Leafs in 1962, 1963, 1964, and 1967. (Shack was also an NHL All-Star from 1962-1964.)

Pat Hannigan, also a left-winger, played in two seasons with the Rangers (1960-61 and 1961-62.) After picking up 44 points with the Rangers, the native of Timmins, Ontario, then spent the next ten years of his career mainly at the WHL and AHL levels - sans a 72-game stint with the then-new expansion Philadelphia Flyers. Needless to say, Hannigan wasn't Shack.

Johnny Wilson, from Kincardine, Ontario, is the third and final left-winger involved in this trade. Similar to Hannigan, Wilson spent parts of the next two seasons with the Rangers, too - his last two seasons - as he retired following the 1961-62 season.

By the time Wilson arrived in New York, he had already amassed four Stanley Cups (all with Detroit - 1950, 1952, 1954, and 1955), but as was evident based on his 1962 retirement - he was at the end of the line.

Following Wilson's retirement, he would later get into coaching at the collegiate and WHA levels. He would also coach at the NHL level, including stints with the Los Angeles Kings, Detroit Red Wings, Colorado Rockies, and Pittsburgh Penguins.

There's no easy way to say this - this trade was an absolute bust.

Even if Eddie "The Entertainer" was considered to be *"tempestuous,"* as he was branded at the time - the Rangers should have either embraced that or asked for a better return.

**DATE OF TRADE: June 12th, 1961**

**RANGERS ACQUIRE: Les Hunt and Cash**

**DETROIT RED WINGS ACQUIRE: Bill Gadsby**

This trade was another bomb - the second of two-consecutive huge mistakes from the office of Muzz Patrick.

After being dealt to Detroit, Gadsby would play for the Red Wings for five more seasons. He would later become the head coach of the club too.

Les Hunt, a defenseman from Schreiber, Ontario, never played one game in the NHL. Instead, he spent most of his career, thirteen seasons, in the WHL.

It's tough to say which trade was worse - this one or the one that preceded it.

On the one hand, Eddie Shack became a legend in Toronto. At least the Rangers got parts of two seasons out of Hannigan and Wilson - a silver lining for sure.

On the other hand, the Rangers received nothing of value in return for their Hall of Fame player.

These two trades were pretty much the beginning of the end for Patrick, but he extended his stay for a bit following his next moves.

**DATE OF TRADE: June 13th, 1961 (Separate Trades)**

**RANGERS ACQUIRE: Doug Harvey and Albert Langlois**

**MONTREAL CANADIENS ACQUIRE: Lou Fontinato and John Hanna**

"Leapin" Louie Fontinato, a fan favorite in his day, is most famously known for a February 1st, 1959 fight with Gordie Howe - a fight that "Mr. Hockey" easily won. In fact, that tilt, to this day, is still considered to be one of the most vicious fights in NHL history.

Fontinato, who was featured in my first book, was born in Guelph, Ontario. Later on, he would become known as the great-uncle of two-time Ranger, Greg McKegg.

The defenseman would play for the Canadiens for the next two seasons. He was forced into retirement after a March 9th, 1963 game with the Rangers, when he missed a check on Vic Hadfield and went directly head-first into the boards. This injury paralyzed the bruiser for a month and ended his days as a player.

John Hanna, a defenseman from Sydney, Nova Scotia, played on some lean Ranger teams. Following this trade, he spent the next fourteen seasons primarily at the minor-league level. He also played six games for the Habs in the 1963-64 season and then in fifteen more games with the expansion Flyers for the 1967-68 season. Most of his career was with the Quebec Aces (AHL) and the Seattle Totems (WHL).

Albert Langlois, a defenseman from Magog, Quebec, was a three-time Stanley Cup champ with the Canadiens (1958, 1959, and 1960). He had three solid seasons with the Rangers before moving on to the Detroit Red Wings organization.

His last season in the NHL took place in the 1965-66 campaign, where he played in Boston, where in a "fun fact," he was the second-last Boston Bruin ever to wear the number four. But, as you may have figured out, Bobby Orr soon took over the Bruins' blue line and made #4 synonymous with himself.

The star of this trade was Doug Harvey, who, like Bobby Orr, is considered one of the greatest NHL defensemen of all time. Whenever fans, players, or anyone else discuss who the greatest defenseman of all time was, it boils down to a discussion between Harvey and Orr.

Before joining the Rangers, Harvey, born in Montreal, Quebec, was a season-in-season-out All-Star, playing in the All-Star Game eleven times. (He would play in two more, one with the Rangers in 1962 and one with the St. Louis Blues in 1969.)

More impressively, Harvey also won six Norris Trophies, adding a seventh to his mantle as a Ranger in 1962.

Harvey was also a six-time Stanley Cup champion, winning the biggest prize in hockey in 1953, 1956, 1957, 1958, 1959, and 1960.

So why would the Montreal Canadiens want to trade one of the greatest, if not *the* greatest, defenseman of all time, a hometown hero, and a defenseman who was eventually inducted into the Hockey Hall of Fame in 1973? One word - "money."

As one of the best players in the NHL, Harvey was grossly underpaid - just like every other player in this era and the eras that preceded him. (It wasn't until the "Great Expansion," the advent of the WHA, and an NHL Players' Union that players started to see real money. After all, most NHLers had off-season jobs prior to these three events.)

Things first started going south when before the 1960-61 season, Doug Harvey was named as Montreal's team captain - a decision that didn't sit well with Habs' General Manager Frank Selke.

Despite winning a load of Stanley Cups with Harvey on the Montreal blue line, Selke blamed Harvey for the Habs' six-game 1961 playoff semifinal loss to the Chicago Blackhawks - a Chicago team that went on to win the Stanley Cup in six games, too, when they knocked off the Detroit Red Wings.

Keep in mind - prior to this 1961 loss, the Canadiens had just won five-straight Stanley Cups. What would Selke have done if he was in charge of the Rangers?!?!

Like all NHL general managers of this era, Harvey also got on Selke's nerves and mentioned the "u" word, as in union. As one of the league's top stars, Harvey was not happy about his paltry salary, a figure slightly under $27,000 in his peak years.

Harvey was also loudly advocating for the NHL to eliminate the reserve clause, a one-sided clause that allowed NHL teams to control players' rights for as long as they wanted. The NHL owners and general managers had all the power, and Harvey was one of the most vocal critics of this unfair condition.

Fed up with Harvey's often (and powerful) complaints, Selke decided to move on from Harvey - despite his team's captain still playing at a remarkably high level.

Muzz Patrick, who saw the opportunity, took Selke's call, where the Rangers' general manager also wondered if Harvey would be interested in becoming head coach of the Blueshirts.

After all, Patrick, just two years prior, had to fire one of his best friends, the "Fiery" Phil Watson, after his buddy's never-ending battles with both his players and the media.

Following Watson's firing, Patrick jumped in and out from behind the Rangers' bench and had problems with Watson's replacement, former Ranger Alf Pike. In a complete 180 from Watson, it was thought that Pike was "too nice" and not stern enough as an NHL head coach.

(Of course, missing the playoffs more times than not, and not having won a Stanley Cup in 21 years at this point didn't help matters either.)

After negotiating with both Selke and Harvey, Harvey accepted Patrick's dual-role offer as a player-coach under one condition - he wanted a three-year contract as opposed to the standard two-year contract that was offered. Patrick quickly agreed, signing Harvey for three years at $25,000 per season ($75,000 overall guaranteed).

In Harvey's first season with the Rangers (where he was also the team's head coach), he won the Norris Trophy and was named to the All-Star Game. Even better for the franchise, the Rangers snapped a three-season playoff drought, their season ultimately ending in the first round after a six-game series loss to the Toronto Maple Leafs.

Even with the playoff loss, Harvey had already accomplished more than Watson and Pike did as head coaches. Heck, he performed better than Muzz Patrick too!

However, Harvey wasn't a fan of coaching. The 1961-62 season would be his first and last season as bench boss. Former Ranger (and as mentioned earlier) Red Sullivan would replace Harvey, creating an interesting dynamic - as the new head coach was coaching the team's previous head coach!

With Harvey still in the lineup, the Rangers would miss the playoffs the next two seasons.

However, during the 1963-64 campaign, Harvey's last season as a Ranger, he grew disinterested in the pro game and returned to his native Montreal, Quebec, to join the Quebec Aces. He would return to the NHL three years later with a quick two-game stint with the Detroit Red Wings. Two seasons later, in the 1968-69 season, he would retire after playing seventy games with the St. Louis Blues.

Going into this trade, Muzz Patrick held all the cards since Selke wanted Harvey away from him. This trade was an easy win for Patrick, as not only was Harvey successful, but Langlois played better than expected. With Fontinato's injury and Hanna's status as mostly a career minor leaguer - Patrick won this trade in a landslide.

**DATE OF TRADE: September 1st, 1961 (Approximate date, exact date unknown)**

**RANGERS ACQUIRE: Cash**

**CHICAGO BLACKHAWKS ACQUIRE: Art Stratton**

This wasn't much of a trade, as Art Stratton, a southpaw center from Winnipeg, Manitoba, only played in two games for the Blackhawks after returning to the club following a short stint with the Detroit Red Wings.

Most of Stratton's success took place in the minor leagues, where he won various league MVP awards and championships. It wouldn't be until the "Great Expansion" when Stratton became a full-time NHLer, playing 58 games for the Pittsburgh Penguins in the 1967-68 season.

Long story short, this was a financial transaction and a "ho-hum" small win for Patrick.

**DATE OF TRADE: February 15th, 1962**

**RANGERS ACQUIRE: Pete Goegan and Cash**

**DETROIT RED WINGS ACQUIRE: Noel Price**

As mentioned earlier, Price had his success away from the Rangers. However, he'd have to wait a bit for that, as he only played in twenty games for the Red Wings.

Like Stratton, the "Great Expansion" extended Price's NHL career. (After his time with the Wings, Price spent three seasons at the AHL level before resuming his NHL career in Montreal.)

Pete Goegan, a defenseman like Price from Fort William, Ontario, played in only seven games for the Rangers. Following his short stint on Broadway, Goegan spent the next four seasons bouncing back and forth between the Detroit Red Wings and their AHL affiliate, the Pittsburgh Hornets. And, like Price, NHL expansion also kept Goegan going, as he played for the Minnesota North Stars for their 1967-68 inaugural season.

This was another wash of a trade. While Price had the better career of the two, neither the Rangers or the Wings got burnt here.

**DATE OF TRADE: February 6th, 1963**

**RANGERS ACQUIRE: Don McKenney and Dick Meissner**

**BOSTON BRUINS ACQUIRE: Dean Prentice**

Similar to the Shack and Gadsby trades, this was another nail in Patrick's coffin, although not the final one.

In this transaction, Patrick dealt away a huge fan favorite, left-winger Dean Prentice who had played for the club for eleven-consecutive seasons before this deal.

(Of note: while I did mention Dean Prentice's name in my "New York Rangers Rink of Honor and the Rafters of Madison Square Garden" book in the omissions segment, many people who told me that I erred big-time. They all felt that Prentice was a no-doubt candidate.

One of those people? Walt Tkaczuk himself!

And perhaps once this particular book you're reading is published, I'll publish an updated version of the Rink of Honor, as there are about fifty or so names that can be included!)

Prentice, a native of Schumacher, Ontario, ultimately finished his NHL career with 1,378 games played (a devilish 666 games with the Rangers). Following this deal, Prentice spent the next eleven seasons of his career with the Bruins, Red Wings, Penguins, and North Stars.

While not posting similar numbers in Boston as he did in New York, as is evident having played in 712 more games in the NHL once leaving the Rangers, he was far from done. (Ironically, Prentice's best offensive season statistically was in the final half of his career in Detroit, with 55 points in the 1967-68 season.)

Don McKenney, who was already souring in Boston, was a center from Smith Falls, Ontario. He played in 76 games for the Rangers in parts of two seasons, finishing with a points total of 50. McKenney's place in Rangers' trading history would eventually become more profound with Patrick's second-to-last trade as the club's general manager.

After 36 games played in parts of two seasons with the Rangers, Dick Meissner, a right-winger from Kindersley, Saskatchewan, would soon be traded again. More importantly, Meissner's one game from the 1964-65 season would be his last NHL game, as he returned to the minor leagues. Once there, he extended his professional career for ten more seasons.

This was another big-time fail from Patrick. It was also another trade that soon led to the end of his tenure.

**DATE OF TRADE: June 4th, 1963**

**RANGERS ACQUIRE: Phil Goyette, Don Marshall, and Jacques Plante**

**MONTREAL CANADIENS ACQUIRE: Dave Balon, Leon Rochefort, Len Ronson, and Lorne "Gump" Worsley**

While not exactly "The Trade" of 1975, when Phil Esposito, Jean Ratelle, and Brad Park were the biggest names to trade locations, this was also a blockbuster trade. It was also somewhat of a last-ditch effort to change the club's fortunes.

Lorne "Gump" Worsley and Phil Goyette are extensively featured in "The New York Rangers Rink of Honor and the Rafters of Madison Square Garden." I will try not to repeat what I wrote in that book here.

When it comes to Worsley, born in Montreal, Quebec, the biggest principle of this trade going to Montreal is much irony. For starters, he and Jacques Plante, the other big name in this trade, did not get along. While the word "despise" may be a severe exaggeration, regardless, the two could not be any more like night and day.

Also ironic was that Worsley in New York was like Doug Harvey in Montreal - he wanted an NHL Players' union. Once that "u" word was mentioned, Patrick quickly looked to get Worsley out of town, where, after trading him, Patrick didn't tell Worsley that he was traded.

Patrick's failure to let his goalie know that he was traded ultimately led to Worsley never having anything to do with the Rangers again - despite his status as one of the few franchise goaltenders in team history. Worsley said as much in his autobiography, "They Call Me Gump."

134

Another thing mentioned in Worsley's memoirs - his never-ending battle to get a pay raise, where over $500, the Rangers, during the 1953-54 season, sent him to the Vancouver Canucks, one of their affiliates at the time, as a form of punishment. The season prior, Worsley won the Calder Trophy, making this demotion over a $500 squabble even more insulting.

Many hockey historians and Ranger fans consider this trade a loss because Jacques Plante, born in Shawinigan Falls, Quebec, didn't pan out with the Rangers, while Worsley won all his hardware in Montreal.

In comparison, Plante won six Stanley Cups and six Vezina Trophies in Montreal. He also won the Hart Trophy in 1962. Following the trade, Plante would win one more Vezina in 1969 - in St. Louis - where he shared the trophy with teammate Glenn Hall.

The other Hall of Fame goalie (Plante and Hall, too, for that matter, were eventually enshrined), Gump Worsley, went on to win four Stanley Cups and two Vezina Trophies in Montreal. Previously, the only hardware he had with the Rangers was the aforementioned Calder Trophy - and look where that got him! A one-way ticket to Vancouver!

What's often lost in the Plante vs. Worsley debate following this trade is that the Montreal Canadiens were world-beaters and had every advantage of the league in their favor. Any halfway decent goalie would have won multiple Stanley Cups and Vezina Trophies with the Habs in this era. The New York Rangers were in a dark age, which rocked Plante's world.

After all, there is a reason why Worsley, in his Ranger years, when asked, *"what team gives you the most trouble?"* - promptly replied with *"The Rangers!"*

Plante's two seasons with the Rangers were the worst of his career, which was truly an indictment on the team in front of him. Once leaving New York, Plante would return to prime form, where he had outstanding seasons in both St. Louis and Toronto, where his goals-allowed average and save percentage were actually better than the numbers he posted in his glory years in Montreal.

So yeah - Plante's run in New York was his worst, but the Rangers were much worse at the time.

As far as the skater faces trading places, Phil Goyette, a center from Lachine, Quebec, had six strong seasons with the Rangers. Lost in Montreal's depth (where he was part of a checking line), Goyette thrived in New York. He was a tremendous acquisition on behalf of Patrick.

Donnie Marshall, from Verdun, Quebec, was Goyette's left-winger in Montreal. Marshall won the Stanley Cup with his centerman four times, in 1957, 1958, 1959, and in 1960. Marshall also won another Stanley Cup with the Habs in 1956 as well, which made him a five-time Stanley Cup champ at the time of this trade.

Just like Goyette, Marshall also had an impressive run in New York, playing for the Rangers in seven different seasons. Marshall also set career highs with the Rangers, where during the 1965-66 season, he had 26 goals, 28 assists, and 54 points - the best scoring totals of his career.

Yes, while Plante didn't have the best defensive teams in front of him, offensively, both Marshall and Goyette thrived in New York.

Going to Montreal was left-winger Len Ronson, who, aside from five games with the Oakland Seals during the 1968-69 season (where he didn't record a single point while playing on a historically bad team), the native of Brantford, Ontario, never played in the NHL again.

Centerman Leon Rochefort, from Cap-de-la-Madeleine, Quebec, couldn't crack Montreal's deep lineup until many years later, although with one game played in the 1965-66 season and four more games played in the 1966 Stanley Cup Playoffs, he did get his name on the Stanley Cup. He'd win it again in 1971 as a regular roster member, but following the parade, he soon found himself with the Red Wings.

Dave Balon, a left-winger from Wakaw, Saskatchewan, was the most successful skater of the Rangers going to Montreal. Balon first became a full-time Ranger during the 1961-62 season. Now in Montreal, he would win two Stanley Cups (1965 and 1966). Ironically, Balon would eventually find himself back in New York for the Emile Francis era.

After being claimed by the Minnesota North Stars during the 1967 expansion draft, Francis traded for Balon, where the left-winger returned to his first club at the start of the 1968-69 season. Along with Bill Fairbairn and Walt Tkaczuk, Balon would become one-third of the famous "Bulldog" line, a featured trio in the peak Francis years.

In summary, while the Canadiens would continue their winning ways (something that the Rangers couldn't prevent), the Rangers received two outstanding players in Goyette and Marshall. And since Balon eventually returned to the Blueshirts, it's tough to claim this trade was a flat-out loss like others do.

In my eyes, this trade is a win - even if the standings wouldn't suggest as much. After all, it just wasn't the Rangers - not many teams could impede all the winning in Montreal.

**DATE OF TRADE: February 14th, 1964**

**RANGERS ACQUIRE: Ron Ingram**

**DETROIT RED WINGS ACQUIRE: Albert Langlois**

As mentioned earlier, Albert Langlois had three decent seasons in New York. He'd hang on with the Red Wings for parts of two seasons before ultimately finishing his NHL career with the Bruins, which took place following the 1965-66 season.

Defenseman Ron Ingram, from Toronto, Ontario, finished out the 1963-64 season with the Rangers. He played three games with the Rangers in the following season - the final three NHL games of his career.

Since Langlois had a longer career (and better stats), this trade was a loss, but not a major loss on Patrick's record.

**DATE OF TRADE: February 22nd, 1964**

**RANGERS ACQUIRE: Bob Nevin, Dick Duff, Bill Collins, Arnie Brown, and Rod Seiling**

**TORONTO MAPLE LEAFS ACQUIRE: Don McKenney and Andy Bathgate**

Despite Patrick's previous trades involving Eddie Shack, Bill Gadsby, Gump Worsley, Dean Prentice and others, this trade was the biggest - especially when it comes to a Ranger going the other way. After all, Andy Bathgate's jersey (#9) remains in the rafters of Madison Square Garden to this day.

Throughout Bathgate's run in New York, the media considered him to be the best Ranger since the days of "The Bread Line" Blueshirts - Frank Boucher and the Cook brothers, Bill and Bun.

By the time this trade occurred, Bathgate, the center from Brampton, Ontario, had accumulated 272 goals, 457 assists, and 729 points in his 719 games played throughout twelve seasons of work with the Rangers. In other words - he averaged more than a point per game in his legendary run on Broadway - although a dark period of franchise history.

More impressive was that Bathgate was at the top of every pertinent all-time franchise scoring category at the time of this trade. Whether it was goals, assists, points, power-play goals, power-play assists - you name it - Bathgate's name was at the top of all scoring categories.

Of note: while this isn't a knock on Bathgate, he also played in an era of 70-game seasons as opposed to 48-games or fewer seasons than "The Bread Line" players played in, whose numbers Bathgate would eventually, and easily at that, blow by. The same logic also applies to the players who later broke Bathgate's records, as they played 80 games or more in seasons. This gives you the complete story. Either way, Bathgate was a generational Ranger - and that's a fact, not an opinion.

At the time of this trade, the Class of 1978 Hall of Famer had done it all with the Rangers; he won a Hart Trophy in 1959, played in All-Star Games (eight in all), and broke every scoring record possible. The only thing missing was the Stanley Cup.

As mentioned throughout this Muzz Patrick era, the Rangers weren't good. (I may have mentioned this once or a thousand times!)

In Bathgate's twelve seasons in New York, he only reached the playoffs four times - in a six-team league nonetheless! Even worse, in these four playoff appearances, the Rangers never got out of the first round.

Had Bathgate started his career anywhere besides New York, he would likely have multiple Stanley Cup wins in the first twelve years of his career.

Before this trade-deadline deal, it was widely known that Bathgate wanted a chance to play for the Stanley Cup. He started to get fed up a bit due to nagging injuries (mainly his knee), and like other long-time Rangers from this era - he was sick and tired of losing. (And while the phrase "mental health" was not a thing at the time, losing was, is, and always will be draining on one's psyche.)

Moving a fan favorite (the greatest Ranger of the last 25+ years) was no easy task at this point. This trade of Bathgate was even somewhat above Patrick's paygrade, as just two months before the deal, then-President of the Rangers William M. Jennings told the media that he would move Bathgate if he could get a fair return for him. (Jennings wanted established NHL players in exchange, not a bunch of young minor leaguers with potential.)

And have I mentioned yet that Andy Bathgate was the Rangers' captain at the time of this trade?

While Bathgate did have his injuries to contend with and expressed an interest in winning the Stanley Cup, following the trade, Bathgate said the following to the media:

*"Look what happened to me when the Rangers wanted to trade Jean Ratelle. I was captain at the time and I felt that I had something to say. I really put forth a case for keeping Ratelle, and Muzz Patrick told me right then and there, 'you're getting too big for your britches'. Right after that, I was history. I was traded because I spoke up for a guy who they didn't think was tough enough."*

The above quote may have been Bathgate speaking from an emotional standpoint. It's also a spoiler, as with one legend leaving, a new legend would soon be born, in "Gentleman" Jean Ratelle, who would soon become the center of the iconic "Goal a Game" (GAG) line.

But enough about Ratelle for now because you know he will take up a significant portion of this book once we get to 1975!

Two months and three days following this trade, Bathgate accomplished his goal - he won the Stanley Cup, as his new team, the Toronto Maple Leafs, defeated the Detroit Red Wings in seven games to take home the chalice.

After winning the Stanley Cup, Bathgate would spend one more season in Toronto. Following the 1964-65 season, Bathgate moved on when he was traded to the Detroit Red Wings. One of the greatest Rangers of all time would then spend two seasons in the Motor City. He'd ultimately end his NHL career with the Pittsburgh Penguins, which took place following the 1970-71 season.

140

Now retired, Bathgate switched leagues when he coached the Vancouver Blazers of the WHA for the 1973-74 season. He'd then play for the team in the 1974-75 season, thus briefly ending his retirement. However, he'd only play in eleven games for the Blazers before retiring for good.

Bathgate's career, which could fill a whole book in itself, was one of the best careers in NHL history, finishing with 349 goals and 624 assists, good for a point total of 973.

Just like how he could have won multiple Stanley Cups had he not spent most of his career with the Rangers, if Bathgate played his first twelve seasons elsewhere, he likely would have easily smashed the 1,000 career-points total.

One must truly understand how bad the Rangers were in Bathgate's heyday. Even on February 26th, 2016, when Bathgate passed away, his New York Times obituary headline read, *"Andy Bathgate, Standout on Dismal 1950s Rangers, Dies at 83."*

So that's Bathgate. How about everyone else?

Don McKenney, previously acquired in the big Dean Prentice trade (just like Bathgate), would remain in Toronto for the Stanley Cup victory and the season that followed.

After 24 games played with the Red Wings for the 1965-66 season, with some stops in between in the minors, McKenney finished his NHL career with the St. Louis Blues in their expansion/debut season.

Obviously, with Bathgate being the big name here, McKenney was kind of a "throw-in," as a way to balance out this trade.

While the Rangers lost the face of their franchise, they didn't come out as losers. Put it this way: of the five players acquired, two of them made my "New York Rangers Rink of Honor." Those two players were right-winger Bob Nevin from South Porcupine,

Ontario (who served the team as captain), and defenseman Rod Seiling from Elmira, Ontario.

Once the trade was complete, Patrick said the following to the media about his newest players:

*"We got two established hard-checking forwards in Nevin and Duff, plus three of the greatest prospects in Canada. We still think we can make the playoffs.*

*"Seiling is an outstanding junior player in Canada. I expect to keep him with the Marlboros for the remainder of the season before turning him professional."*

Nevin and Seiling are extensively covered in my first book. Both were excellent Rangers and would later become signature cogs in the Emile Francis era.

Center Bill Collins, from Ottawa, Ontario, would never play for the Rangers. He was later selected by the Minnesota North Stars in the "Great Expansion" draft of 1967 - a small piece to give up in the grand scheme of things.

Collins, who would go on to have a ten-year career in the NHL, later returned to the Rangers for the 1975-76 season - a catastrophic and changing-of-the-guard season for the Blueshirts. He retired following the 1977-78 season as a Washington Capital, where he finished his career with 311 points tallied up in 768 career NHL games played.

Defenseman Dick Duff, from Kirkland Lake, Ontario, was inducted into the Hockey Hall of Fame in 2006. At the time of this trade, Duff had already won two Stanley Cups with the Maple Leafs (1962 and 1963).

In the season following this mega trade (the 1964-65 season), Duff was traded again - by new general manager Emile Francis. I'll get into that trade soon enough, but as a spoiler - now in Montreal, Duff went on to win four more Stanley Cups.

Arnie Brown, from Oshawa, Ontario, was seldomly used by the Maple Leafs. The defenseman, who had the best seasons of his career with the Rangers, flourished in the Emile Francis era - just like Nevin and Seiling.

Despite the big name of Bathgate changing locations, and all the Stanley Cups that some of these players have to their names - it's tough to say who won this trade. Usually, the rule of thumb is that the team who gets the best player wins the trade.

It would be easy to say that Toronto won this trade. After all, following the trade, they went on to win the Stanley Cup.

That said, prior to this blockbuster, the Leafs had already won the Stanley Cup the past two seasons (1962 and 1963). Would they have won the Stanley Cup in 1964 without making this trade? It's tough to say. What's not tough to say is this trade worked out for them this season for sure. They went all-in and got the job done. That's all that matters from their perspective.

Long term, and with the Rangers always in a perpetual state of failure, Brown, Nevin, and Seiling became a huge part of Rangers' success that was soon to come. Bathgate and McKenney would soon move on from the Leafs, where they weren't part of the franchise's 1967 Stanley Cup victory - the last Stanley Cup that Toronto won.

On the other hand, if the Rangers never made this trade, would Bathgate help the Emile Francis era Rangers win a Stanley Cup - especially when the GAG line gained prominence? We'll never know.

After presenting you with all the facts in assessing this trade, I think this was a rare win-win trade where both teams filled their needs and accomplished what they desired, even if it was the Leafs, not the Rangers, who would win the Stanley Cup.

**DATE OF TRADE: April 19th, 1964**

**RANGERS ACQUIRE: Bev Bell and Ray Brunel**

**MONTREAL CANADIENS ACQUIRE: Howie Glover**

In one of Patrick's final moves as general manager, he sent right-winger Howie Glover, a native of Toronto, Ontario, to Montreal. For the next six years, Glover played for the AHL Cleveland Barons, sans one game with the Habs during the 1968-69 season.

Bev Bell, a center from Regina, Saskatchewan, never made it to the NHL. He retired after the 1964-65 season, where he played for the Vancouver Canucks (WHL).

Ray Brunel, also a center, played with the Canucks. Like Bell, a native of St. Lupicin, Manitoba, never made it to the NHL. Instead, he toiled around inferior leagues such as the CPHL, CHL, IHL, MSHSL, and other alphabet soup leagues.

In turn, this trade was pretty much a fart in the wind, with no gain, no loss. This was also Patrick's second-to-last trade.

**DATE OF TRADE: June 25th, 1964**

**RANGERS ACQUIRE: Lou Angotti and Edward Lawson**

**TORONTO MAPLE LEAFS ACQUIRE: Edward Ehrenverth and Duane Rupp**

Right-winger Ed Ehrenverth, from Peace River, Alberta, never made it to the NHL, as he was a career minor leaguer, where he spent the bulk of his days with the San Diego Gulls of the WHL.

Duane Rupp, a defenseman from McNutt, Saskatchewan, began his professional career in the 1958-59 season. Before this trade, he had only played in two NHL games with the Rangers in the 1962-63 season. Following this trade, he'd play in two games a piece during the next two seasons. Perhaps the number two was his lucky number!

Like other players in this period of time, Rupp benefitted from the "Great Expansion" and the advent of the WHA. Pretty much a career minor leaguer until the 1967-68 season, Rupp went on to play in the NHL up until the 1973-74 season, where he also had stints with expansion clubs such as the Pittsburgh Penguins and Minnesota North Stars.

Center Ed Larson, from Galt, Ontario, who came to New York in this trade - just like Ehrenverth, who shared the same first name - never made it to the NHL either.

Lou Angotti, a right-winger from Toronto, Ontario, was the most successful player of the four involved in this trade. He played two seasons in New York before moving on to Chicago, where he found his most success.

Amassing 653 NHL games in his stints with Toronto, New York, Chicago, Philadelphia, Pittsburgh, and St. Louis, Angotti carved out a solid career for himself.

While Angotti's tenure in New York was short, Patrick easily won this trade - his last - and much to the delight of many Ranger fans from this era.

Emile Francis, known as "The Cat," a nickname he earned in his playing days as a goaltender, was one of the most beloved men in Rangers' history - even if his "rebuild" trades, his final deals as general manager, were panned at the time.

Photo Credit: This signed 8x10 photo is from my memorabilia collection. The name of the photographer is unknown.

## EMILE FRANCIS

Tenure as Rangers' General Manager: October 30, 1964 – January 6, 1976

You know the deal - Emile Francis was covered at length in my first book.

In a "The New York Rangers Rink of Honor and the Rafters of Madison Square Garden" update: Sadly, Francis passed away on February 19, 2022, at the age of 95. Unfortunately, the Rangers never honored him when he was alive, despite yours truly, and many others, campaigning for such an honor. If the Rangers ever decide to do so, it will now be too late.

The arrival of Emile Francis to the big chair in New York City was an interesting tale, or in the case of "The Cat" - a "tail."

Starting in 1943, Francis played professional hockey for sixteen years. During that time, he played in 95 NHL games, mainly for the Blackhawks. Francis also tended the Rangers' net during his epic Hall of Fame career (Class of 1982, as a builder) but primarily plied his trade in the minor leagues. Perhaps in a different era, where there weren't only six NHL clubs, with only one goaltender on their roster - his time spent in the NHL would have been longer.

Following the 1959-60 season, at the age of only 33, Francis traded in his skates for a whistle. After flirting with the Blackhawks organization, instead, Francis accepted a job to coach the Guelph Royals, the Rangers' Ontario Hockey Association (OHA) affiliate.

Now 34 years old, Francis began his head coaching career in Guelph, where he was introduced to two promising Ranger prospects at the time, Jean Ratelle and Rod Gilbert.

While Francis was having success with the Royals, Patrick wasn't having any of that with his Rangers.

Prior to Patrick's dismissal, there were many loud shouts of "FIRE PATRICK" from Ranger fans at Madison Square Garden, a sentiment that was echoed in media reports.

Funny enough, in August 1962, now in need of a head coach following Doug Harvey's request to remove the title "coach" from his player-coach title, Patrick told the Ranger scribes that he was interested in promoting Francis from Guelph to New York.

That's what happened - in a way.

Instead of awarding Francis the head coach job, "The Cat" was named the Rangers' assistant head coach. In hindsight, this worked out for Francis, as not only did Patrick hear the jeers for his team's failures, but so did Patrick's new head coach, Red Sullivan.

When Rangers' ownership finally gave in to their fans and admitted the inevitable in their firing of Patrick, it was Francis, not Sullivan, who became the new general manager. By December of 1965, Francis, who was now calling the shots, got rid of Sullivan, too, and began his first of three separate stints in his dual role of head coach and general manager.

As author George Grimm eloquently stated in his book, which covered Emile Francis and his era, *"We Did Everything But Win,"* those five words (which are also the title of his excellent book) are the most accurate description of Francis' tenure.

For a Ranger franchise that was so bad and for so long, Francis rebuilt the team and turned them into a perennial playoff contender. Aside from his hockey genius and knowledge of the game, one of the reasons why the Rangers were able to turn it around was because Francis would only accept the job under the condition that every home playoff game had to be played at MSG - the elephants, trapeze artists, and clowns be damned.

While Francis made organizational (and roster) changes, many changes throughout the league also took place.

The first incarnation of the NHL Draft was held in 1963. In 1965, Francis took part in the third-ever NHL Amateur Draft, where - wouldn't you know it - he had the first-overall selection. In what was only a three-round, eleven-player draft, Francis selected André Veilleux first overall, a player who never made it to the NHL.

As the NHL Draft evolved, so did the league.

When Francis first became general manager, there were only six NHL teams. When he was fired in 1976, the league had tripled in size and now fielded eighteen clubs. While the league had always planned to expand, the emergence of the WHA in 1972 hurried those plans. (One of the NHL's expansion teams at the time, in a move to prevent the WHA from fielding a Long Island team? The Islanders.)

Not only did Francis have to worry about a bigger league - he had to worry about a second league, too, concerns that his predecessors never had.

If that wasn't enough on "The Cat's" food dish, player salaries significantly increased due to the two warring leagues competing for talent.

Ironically (when you consider Francis' playing career), a new position, roster spot, and player salary had also emerged - a team's need for (and I know this is an oxymoron) a "full-time" backup goaltender.

And, oh yeah, that pesky "u" word, as in the word "union," that was attempted so many times before, finally came to light as the NHLPA was founded in 1967.

While the NHL would continue to evolve after Francis' dismissal, at the time, general managers of his era had more to concern themselves with than ever before.

In eleven full seasons as general manager (he was fired in the middle of his twelfth season), the Rangers reached the playoffs nine times and also made a Stanley Cup Final appearance in 1972 that many believe the Rangers would have won had Jean Ratelle not been injured.

Francis was the architect of many big trades, but it's the trades that he made in his effort to rebuild that he'll always be remembered for.

"The Cat" was the catalyst behind the biggest trade in NHL history, where Phil Esposito and Carol Vadnais became Rangers, while long-time Blueshirt favorites Brad Park and Jean Ratelle became Bruins.

As of this 2022 writing, only two Ranger general managers have won the Stanley Cup, Lester Patrick, and Neil Smith. If you rank

149

general managers based solely on their ability to win championships (and that's rational to me), Francis is the third-best general manager in all of club history.

During Francis' run, not only did he change the culture for the better, the team enjoyed many glory years; while fans were upset with his rebuild trades at the time, these trades set the Rangers up for future success - as Francis, as early as 1979, was proven correct in his assessment to reconstruct the Rangers' roster.

Let's now take a look at how "The Cat" scratched and clawed his way into the hearts of Ranger fans. (Yes, I know I have overdone these puns - go with it!)

Yours truly with Eddie Giacomin in 2015. As they say, "goalies know goalies." Francis knew how good Giacomin could be, despite much skepticism at the time when Francis first acquired him. By the end of Giacomin's tenure on Broadway, #1 was arguably the biggest fan favorite in Rangers' history, while Francis was viewed as a villain for moving on from him.

Photo Credit: My buddy YOFFREY!

## DATE OF TRADE: December 21st, 1964

## RANGERS ACQUIRE: Bill Hicke and Jean-Guy Morissette (Loan)

## MONTREAL CANADIENS ACQUIRE: Dick Duff and Dave McComb

In "The Cat's" first trade as general manager of the Rangers, he sent Dick Duff (as previously acquired by Muzz Patrick in the Andy Bathgate trade) to Montreal. Duff then won the Stanley Cup with the Habs in 1965, 1966, 1968, and 1969.

Duff, following his time in Montreal, rounded out his career by playing for expansion franchises such as the Los Angeles Kings and the Buffalo Sabres. However, he cemented his status as a Hall of Famer in Montreal. Oops.

Dave McComb, a center from Toronto, Ontario, never made it to the NHL. Instead, outside of a short stint in the AHL, he was mostly a men's senior league player, spending most of his career in the OHA.

Bill Hicke, a right-winger from Regina, Saskatchewan, had previously won two Stanley Cups in Montreal (1959 and 1960).

Hicke played in 729 NHL games throughout his lengthy career (he also skated in 73 WHA contests with the Alberta Oilers) and played 137 of these matches with the Rangers across three seasons. The Oakland Seals would later draft him in the 1967 expansion draft, where in the 1968-69 season - he would represent the club as an All-Star.

Jean-Guy Morissette, a goalie from Causapscal, Quebec, played one game for the Montreal Canadiens in the 1963-64 season. This was his first and only game in the NHL, as he, too, is part of an ever-growing list of one-and-done NHLers.

While Hicke was serviceable for his brief stint in New York, Duff went on to win four Stanley Cups and became a Hall of Famer. Of course, and as previously noted, playing for the Canadiens sure bolstered Duff's career, but in any event - Francis' first trade was a loss.

Furthermore, while Montreal had every advantage going for them - perhaps Duff could've helped the Rangers in their Stanley Cup bids at the height of the Francis era.

**DATE OF TRADE: February 4th, 1965**

**RANGERS ACQUIRE: John Brenneman, Wayne Hillman, and Doug Robinson**

**CHICAGO BLACKHAWKS ACQUIRE: Wally Chevrier, Camille Henry, Don Johns, and Billy Taylor Jr.**

In a rare seven-player trade from this era, left-winger John Brenneman, from Fort Erie, Ontario, played 33 of his career 152 games with the Rangers. In a cruel twist of events, following the 1967 intra-league draft, Brenneman now had the blue Leaf on the crest of his sweater. However, since he was sent down to the minors before the playoffs - his name was omitted from the Leafs' 1967 Stanley Cup victory.

Following the Leafs' championship, Brenneman bounced in and out of the minors and the NHL, where his final games at the top level of hockey took place in the 1968-69 season with the Oakland Seals.

Ironically (as opposed to Brenneman), Wayne Hillman, a defenseman from Kirkland Lake, Ontario, got his name etched onto the Stanley Cup with the Blackhawks - despite playing in only one game during the 1961 Stanley Cup Final. Go figure.

Hillman spent parts of four seasons with the Rangers, where in his last season in New York (1967-68), the Chicago Blackhawks, Hillman's former club, knocked off the Rangers in six games in the first-round series. Following the playoff loss, Hillman moved on to expansion franchises such as the Minnesota North Stars and Philadelphia Flyers.

Doug Robinson, a left-winger out of St. Catharines, Ontario, spent parts of three seasons with the Rangers, where he spent nearly half of his career with the Baltimore Clippers (AHL). He'd later be claimed by the Los Angeles Kings in the 1967 expansion draft, where he finished his career following the 1970-71 season.

Going to Chicago was center Billy Taylor Jr., who after two games with the Rangers in the 1964-65 season, would never play in the NHL again. Taylor Jr., born in Kincaid, Saskatchewan, was the son of the previously discussed Taylor Sr. Sadly, the father outlived the son, as Junior passed away in 1979 at the age of 36. Senior lived until 1990 when he passed away at the age of 71.

Defenseman Don Johns, from Saint George, Ontario, would never play for the Blackhawks either. Four months after this trade, the

Hawks flipped him to the Canadiens, where he played only one game in the 1965-66 season. He then played four more NHL games in the expansion season with the Minnesota North Stars.

Wally Chevrier, a southpaw defenseman from South Porcupine, Ontario, never played in the NHL. He spent his fifteen-season professional career at the minor-league level, including stops in the AHL, WHL, EPHL, and in the CPHL. At the time of this trade, Chicago received "future considerations," who Chevrier turned out to be.

Camille Henry, known as "The Eel," was ironically the "big fish" of this trade. (He's also heavily featured in "The New York Rangers Rink of Honor and the Rafters of Madison Square Garden.")

At the time of the trade, Henry, who had already spent parts of eleven seasons with the Rangers (including a Calder Trophy win in 1954, and a Lady Byng Trophy in 1958) was the team's captain.

Acquired in order to help Chicago's playoff hopes, Henry was part of the Blackhawks' losing effort in the 1965 Stanley Cup Final when his team was defeated by the Canadiens in seven games. Following the loss, he spent the next season with the St. Louis Braves (CPHL) before Francis re-acquired him before the start of the 1967-68 season.

Chicago tried to boost their chances of winning the Stanley Cup with this trade. However, despite the Blackhawks losing the series in seven games, the Rangers won this trade, especially since Francis received more games and production from the players he acquired.

Had Chicago won the Stanley Cup following this trade, this would have been a win-win type of deal. They didn't, which is why Emile Francis is the victor here.

**DATE OF TRADE: May 17th, 1965**

**RANGERS ACQUIRE: Eddie Giacomin**

## PROVIDENCE REDS ACQUIRE: Aldo Guidolin, Jim Mikol, Marcel Paille, and Sandy McGregor

In a rare NHL/AHL trade, Emile Francis did pretty well for himself here - as you'd imagine. None of the four players who joined the Reds full-time ever did much damage in the NHL, much less played in the NHL again. Furthermore, not one member of this quartet went on to have a Hockey Hall of Fame career like Giacomin did.

We'll get more into Giacomin (and in depth) once we get to the end of the Francis era, as #1's exit was much more emotional and impactful than his arrival.

As far as everyone else, Aldo Guidolin, a defenseman from Forks of Credit, Ontario, played in 182 NHL games, all with the Rangers, from the years 1952 through 1956. Following this trade, he'd never play in the NHL again. However, he'd continue his hockey career until 1969, when, in those thirteen years, he skated in 879 AHL contests.

Once retiring as an active player, Guidolin got into coaching and later coached the Colorado Rockies during the 1978-79 season. When he passed away in 2015, Guidolin ranked eighteenth all-time in most AHL games played.

Jim Mikol, a defenseman from Kitchener, Ontario, played in four games with the Leafs in the 1962-63 season. Once in New York, the career minor leaguer played in thirty games for the Rangers in the 1964-65 season - the final games of his 34game NHL career. Following this trade, Mikol remained in the AHL until his retirement in 1970.

Marcel Paille, a goalie from Shawinigan Falls, Quebec, played professional hockey for nearly 25 seasons, including in the QHL, AHL, NHL, WHL, and the WHA.

From 1957 to the time of this trade in 1965, Paille filled in for the Rangers whenever the team needed someone to relieve their starter. During these eight years, Paille played in 107 games for the club, where he totaled a record of 32-52-22, a GAA of 3.42, and a save percentage of .896. When he wasn't playing for the Rangers, Paille played for their AHL affiliates.

It was in the AHL where Paille made his name, as he'd never play in the NHL again after this transaction.

Paille, who first turned pro in 1949, by the time he retired in 1974, was known as the greatest AHL goalie of all time.

The Class of 2010 AHL Hall of Famer and Calder Cup winner still holds many AHL records to this day, including most regular games played (765), most playoff games played (87), most playoff wins (49), longest playoff shutout streak (207:27), and most playoff minutes (5,368).

Donald "Sandy" McGregor was a right-winger from Toronto, Ontario. Another career minor leaguer, he played in two call-up games for the Rangers during the 1963-64 season - the extent of his NHL career. The longtime Baltimore Clipper (AHL) retired following the 1968-69 season.

As mentioned, we'll later get into Giacomin, but for now, I'm assuming you're aware of his legacy with the Rangers, especially since his jersey number is retired by the club.

In any event, this trade was a landslide victory for "The Cat."

**DATE OF TRADE: June 4th, 1965**

**RANGERS ACQUIRE: Ray Cullen and John McKenzie**

**CHICAGO BLACKHAWKS ACQUIRE: Dick Meissner, Mel Pearson, Tracy Pratt, and Dave Richardson**

Ray Cullen, a right-handed center from St. Catharines, Ontario, played in only eight games for the Rangers during the 1965-66 season. A year later, he was selected by the Detroit Red Wings at the NHL's 1966 intra-league draft. He'd then find his most success a season later when the Minnesota North Stars picked him at the league's expansion draft. A veteran of 313 NHL contests, he retired in 1971.

Right-winger John McKenzie, from High River, Alberta, appeared in only 35 games for the Rangers in the 1965-66 season. He'd later be moved to Boston, where he soon became part of the Bruins' 1970 and 1972 Stanley Cup winning teams.

McKenzie, whose run in New York was obviously short, went on to have the best years of his career after leaving the city that never sleeps. So, yeah - trading him later on wasn't a wise move.

In total, he'd play in 691 NHL games and 477 WHA games, where the money in the WHA was too good to refuse. In fact, after winning the Stanley Cup in 1972, he'd never play in the NHL again, as he became a richer man by playing for the inferior professional league. In total, his career spanned 21 professional seasons.

Dick Meissner, a right-wing from Kindersley, Saskatchewan, would never play in the NHL again following this trade. Instead, he spent the final nine seasons of his career at the minor-league level - despite NHL expansion and the WHA creating more professional opportunities for players.

Center Mel Pearson, from Flin Flon, Manitoba, would never play for the Blackhawks. The Pittsburgh Penguins would soon secure his rights at the 1967 expansion draft. Pearson only played in two games for the Penguins while mainly playing the next five seasons of his career at the WHL level for the Portland Buckaroos. He'd ultimately put a bow on his career following the 1972-73 season after seventy games played with the WHA Minnesota Fighting Saints.

Dave Richardson, a left-wing from St. Boniface, Manitoba, played for the Blackhawks in three games during the 1965-66 season. He'd later play in one game for the Red Wings during the 1967-68 season and that would be a wrap on his NHL career.

Tracey Pratt, son of 1940 Stanley Cup champion Babe Pratt, was also a defenseman like his father. Born in New York while his dad played on the Blueshirts' blue line, the American by birth never played for the Blackhawks. Instead, he was drafted by the Oakland Seals at the 1967 expansion draft.

Starting his NHL career in Oakland, Pratt would later play for the Penguins, Sabres, Canucks, Rockies, and Maple Leafs. In total, he'd amass 580 games in the NHL - just none with the Rangers or Blackhawks!

It's tough to call this specific trade a loss, but due to the careers that McKenzie and Pratt would have (especially McKenzie), this wasn't a good trade for "The Cat" either.

**DATE OF TRADE: June 8th, 1965**

**RANGERS ACQUIRE: Dunc McCallum**

**DETROIT RED WINGS ACQUIRE: Bob Cunningham**

Defenseman Dunc McCallum, from Flin Flon, Manitoba, played in two games for the Rangers during the 1965-66 season. He'd later play in 285 professional games, between the NHL and WHA, which first began at the start of expansion.

Center Bob Cunningham, from Welland, Ontario, who played his fourth ever game in the NHL with the Rangers during the 1961-62 season, would never play in the NHL again after this trade. Instead, the career minor leaguer skated in the AHL, IHL, WHL, and CPHL.

This was Francis' first "no harm, no foul" trade.

**DATE OF TRADE: June 8th, 1965**

**RANGERS ACQUIRE: Cesare Maniago and Garry Peters**

**MONTREAL CANADIENS ACQUIRE: Earl Ingarfield Sr., Gord Labossiere, Dave McComb, Noel Price, and Cash**

Francis, looking to overturn the roster Patrick left him, put forth another huge multi-player deal here, his fourth trade at this point in time.

Earl Ingarfield Sr., a center from Lethbridge, Alberta, who would later replace former teammate Phil Goyette as the head coach of the expansion New York Islanders (yuck), was sent to Montreal in this trade. Following this trade, very quickly - a day later - on June 9th, 1965, the Rangers reclaimed their "former" center during that year's intra-league draft.

Come the 1967 expansion draft, the Rangers would move on from Ingarfield for good when the Pittsburgh Penguins claimed him. However, during this particular transaction, Ingarfield never wore a Habs sweater, as he continued his career with the Rangers following this deal.

Defenseman Noel Price, as discussed earlier, would go on to win the Stanley Cup with Montreal in 1966. He would also later join Ingarfield in Pittsburgh during expansion.

Center Dave McComb, also as discussed earlier, never reached the NHL level.

Center Gord Labossiere, from St. Boniface, Manitoba, would never play for the Canadiens. However, he would later play for the Los Angeles Kings in their inaugural season, and following NHL time in both LA and Minnesota - he went on to win two WHA Avco Cups with the Houston Aeros (1974 and 1975).

Garry Peters, a center from Regina, Saskatchewan, played in one season for the Rangers during the 1965-66 campaign. He returned to Montreal in the season that followed, before moving on to the expansion Philadelphia Flyers. He then finished his professional career in the WHA, where he last played for the New York Golden Blades/New Jersey Knights during the 1973-74 season.

In hockey-happy Montreal, goaltender Cesare Maniago, from Trail, British Columbia, would never be able to wrest the starter's job from Gump Worsley. The same would also apply in New York, as Eddie Giacomin, in Maniago's second season with the Rangers, would take full control of the barrel.

Ironically, Maniago's greatest NHL success would take place with the Minnesota North Stars, where he was part of a tandem with "The Gumper" himself.

After nine solid seasons in Minnesota, Mangiao played in two more seasons with the Vancouver Canucks.

The Rangers got the better end of the deal here, but not by much, especially since Price would go on to win the Stanley Cup with the *Bleu Blanc et Rouge.*

**DATE OF TRADE: January 7th, 1966**

**RANGERS ACQUIRE: Cash and Considerations (Larry Mickey)**

**CHICAGO BLACKHAWKS ACQUIRE: Lou Angotti**

The story of Larry Mickey, a right-wing from Lacombe, Alberta, is a sad one. On July 23rd, 1982, at 38, he committed suicide due to carbon monoxide poisoning while sitting in a parked car in his garage.

At the time, he was just served divorce papers from his soon-to-be ex-wife, Lynda, who called him "weak" and showed no compassion when she said he was a "failure" following his death. (Lynda was his second spouse, as his first wife Eleanor, was tragically killed in a 1967 auto accident.)

As a player, Mickey was known for his hard work and grit more than for his skill and ability. Over parts of three seasons, he played in nineteen games for the Rangers, where he picked up two points.

However, following twenty games combined with the Blackhawks and Rangers, he'd later play in 272 more NHL games with the Maple Leafs, Canadiens, Kings, Flyers, and Sabres. However, in New York, he had trouble cracking into the lineup.

160

Lou Angotti, who was first acquired by Muzz Patrick in his final trade as general manager, had a good run in Chicago, with stints in Philly and Pittsburgh. He played the 1973-74 season with the St. Louis Blues before finishing his professional career in the season following for the Chicago Cougars of the WHA.

While not a big loss, this was a loss for Emile Francis, as Angotti went on to have the better career.

**DATE OF TRADE: January 10th, 1966**

**RANGERS ACQUIRE: Reggie Fleming**

**BOSTON BRUINS ACQUIRE: John McKenzie**

As mentioned earlier, John McKenzie went on to have a great career in Boston, winning two Stanley Cups (1970 and 1972).

Reggie Fleming, a tough-guy defenseman from Montreal, Quebec, had previously won the Stanley Cup in 1961 with the Chicago Blackhawks. He had a decent run in New York over parts of four seasons, but he wasn't John McKenzie. That said, Fleming, who had a reputation as a hard-nosed customer, would quickly endear himself into the hearts of Ranger fans.

However, due to McKenzie's success, despite how well Fleming played - this trade is a loss on Francis' ledger.

**DATE OF TRADE: June 13th, 1966**

**RANGERS ACQUIRE: Red Berenson**

**MONTREAL CANADIENS ACQUIRE: Garry Peters and Ted Taylor**

Garry Peters, as previously mentioned, was first acquired a year prior to this deal. He played in the 1965-66 season with the Rangers and then bounced around.

Two days following this particular trade, Montreal exposed left-winger Ted Taylor from Oak Lake, Manitoba, in the 1966 NHL intra-league draft. The Detroit Red Wings claimed Taylor a year later, and they exposed Taylor themselves during the 1967 expansion draft, where the Minnesota North Stars claimed him.

Before joining the North Stars, Taylor had played in only eight NHL games. He then played in 31 games during the expansion season, where following it, he went to the WHL, where he soon joined the Vancouver Canucks.

Once the Canucks became an NHL team after another league expansion (1970-71), Taylor was one of the six holdovers from the WHL incarnation of the team.

However, once the WHA came knocking, Taylor answered the door and spent the final six seasons of his career with the Houston Aeros. With the Aeros, he won two Avco Cups (1974 and 1975).

Coming to Broadway was Gordon "Red" Berenson, a center from Regina, Saskatchewan, where the collegiate star (University of Michigan) took his Stanley Cup winning experience with him (1965 with Montreal).

Berenson wouldn't stay with the Rangers for long, as after one season in New York, he was traded again in the early stages of the 1967-68 season.

Once leaving New York, Berenson became part of the expansion St. Louis Blues and their three-consecutive Stanley Cup runs (runs that happened only because one expansion team was guaranteed a spot in the Stanley Cup Final in the NHL's attempt to grow the sport in the league's six new markets). The Blues were swept in every Stanley Cup Final; 1968 and 1969 vs. Montreal, and 1970 vs. Boston.)

Berenson spent the first half of the 1970s in Detroit before returning to St. Louis in 1975. He finished his career as a Blue note and retired following the 1977-78 season.

Following retirement, Berenson would not only become the head coach of his college alma mater but of the St. Louis Blues too. As one of the most successful coaches in hockey, Berenson won the Jack Adams award in 1981. He also won numerous championships in addition to receiving many individual accolades at the University of Michigan.

After 33 seasons as the head coach of the Wolverines, on April 10, 2017, Berenson, then approaching the age of 78, announced his retirement.

Perhaps by the time you read this book, Berenson will have rightfully been inducted into the Hockey Hall of Fame in Toronto.

As far as this particular trade goes, Berenson had the best career of the three men involved, but this trade also didn't backfire. This is a wash.

**DATE OF TRADE: June 6th, 1967 (Expansion Draft Claim and Trade)**

**RANGERS ACQUIRE: Rod Seiling**

**ST. LOUIS BLUES ACQUIRE: Tim Ecclestone, Gord Kannegiesser, Bob Plager, and Gary Sabourin**

Similar to the Vegas Golden Knights during their 2017 NHL Expansion Draft, which took place fifty years following the "Great Expansion of 1967," former Ranger, the son of Lester and the brother of Muzz, Lynn Patrick, was the general manager of the St. Louis Blues at this time.

The 1940 Stanley Cup champion, as Vegas would later do, used the advantages that expansion afforded him when he selected Rod Seiling in the sixth round (36th overall) of a twenty-round draft.

Following the draft, Patrick flipped Seiling back to the Rangers for a collection of four players, including Bob Plager, who was reunited with his brothers Bill and Barclay in St. Louis.

Bob Plager, a defenseman from Kirkland Lake, Ontario, became a legend in St. Louis following this trade and spent the final ten seasons of his career with the Blues. In retirement, Plager, who finished his career with 644 NHL games under his belt, briefly coached the team for the 1992-93 season.

Tim Ecclestone, a right-winger from Toronto, Ontario, was also an original Blue, where he challenged for the Stanley Cup in 1968, 1969, and 1970. While he never suited up for the Rangers, Ecclestone went on to spend ten seasons in the NHL, where he also played for the Red Wings, Maple Leafs, and Flames (the Atlanta incarnation). Overall, he played in 692 NHL games.

Prior to beginning his NHL career, Ecclestone was drafted by the Rangers in the second round (ninth overall) of the 1964 NHL Amateur Draft.

Gord Kannegiesser didn't have as much luck as Plager and Ecclestone, as he only played in nineteen games for the Blues during the 1967-68 season. He played in four more games during the 1971-72 season in St. Louis - his last NHL season. Once done in Missouri, the defenseman from North Bay, Ontario, would hook up with the WHA, spending the final three seasons of his career playing for the Houston Aeros and the Indianapolis Racers.

Right-wing Gary Sabourin, from Parry Sound, Ontario, carved out a great career for himself in St. Louis, where he also represented the Blues in the 1970 and 1971 NHL All-Star Games.

Of Sabourin's 627 games played in the NHL, the bulk of them took place during his seven-year run in St. Louis.

After playing in the 1974-75 season with the Toronto Maple Leafs, he joined the California Seals for the 1975-75 campaign. He followed the Seals to Cleveland when they rebranded as the Barons for the 1976-77 season - Sabourin's last season before retiring.

While Emile Francis gave up a lot to retain Seiling, it was well worth it. No one can argue that, as Seiling was there for all the peak years.

164

The defenseman lasted throughout the entire height of the Francis era, the "We Did Everything But Win" era of Rangers, where at the tail end of it, Seiling was claimed on waivers by the upstart Washington Capitals in 1974.

Both general managers won here. Lynn Patrick turned Rod Seiling into three key pieces of a team (despite the advantage of playing in the newly created West division) that would "contend" for the Stanley Cup for three consecutive seasons.

Francis retained one of his best defensemen for perhaps three players, who, while helping out in St. Louis, may not have received significant time in New York.

**DATE OF TRADE: June 6th, 1967**

**RANGERS ACQUIRE: Larry Jeffrey**

**PITTSBURGH PENGUINS ACQUIRE: Paul Andrea, Frank Francis, George Konik, and Dunc McCallum**

Larry Jeffrey, a left-winger from Goderich, Ontario, had previously won the Stanley Cup with the Toronto Maple Leafs in 1967. Following the championship, the Penguins selected him during the expansion draft and then flipped him to the Rangers in this trade for four bodies.

Jeffrey would play in the next two seasons with the Rangers, 122 games in all, picking up only thirteen points. Once the 1968-69 season concluded, he retired.

Paul Andrea, a right-winger from North Sydney, Nova Scotia, would spend the next two seasons with his new club. Having played only four games with the Rangers in the 1965-66 season, Andrea eventually played 280 professional games between the NHL and WHA combined. Expansion most certainly extended his career as a major leaguer.

The man with two first names, Frank Francis, never played in one professional game. Not much is known about what the forward from Toronto, Ontario, did after this trade.

George Konik, a left-winger from Flin Flon, Manitoba, played in 106 professional games, where, like Andrea, he split time between the NHL and WHA.

Konik, an original Penguin, played the entire 1967-68 season in Pittsburgh. Following the season, he spent the next four years of his life playing for the United States national team and in their league (USHL).

Konik's final professional season took place in the 1972-73 campaign, where he skated in 54 games for the Minnesota Fighting Saints (WHA).

Dunc McCallum, as discussed earlier, was the biggest name in this trade. After two games with the Rangers during the 1965-66 season, he amassed 185 more games as a Penguin.

Like many fringe players of this era, McCallum would also make the jump to the WHA, where he last played for the Chicago Cougars in the 1974-75 season.

Jeffrey had the best career of the players involved in this trade, but his final two seasons weren't his best. Everyone Pittsburgh acquired here was a product of expansion, but even with Jeffrey's down seasons, he still remained as the best player of the lot.

This trade is an ever-so-slight victory for Francis.

**DATE OF TRADE: June 16th, 1967**

**RANGERS ACQUIRE: Barclay Plager**

**LOS ANGELES KINGS ACQUIRE: Trevor Fahey, Jim Murray, and Ken Turlik**

Defenseman Barclay Plager, from Kirkland Lake, Ontario, was the most successful of the Plager brothers, but he wouldn't last long in

166

New York. More on that in a bit. However, it should be mentioned that at this period of time, Plager, now 26 years old, was a career minor leaguer.

Left-winger Trevor Fahey, from New Waterford, Nova Scotia, played in only one career NHL game - with the Rangers during the 1964-65 season. Aside from that one game, he was a career minor leaguer, where he played in such leagues as the EHL, IHL, and CPHL.

Ken Turlik, a right-winger from Lethbridge, Alberta, played in one less NHL game than Fahey did - as in zero. He, too, was a career minor leaguer.

Defenseman Jim Murray, from Virden, Manitoba, played in thirty games for the Kings in their inaugural season. These would be the final thirty games of his NHL career, as he, too, was a career minor leaguer. He spent most of his time at the WHL level for the Phoenix Road Runners.

This trade was a win for Francis, although he wouldn't hold on to Plager for long.

**DATE OF TRADE: August 17th, 1967**

**RANGERS ACQUIRE: Camille Henry**

**CHICAGO BLACKHAWKS ACQUIRE: Paul Shmyr**

Camille Henry, from Quebec City, Quebec, the former captain and a beloved fan favorite of Ranger fans, was traded to Chicago prior to the 1965 NHL trade deadline. Two years later, he was back in New York. However, this stint was nowhere as successful as the first one for the left-winger.

Henry split time with the Rangers and the Buffalo Bisons (AHL) in his return season on Broadway. These 36 games in blue from this 1967-68 season would be Henry's final contests as a Ranger.

Following the 1967-68 season, Henry was still in blue - this time in St. Louis.

Paul Shmyr, a defenseman from Cudworth, Saskatchewan, was 21 years old at the time of this trade. He was also thirteen years younger than Henry. After a season in the minors, he'd crack into the Blackhawks lineup during the 1968-69 season. Then, once the calendar flipped to a new decade, the 1970s, Shmyr became a full-time professional player.

All in all, following this trade, Shmyr would play in parts of thirteen professional seasons, including stops in both the NHL and WHA. He played a whopping 854 games in all - 343 in the NHL and 511 in the WHA.

While not a mitigated disaster of a trade, especially since the Rangers would have some great seasons in the years ahead, this one was easily a loss, as Henry couldn't regain the form he once had in his prime years in the Big Apple.

**DATE OF TRADE: November 29th, 1967**

**RANGERS ACQUIRE: Ron Attwell and Ron Stewart**

**ST. LOUIS BLUES ACQUIRE: Red Berenson and Barclay Plager**

Barclay Plager, just acquired in the summer, was flipped five months later. He would spend the next decade in St. Louis, where, along the way, he appeared in four All-Star games (1970, 1971, 1973, and 1974).

A Blues legend, Plager would later coach the franchise through parts of four seasons. In addition, his #8 hangs in the rafters of St. Louis to this day.

Red Berenson, as mentioned earlier, had a long career and eventually put forth a coaching resume worthy of the Hall of Fame.

Right-wing Ron Attwell, from Humber Summit, Ontario, was a career minor leaguer, where aside from four games played with the Rangers for the 1967-68 season (no points recorded), he had spent thirteen years at inferior levels.

168

Prior to this trade, he also played eighteen games for the expansion Blues this same season. Atwell played in only 22 NHL games.

Atwell would eventually retire following the 1969-70 season, where he last wore a Buffalo Bison sweater.

At this point, Ron Stewart, a center from Calgary, Alberta, was 35 years old. During his thirteen seasons in the Leafs' blue and white, he had previously won three Stanley Cups in Toronto (1962-1964). He would later be moved to Boston, where, after two seasons in Beantown, the Blues drafted the center in the fifteenth round of the 1967 expansion draft (90th overall).

Despite his age, Stewart continued to play at a high level, where he remained with the Rangers for parts of six seasons - including the peak years of the Emile Francis era.

Stewart, who Francis once praised as one of his best penalty killers, would later be involved in a tragic off-ice incident. More on that to come once we hit the date of November 14th, 1972.

Like many trades made throughout this era, while Plager went on to have a longer and better career from this point forward - Stewart filled a need. Francis wanted Stanley Cup experience on his roster, and he got it with Stewart. In addition, no one could have predicted the career Plager would have.

On paper, this trade is a loss, but it was anything but on the ice.

**DATE OF TRADE: December 1st, 1967 (Approximate date, exact date unknown)**

**RANGERS ACQUIRE: Cash**

**CALIFORNIA GOLDEN SEALS ACQUIRE: Larry Popein**

Larry Popein, aka "The Pope," is another player featured in my first book.

The native of Yorkton, Saskatchewan, had the best years of his career with the Rangers from 1954 through 1961, where the stoic and admirable center played for the club through some very lean years.

Despite a reputation of being well-liked and hard-working, following the 1960-61 season, in a six-team league, Popein never played for the Rangers again. Instead, Popein toiled around for the next six plus seasons in Vancouver, playing for the Rangers' affiliate at the time, the Canucks.

As already mentioned (and repeatedly at that), expansion, which doubled the number of teams in the league, would benefit many. Popein was one of these players, as he would skate in 47 games for the Seals in their debut season - Pope's last season as an NHLer.

Even without knowing the number of dollars exchanged - this was a win for Francis, as Popein was way past his prime at the time of this trade and soon retired. It was a win for the Seals, too, as it gave them veteran experience for as limited of a time as it was.

Ironically, Popein would soon rejoin the Rangers organization. In fact, he was involved in the very next trade that Francis made!

**DATE OF TRADE: May 14th, 1968**

**RANGERS ACQUIRE: Larry Popein**

**CALIFORNIA GOLDEN SEALS ACQUIRE: Cash**

After his 47-game stint with the Seals, Francis reacquired "The Pope." However, Popein was then relegated to the Omaha Knights of the Central Hockey League. And, as you may imagine, Omaha is not exactly "Hockeytown, USA," nor is it the "city that never sleeps."

However, after his playing days, Popein wasn't out of work for long.

Following the 1969-70 season, Popein would spend the next twenty-two years of his life in hockey in various coaching, scouting, and front office roles. Not only did he serve as an interim coach for the Rangers during the 1973-74 season (18-14-9 in 45 games), but he was also a scout for the Calgary Flames when they won the Stanley Cup in 1989.

This trade was much ado about nothing, where its biggest impact was that it kept Popein around the organization until he moved on to the Vancouver Canucks (director of player development), a long-time western Canadian franchise that moved up from the WHL to the NHL.

**DATE OF TRADE: June 12th, 1968**

**RANGERS ACQUIRE: Dave Balon**

**MINNESOTA NORTH STARS ACQUIRE: Wayne Hillman, Joe Johnston, and Dan Seguin**

As mentioned during the Plante and Worsley goaltender mega-swap under Muzz Patrick, Balon went off to Montreal and, while there, won two Stanley Cups. After Minnesota drafted him in the 1967 expansion draft, he was back home in New York five years later.

However, just like Patrick before him, Francis would soon trade the left-winger out of New York again. More on that to come.

The Stars traded their 1968 All-Star for three players.

Left-wing Dan Seguin, from Sudbury, Ontario, played in only eleven games for the Stars before the Vancouver Canucks claimed him. In all, Seguin, mainly a minor leaguer, played in 37 NHL games during his eight-year professional career.

Ironically, Joey Johnston, another left-winger, would also play in only eleven games for the Stars. He would later move on to the California Golden Seals, where he played for four seasons before ultimately retiring as a Blackhawk following the 1975-76 season.

Previously, Johnston, a native of Peterborough, Ontario, was the Rangers' second-round selection (eighth overall) of the 1966 NHL Amateur Draft.

Wayne Hillman, first acquired by Francis three years prior, was the most successful player on the Minnesota side of things, playing in fifty games for the North Stars during the 1968-69 season.

Following Hillman's one-and-done season with the North Stars, he'd catch on with the Philadelphia Flyers for four seasons. After that, he jumped ship to the WHA, skating the final two years of his career with the Cleveland Crusaders. He retired after the 1974-75 campaign.

This trade was a win for Francis, solely because Balon soon became an integral part of Ranger success.

**DATE OF TRADE: June 13th, 1968**

**RANGERS ACQUIRE: Don Caley and Wayne Rivers**

**ST. LOUIS BLUES ACQUIRE: Camille Henry, Robbie Irons, and Bill Plager**

"The Cat," who loved his multi-player deals, made another one here.

Camille Henry, as previously mentioned, was off to St. Louis. As he did in Chicago four years prior, he'd help the Blues challenge for the Stanley Cup in 1969. A season later, the 1969-70 season, "The Eel" played four more games before retiring for good.

Bill Plager, a defenseman and the last of the three Plager brothers to be mentioned in this book (he, too, was from Kirkland Lake, Ontario), was the least successful of the trio, but he still had his prime seasons in St. Louis.

Go figure - the Rangers had all three Plager brothers under contract at one point, and then all three men would play together in St. Louis.

As Alanis Morissette once asked - *"isn't it ironic, don't ya think?"*

Goaltender Robbie Irons, from Toronto, Ontario, and the last piece of the puzzle heading to St. Louis, had a professional hockey career that spanned fourteen seasons. However, he's also on the "one-and-done" NHL list.

Irons' lone NHL game took place during the 1968-69 season under special circumstances to boot - as his one game of NHL experience lasted for all of three minutes.

To continue the theme of irony (as Irons' one game featured the Rangers as the opponent), Blues' goalie Glenn Hall was ejected from a November 13th, 1968 game between the two teams.

At this point in time, former Ranger Jacques Plante split the net in St. Louis with his brother of the barrel. Whichever goalie had the night off, that man would sometimes sit in the press box or be elsewhere.

When Hall was booted from the game, the Blues had to fill their net. However, Plante needed time to get ready and the officials weren't going to afford the Blues that time.

As Plante suited up, Robbie Irons temporarily backstopped. Three minutes later, once Plante was ready to go, Irons returned to his spot on the bench.

Irons never faced a shot. So, hey - he finished his NHL career without ever giving up a goal.

For the record, once Plante entered the game, he made 23 saves on 23 shots faced. The Blues won 3-1 in this rare game where three different goalies got ice time. (Plante, ever eccentric, also half-joked that he deserved another shutout on his record - something that did not happen!)

The irony doesn't stop there.

Goaltender Don Caley, from Dauphin, Manitoba, who the Rangers received in this trade (and like Irons), also finished his career with only one game of NHL experience (with the Blues) during a game which took place on December 30th, 1967, against the Toronto Maple Leafs.

In a blowout that the Leafs eventually won by a final score of 8-1, starting goaltender Seth Martin was pulled in the second period after giving up a five-spot. Caley would play during the second half of the game, where he gave up three goals in all - three more than Irons ever gave up!

Wayne Rivers, a right-wing from Hamilton, Ontario, played professional hockey for seventeen seasons. Until the advent of the WHA - he was mainly a minor leaguer.

Rivers skated in four games for the Rangers in the 1968-69 season, failing to pick up a point in this quartet of contests. Rivers, who then played in the AHL until the inception of the WHA, in 1972 joined the NHL's competitor, playing in 357 WHA games.

Since Plager went on to have the best career of the lot at this point, St. Louis won this trade - even if the goaltenders washed each other out.

**DATE OF TRADE: September 13th, 1968**

**RANGERS ACQUIRE: Ron Boehm**

**CALIFORNIA GOLDEN SEALS ACQUIRE: Cash**

Ron Boehm, a left-winger from Allan, Saskatchewan, played in sixteen games for the expansion Seals in the 1967-68 season. These contests would be his last sixteen games too.

Following the trade, Boehm bounced around the minor leagues for six seasons, where he had stints in the AHL, CHL, and NAHL.

This trade was essentially a minor cash loss for the Rangers - a franchise who could afford it.

**DATE OF TRADE: May 13th, 1969**

**RANGERS ACQUIRE: Norm Beaudin**

**ST. LOUIS BLUES ACQUIRE: Cash**

Norm Beaudin, the right-wing from Montmartre, Saskatchewan, would never play for the Rangers. Instead, prior to the inception of the WHA, he mainly was a minor leaguer, where he played in thirteen games for the Blues in the 1968-69 season. He played twelve more games for the North Stars during the 1970-71 season. These twenty-five games were the only NHL games that Beaudin ever played.

However, Beaudin's career would be saved by the WHA, where in 1972, he joined the Bobby Hull-led Winnipeg Jets. In his first season in Winnipeg, Beaudin recorded 38 goals and 65 assists for 103 points. This would be the best professional stat line of Beaudin's career.

Following his career-best season, Beaudin's numbers dropped off. He'd eventually become a victim of the "Swedish Invasion" due to the soon-to-be Rangers - Ulf Nilsson and Anders Hedberg.

After winning the Avco Cup in 1976, Beaudin played one season in Switzerland and then retired in 1977.

The above is just a long way of saying that this trade was another small financial loss for Emile Francis.

**DATE OF TRADE: June 6th, 1969**

**RANGERS ACQUIRE: Don Blackburn and Leon Rochefort**

**PHILADELPHIA FLYERS ACQUIRE: Reggie Fleming**

Francis, as he previously did when he first traded for Reggie Fleming - lost this trade featuring Fleming too.

Following this trade, Fleming would go on to play in four more professional seasons, with stops in Philadelphia, Boston, and with the Chicago Cougars of the WHA.

At 42 years old, in 1978, and after playing for small minor league teams, Fleming called it a career, and what a great one it was.

Don Blackburn, a left-winger, played in three games for the Rangers during the 1969-70 season and spent the rest of the season with the Buffalo Bisons (AHL).

A season later, the 1970-71 campaign, Blackburn's NHL ice time was sliced down to a third, where he only played in one game and then spent the rest of the season with the Rochester Americans (AHL). Following that season, the New York Islanders claimed the unprotected player out of Kirkland Lake, Ontario.

Blackburn would then split time with both the Islanders and the North Stars during the 1972-73 season. He'd then finish his career by playing in the WHA for three seasons, as a New England Whaler, where he retired after the 1975-76 season.

Former one-time Ranger, Leon Rochefort, was flipped to Los Angeles just three days following this deal.

This trade was a loss, but none of any true significance.

**DATE OF TRADE: June 9th, 1969**

**RANGERS ACQUIRE: Real Lemieux**

**LOS ANGELES KINGS ACQUIRE: Dennis Hextall and Leon Rochefort**

Right-winger Real Lemieux, from Victoriaville, Quebec, played in 55 games for the Rangers during the 1969-70 season, but by the end of the season, he would find himself back in Los Angeles. He would later find himself back with the Rangers for the 1973-74 season too.

As mentioned in the Worsley/Plante trade, Leon Rochefort played in one season for Los Angeles before returning to Montreal, where he won the Stanley Cup in 1971. He would remain in the NHL until 1976, finishing his career with stops in Detroit, Atlanta, and Vancouver.

The seldomly used Dennis Hextall (thirteen games with the Rangers) would play in 28 games for the Kings during the 1969-70 season.

176

The son of Rangers' legend Bryan Hextall, the left-winger from Red Lake, Ontario, would leave one California team for another when he became a Seal for the 1970-71 season.

Following his stint on the left coast, Hextall returned to traditional hockey markets, spending parts of four seasons in Minnesota and likewise, parts of four seasons in Detroit too.

He then played the final two seasons of his career in Washington, where he retired after the 1979-80 season.

While Hextall wasn't his father, he was much better than Lemieux.

For comparison: Lemieux picked up 155 points in 457 games. Hextall picked up 503 points in 681 games played.

With the addition of Rochefort in this trade, simply put - Francis gave up way too much for Lemieux. This trade is a loss.

Up next, a trade that truly ended an era and brought tears to the eyes of Ranger fans.

(Of note: the next three out of four trades were massive and soon created a whole litany of "what if" questions.)

**DATE OF TRADE: June 10th, 1969**

**RANGERS ACQUIRE: Cash**

**CALIFORNIA GOLDEN SEALS ACQUIRE: Harry Howell**

Harry Howell, one of the greatest Rangers ever to adorn their sweater, was moved for chump change in a trade that signaled the end of an era.

While the 1950s and 1960s were lean times for the franchise, three homegrown stars shone brightly. Gump Worsley, previously traded six years prior, was one of those stars. Andy Bathgate, traded eight months after Worsley, was the other. And, of course, there was #3 himself, the pride of Hamilton, Ontario, Harry Howell.

Sometimes, people, including yours truly in this very book, liberally and loosely throw around the word "legend." However, without a shadow of a doubt, Howell was not only Rangers' royalty - he was a legend.

Unfortunately for Howell (and Worsley and Bathgate), he is also the face of a dark age in franchise history, albeit through no fault of his own.

For example, Howell began his career during the 1952-53 season and remained with the team until the time of this trade. During his seventeen years on Broadway, Howell's Rangers qualified for the playoffs only seven times (where two of those appearances took place AFTER expansion), and in each postseason - the Rangers were eliminated in the first round.

As mentioned earlier in this book, like most excellent Rangers from this era - Howell would have a collection of Stanley Cups had he played elsewhere in his prime. While Ranger fans loved him (and these feelings were reciprocated), he would have been a multiple Stanley Cup champion had he played in Montreal.

"Harry the Horse" was a moniker bestowed upon him due to his "iron-man" status. In seventeen seasons with the Rangers, Howell played in a whopping 1,160 games - a record at the time and still holds to this day.

(Brian Leetch, another defenseman, has played the second-most games for the Rangers, 1,129 in all. And had Glen Sather not foolishly traded Leetch - barring injury, Leetch would have caught and surpassed Howell.)

Howell's consistency is a testament to his eliteness. In an era where players were lucky if they amassed even eight or ten seasons, he only missed seventeen games during Howell's first sixteen seasons. Howell only missed forty games during his entire tenure in New York.

Howell's durability wasn't lost on anyone at the time either. On January 25th, 1967, the Rangers celebrated Howell's 1,000th-game milestone, where the franchise *"flew in two plane-loads"* (his words) of his friends and family into New York from Canada.

What's perplexing is that it would take 42 years for the Rangers to retire his #3 jersey, which took place on February 22nd, 2009. (Bathgate's #9 was also retired on this day.)

(Of course, the topic of the Rangers honoring their history (and their failures to do so) is another topic for another time. And have I mentioned yet that I once wrote a book entitled "The New York Rangers Rink of Honor and the Rafters of Madison Square Garden"? I may have!)

Howell, who became a no-doubt-about-it Hall of Famer after retiring (Class of 1979), was a perennial All-Star with the Rangers. What was also impressive was that two seasons prior to this trade, he won the Norris Trophy in 1967. And as the well-known story goes, following his win, Howell said he was glad to have finally won it, as he then predicted that Bobby Orr would own the award for the next decade.

That's what happened.

Following Howell's lone Norris Trophy win (before his win, Doug Harvey usually dominated the trophy), #4, Bobby Orr, would win the following eight-straight Norris trophies. Someone keenly aware of this fact was Brad Park. Ironically, Howell helped facilitate Park's entry to the league during #2's rookie season; perhaps more ironically than that - it would be Park himself who ended up playing in Boston (and for a short time with Orr).

But alas, I digress. (Although I will say, like many other legends who are brought up throughout this book, you can write a whole book on just Harry Howell alone. Perhaps a future book idea!)

By now, and if you didn't know it already - Howell was Rangers' royalty. So why did Francis trade him in a trade that would piss off the entire fan base? (And some of Howell's teammates at the time!)

Howell, born on December 28, 1932, was approaching the age of 37. Similar to NHLers today, most players did not play at that age. It was unusual to see players surpass the age of 35 in Howel's era as opposed to today, where we are seeing more and more players play into their late 30s and beyond.

During the 1968-69 season, Howell's last campaign in New York, he suffered a back injury. As a result, despite his impeccable track record, he missed 23 games this season. (As mentioned earlier, prior to this season, he had only missed 17 games throughout his entire career.)

With the thinking that his star was aging out and soon coming to the end, Francis asked Howell about retiring, and if he would consider joining the Rangers' front office. Howell, knowing his body and previous history, thought he still had plenty of hockey left in him.

While Brad Park was a completely different player than Howell (as Park was an offensive wizard as opposed to Howell's strengths as a pure defensive defenseman), Francis thought that he had enough in Park that it was time to move on from Howell. And that's what he did.

In the first of two moves made on this day, Francis sold Howell's rights to the lowly California Seals for cash. It was the wrong move.

For what it's worth - at least Muzz Patrick received incredible talent in return when he traded away both Worsley and Bathgate. All Francis got here for Howell was a few bucks.

Following the trade, Howell played in four more NHL seasons - parts of two seasons with the Seals and then two full seasons with the Los Angeles Kings. He would then play in three more seasons, all in the WHA, where he finally retired as a member of the Calgary Cowboys following the 1975-76 season.

Traded by Francis at the age of 36, Howell played hockey for seven more years and then retired at the age of 43.

Of course, this presents another "what if" question for many. "What if Harry Howell spent those next seven seasons with the Rangers?"

After all, during the bulk of Howell's post-Ranger years, he continued to play in 70+ games per season.

Sure, Howell was regressing, but don't you think he would have made a difference compared to some of the third, fourth, fifth, and sixth defensemen on the Rangers' roster following the trade? Plus, this was the same Howell who just won a Norris Trophy, the last player to ever do so before the emergence of Bobby Orr - a defenseman who was in a class by himself.

In the 1971 Stanley Cup Playoffs, the Rangers lost a crushing seven-game semifinal to the Chicago Blackhawks. They'd reach the Stanley Cup Final a year later, losing the series in six games to the Boston Bruins. A season following the Stanley Cup loss, they lost a five-game semifinal series in the 1973 Stanley Cup Playoffs, where the Blackhawks ousted them again. Conversely, "Harry the Horse" logged 77 games in the 1971-72 season and 73 games in the 1972-73 season in LA.

This trade was a complete and utter failure. Ranger fans didn't like it then, and over fifty years later - this trade still stinks.

After retiring after his 24 professional seasons, Howell got into coaching and served the Cleveland Barons as the team's general manager.

In 1990, Howell finally became a Stanley Cup champion for the first time in his life - as a scout for the Mark Messier-led Edmonton Oilers. Howell was 57 years old, the same Howell who debuted for the Rangers at 19.

On March 9th, 2019, Howell, now at the age of 86, and three years following his long-overdue jersey retirement ceremony, passed away. Following his passing, many members of both the Rangers and NHL alumni wrote touching tributes, all in praise of one of the greatest Rangers to ever lace a pair of skates.

None of those tributes paid homage to his years with the Seals.

**DATE OF TRADE: June 10th, 1969**

**RANGERS ACQUIRE: First-Round Pick of the 1969 NHL Amateur Draft (#8 - Andre Dupont)**

**ST. LOUIS BLUES ACQUIRE: Phil Goyette**

Following the shocking trade of Howell, Phil Goyette, aka "The Professor," aka "The Thin Man," was dealt himself. As mentioned earlier, Goyette was a part of the Worsley/Plante trade from six years prior and thrived in the Big Apple.

And a quick spoiler alert for you: Goyette would eventually return to Broadway, but more on that later.

Similar to Howell, Francis thought Goyette's best days were behind him, as the center was set to turn 36 years old during the 1969-70 season.

In a trade that shows you how much the league had changed in this period of time (as six years prior, on June 5, 1963, the NHL held their first version of an entry draft, the 1963 NHL Amateur Draft), this was the first time the Rangers ever traded a player for a draft pick.

(This practice of trading players for draft picks, like today, would soon become commonplace. Soon, general managers would try to influence future drafts with slick maneuvers. But more on Guy Lafleur later, where I'll explain how his draft changed the way NHL general managers operated.)

This trade took place less than twenty-four hours prior to the commencement of the 1969 NHL Amateur Draft. (The word "amateur" would be replaced by the word "entry" in 1979.)

(Also of note, as we're now in an era where draft picks were frequently traded - the name of the draft, the rules of the draft, and everything else draft related would change throughout the years - just like anything else, especially in the land of the NHL.)

Francis, now with the eighth overall pick of the draft (he had the twelfth-overall pick, too, where he used that pick to draft Pierre Jarry), selected defenseman Andre Dupont.

(And, yes, another future book project could be examining every Rangers draft pick ever made! Like this and my first book - that would be another challenging project, but I enjoy such tasks!)

What did Francis do with his young, fresh-faced draft pick? After seven games with the Rangers during the 1970-71 season, "The Cat" dealt Dupont away. In time, Dupont would win two Stanley Cups with the "Broad Street Bullies" Philadelphia Flyer teams of the mid-1970s. (Like Lafleur, more on Dupont to come.)

Considering that Dupont finished his career with 810 games played and that Francis would later re-acquire Goyette - this trade was another major bomb. However, it wasn't as big of a mistake as the Howell trade.

**DATE OF TRADE: June 12th, 1969**

**RANGERS ACQUIRE: Cash**

**ST. LOUIS BLUES ACQUIRE: Sixth-Round Pick of the 1969 NHL Amateur Draft (#70 - Dale Yutsyk)**

Of these four-consecutive trades mentioned earlier, this was the one that had no impact whatsoever.

Left-winger Dale Yutsyk, from Calgary, Alberta, never made it to the NHL. Instead, he played for three more years at the CHL and WHL levels with five different teams.

That said, Francis did give up some bucks here, so this is a loss, for as minuscule as it was.

183

**DATE OF TRADE: June 17th, 1969**

**RANGERS ACQUIRE: Terry Sawchuk and Sandy Snow**

**DETROIT RED WINGS ACQUIRE: Larry Jeffrey**

Larry Jeffrey, as discussed earlier, retired after the 1968-69 season.

However, since right-winger Bill "Sandy" Snow, from Donkin, Nova Scotia, didn't have much NHL potential, and because Terry Sawchuk was damaged goods at this point - this trade wasn't voided as previous trades were.

(As a call-up for the Wings, he only played in three NHL games in his career, which took place during the 1968-69 season - he finished out the final four years of his career in the minors.)

Obviously, Terry Sawchuk, arguably the greatest goaltender of all time, was the big fish here.

(While I won't be going through Sawchuk's entire career here, if you haven't already, you owe it to yourself to read *"Sawchuk: The Troubles and Triumphs of the World's Greatest Goalie,"* as written by David Dupuis. In 2019, the film "Goalie" was released, a movie that loosely adapted Dupuis' 1998 tell-all and used the book as its main source material.)

Towards the end of Sawchuk's career, he enjoyed and thrived with less playing time. In fact, when splitting the net with Johnny Bower, Sawchuk helped the Maple Leafs win the Stanley Cup in 1967 - their last championship as of this (2022) writing.

At this point in his Hall of Fame career (Class of 1971), Sawchuk was also a troubled man. While he could still tend the net, he couldn't do so full time.

Even worse for the Ukrainian-Canadian (Sawchuk was born in Winnipeg, Manitoba, but his father was from Ukraine) was a litany of off-ice issues, which stemmed from his philandering, spousal abuse (often physical), and chronic alcoholism.

184

Sawchuk himself knew that he could no longer endure a full-time NHL schedule. Now approaching the age of forty, the four-time Vezina winner and four-time Stanley Cup champion was looking for a "time-share" situation, to only play sparingly. Such a situation was available in New York.

Now in New York, Sawchuk was looking to play even less than he did during his second stint in Detroit (thirteen games). Enter Eddie Giacomin, now in the prime of his career - and a goalie who wasn't looking to vacate his net. The situation worked out splendidly for the two Hall of Famers, as Giacomin handled the lion's share of the work, and Sawchuk was only used whenever Eddie needed a break.

(It should be stated here that Gilles Villemure, who would later backup Giacomin, and win a Vezina Trophy in the process, too, was also in the Rangers' farm system at this time. However, Francis thought Villemure needed another year of "seasoning," which is why this Sawchuk option was so attractive. This trade killed two birds with one stone. And who's killing birds with stones these days anyway?)

During the 1969-70 season, Sawchuk's last, Giacomin started 70 of the Rangers' 76 games. Sawchuk took the other six starts and would also play in two more games in relief of Giacomin, as Sawchuk finished the final season of his career with a total of eight games played - eight of 972 NHL contests.

(Of note, in the 1970 Stanley Cup Playoffs, a six-game first-round series loss to the Bruins, Giacomin started five of the games. Sawchuk started the other, and would also play two more in relief of Giacomin.)

On April 16th, 1970, the Bruins closed out the Rangers, thus ending the season for the Blueshirts. Six weeks later, Sawchuk passed away at forty years old.

In a well-known, tragic story that has since been printed thousands of times, on April 29th, 1970, thirteen days following the Rangers' last game, Sawchuk and his teammate & roommate of the time, Ron

Stewart, went out for a night on the town. However, unfortunately, it did not end well.

Sawchuk, who owed Stewart money for rent/housing expenses and disagreed with Stewart about whose responsibility it was to clean the house, got into a shoving match with his housemate at a local Long Beach, NY, watering hole. The physical confrontation led to the removal of both men from the bar.

Once leaving the bar and back at their 83 Bay Street, Atlantic Beach residence, the two continued their argument, and once again - it got physical. Sawchuk, who was already declining in health (he weighed nearly fifty pounds less from the peak of his career at this point of his life), got the worst of it.

As the two men brawled, Sawchuk fell, landing on Stewart's knee or a barbeque grill. (Following the incident, the two men themselves weren't exactly sure what Sawchuk landed on, and as noted, the duo were drinking heavily at the time of the melee, thus impacting their memory.)

Sawchuk was writhing on the ground in complete agony. He was rushed to the hospital, where he was determined to have suffered a laundry list of health problems, including internal bleeding, low blood pressure, and liver problems. In addition, his gallbladder was severely damaged, and an operation had to be performed to remove it.

For three weeks, Sawchuk remained in the hospital - privately.

A week before his passing, he was visited by Shirley Fischler, the wife of Stan, a female pioneer of hockey reporting who at the time didn't identify herself as a reporter. Sawchuk was under the impression that he was talking to a concerned fan, so he opened up to her. Shirley reported the entire story, mentioning how frail the greatest goaltender of all time had looked.

On May 31st, 1970, Sawchuk died. Pulmonary embolism was cited as the cause of death, but he had many health problems before and after the fight with Stewart.

Before his passing, Sawchuck had assumed all the blame for the fight, making it clear that his condition had nothing to do with Stewart. However, a grand jury was put together to see if criminal charges were necessary. The grand jury decided Stewart was in the clear, thus not having to endure a terrible time at trial, where he'd have to relive the incident of his friend's death.

As you can imagine, Stewart took the news very hard, but Francis stood by him. Francis also had to claim/identify Sawchuk's body at the coroner.

Here's George Grimm, a Francis biographer, on the topic of this incident, courtesy of his excellent book (I loved it and highly recommend it) "We Did Everything But Win":

*"The whole Sawchuk affair was one of the toughest things I had ever faced in my whole life," recalled Francis. "They called me back, I was out scouting in Quebec and I had to go to the hospital" Emile recalled. "He underwent a five-hour operation that lasted until midnight and the doctor came out and said 'you might as well go home because there's nothing you can do here, we'll call you if anything changes'."*

*"They called me at six in the morning to tell me he died. I'll never forget it was Memorial Day weekend in New York and I had to go to get his body from the morgue on Second Avenue, and honest to God there were 30 people lying on the floor in bags like we carry hockey sticks in. The guy that took me down there, I could tell he'd been drinking, I could smell it. He said 'Okay which one is the body you came to claim?' I mean I could have nailed him right there. I looked over and I saw Terry's head sticking out from one of the bags with a tag around his neck to identify him. God damn that's where he ended up on the floor in a morgue in New York City on Memorial Day weekend. And I said to myself, if this guy only knew that's the greatest goalkeeper ever. I mean I was sick, believe me."*

187

And now, the analysis of this trade, which yes, I know doesn't mean anything because of the tragedy.

Was this trade a win or a loss?

I'm going to give Francis the win here, although a slight one.

Jeffrey retired so he never came back to burn the Rangers. Sawchuk was a perfect backup for the situation. Giacomin continued to excel, while Villemure gained valuable experience.

It should also be noted that even if this fight and Sawchuk's untimely death had never occurred - that this very likely would have been Sawchuk's last season anyway - a genuine concern from the people who knew him, as no one knew what Sawchuk would do in his life after hockey. Due to his issues, it was doubtful that any team would have given him a coaching or front-office job.

With Villemure soon to be ready (he played in 34 games for the Rangers during the 1970-71 season) and with Francis now embracing a time-share in net - Sawchuk was always going to be a one-year stop-gap type of player for the Rangers.

What Sawchuk would have done had he lived is up for debate, but moving on from him would have never hurt the Rangers.

**DATE OF TRADE: June 27th, 1969**

**RANGERS ACQUIRE: Cash**

**ST. LOUIS BLUES ACQUIRE: Norm Beaudin and Camille Henry**

As mentioned before, Norm Beaudin never played for the Rangers. And as also mentioned, Henry finished his career out in St. Louis, where he wasn't the same player he was in New York.

This trade helped the Rangers' bank account, even if Camille Henry was a major figure in Rangers' history.

**DATE OF TRADE: February 2nd, 1970**

**RANGERS ACQUIRE: Teddy Irvine**

**LOS ANGELES KINGS ACQUIRE: Real Lemieux and Juha Widing**

This was a big trade - and one that Francis easily won.

As mentioned earlier, Real Lemieux, acquired during the offseason, only lasted with the Rangers for 55 games in his first stint with the club before being packaged with the Finnish center Juha Widing (as a young boy, he would also gain Swedish citizenship).

Widing, a rare European player in this era, only played in 44 games for the Rangers in his rookie 1969-70 season. However, he would have a great career in Los Angeles, playing in parts of eight seasons (including five seasons of fifty-five points or better) for the Kings.

Following his work in LaLa Land, Widing played for the Cleveland Barons for one season. He retired after the 1977-78 season after his lone season with the WHA Edmonton Oilers.

While Lemieux and Widing had solid NHL careers, "The Baby-Faced Assassin," Teddy Irvine (who is also part of my "New York Rangers Rink of Honor") soon became a signature component of the Emile Francis era.

The left-wing of the greatest third line in all of Rangers' franchise history (coupled with center Pete Stemkowski and right-wing Bruce MacGregor), Irvine was a major contributor during the deep Ranger playoff runs of the early 1970s. In total, Irvine spent parts of six seasons with the Rangers, where he played in every playoff game during this run.

In the modern day, the native of Winnipeg, Manitoba, Irvine is perhaps now best known as being the father of professional wrestler Chris Jericho.

Following his career with the Rangers, Irvine later became part of a "rebuilding franchise" trade, when he was dealt to the St. Louis Blues. More on that trade once we get to the year 1975.

While Widing posted better offensive numbers than Irvine ever did, the former #27 of the Rangers completely stood out in his well-defined role on the third line.

As mentioned, sometimes general managers trade better players out of roster necessity. Irvine easily made the Rangers better during the GAG Line years.

I wouldn't consider this trade a loss for LA. They did well with what they received in return. However, from a "roster stew" perspective - the Rangers got what they wanted here and more.

**DATE OF TRADE: March 3rd, 1970**

**RANGERS ACQUIRE: Tim Horton**

**TORONTO MAPLE LEAFS ACQUIRE: Future Considerations (Denis Dupere)**

Denis Dupere, a left-wing from Jonquiere, Quebec, who also sported a sweet handlebar mustache in his playing days, never played for the Rangers. However, he did amass 421 games, playing for the Leafs, Capitals, Blues, Scouts (Kansas City), and the Rockies.

One of the highlights of his career took place in the 1974-75 season, as Dupere became the first-ever player to represent the Washington Capitals franchise in an All-Star game.

Defenseman Tim Horton (where I'm obligated by law to mention that he was the founder of the self-named "Tim Hortons" breakfast chain of restaurants. For Americans not familiar, "Tim Hortons" is basically the "Dunkin Donuts" of Canada), prior to this trade, the native of Cochrane, Ontario, had already completed eighteen full seasons with the Leafs. At the time of this trade, Horton had played in 59 more games for the Leafs in his nineteenth season with the club.

During his nineteen years in Toronto, Horton won four Stanley Cups (1962, 1963, 1964, and 1967) and was named to the All-Star game six times.

However, with Toronto struggling during this time and Horton's near-sightedness, the Leafs bid adieu to their two-decade defenseman. Up next was a "cup of coffee" (har-har-har) with the Rangers.

The hard-hitting, yet clean defenseman, played in 93 games for the Rangers over parts of two seasons.

Following the 1970-71 campaign, Horton was claimed by the Pittsburgh Penguins during the NHL's 1971 intra-league draft. Horton would play for the Penguins for one season and would move on with his legendary Hall of Fame career (Class of 1977) to the Buffalo Sabres, which took place during the 1972-73 season. He remained in Buffalo in the season that followed.

However, Horton never finished the 1973-74 season - nor is it truly known if he would have retired following it.

On February 20th, 1974, Horton, then 44 years old (and following a game against the Leafs, nonetheless), started his drive back to Buffalo. Horton was driving his new De Tomaso Pantera sports car. The expensive automobile was given to him by his old friend and boss Punch Imlach, who, just like Horton, had also established his legacy in Toronto.

Imlach, now the Sabres' general manager at this point in time, had previously given Horton the car as an enticement (a successful one) in order to get Horton to continue to play for the Sabres rather than retiring or going elsewhere.

On his trek from Toronto to Buffalo, Horton made a pit stop at an office he shared with Ron Joyce, his business partner in his chain of restaurants. Once there, Horton called his brother Gerry on the phone. During the call, Gerry noticed that his famous sibling was drunk. So Gerry asked his brother to park it and stay overnight.

The Hall of Famer refused both the request and the offer.

At around 4:30 AM, now February 21st, 1974, Horton's lifeless body was found 123 feet away from his crashed car. The car was totaled, and Horton was not wearing a seatbelt.

At the time, the Canadian police did not want to disclose details about Horton's death; instead, they tried to protect his legacy. So while it was assumed at the time that his death resulted from drinking and driving, that wouldn't officially be confirmed until 2005 - over thirty years later.

When Horton's autopsy (and police report) became public three decades following the crash, it was revealed that his blood-alcohol content was twice the legal limit. A bottle of vodka was also reported as one of the items found at the crash site. In addition, Horton also had various drugs in pill form - both in his system and among the debris.

Like Sawchuk, Horton's death was of his own doing. Unfortunately, this sad ending makes it hard to assess the trade and its aftermath.

However, we can say the following: this was another trade where Francis went for an accomplished veteran at the expense of youth. Had the Rangers survived their seven-game penultimate series of the 1971 Stanley Cup playoffs with Chicago, who knows - perhaps Horton would have won a championship with the Rangers too.

**DATE OF TRADE: June 10th, 1970**

**RANGERS ACQUIRE: Cash**

**BUFFALO SABRES ACQUIRE: Ted Hodgson**

This wasn't much of a deal here. Right-winger Ted Hodgson, from Hobbema, Alberta, accumulated only four games of NHL experience throughout his lengthy career, and those games took place in Boston during the 1966-67 season.

192

Following this cash transaction, Hodgson remained at the minor-league level but would later play in 107 career WHA games during the 1972-73 and 1973-74 seasons with the Cleveland Crusaders and Los Angeles Sharks.

After his WHA days ended, he returned to the minors, where he last played in the 1976-77 season with the Oklahoma City Blazers (CHL).

This was another trade that gave Francis more cash on hand.

**DATE OF TRADE: September 9th, 1970**

**RANGERS ACQUIRE: Cash**

**ST. LOUIS BLUES ACQUIRE: Gerald Lemire**

In another deal that put more money in the bank, Francis sent defenseman Gerald Lemire, from Cornwall, Ontario, to the St. Louis Blues.

Lemire would never play in the NHL. In fact, he never played hockey at a major or minor-league level again following this deal, as his 1969-70 season with the Kansas City Blues (CHL) wound up being his last season as a professional hockey player.

**DATE OF TRADE: October 31st, 1970**

**RANGERS ACQUIRE: Pete Stemkowski**

**DETROIT RED WINGS ACQUIRE: Larry Brown**

This was another "home run" (or "hat trick," since we're talking hockey), of a trade by "The Cat." This acquisition of "Stemmer," another featured name in my "New York Rangers Rink of Honor," now gave the Rangers two-thirds of what would become the best third-line in franchise history. And heck, defenseman Larry Brown, from Brandon, Manitoba, would soon be back, too, albeit briefly.

Prior to this trade, center Pete Stemkowski, born in Winnipeg, Manitoba, had won the Stanley Cup in 1967 with the Leafs. Now in Detroit, he had quickly worn out his welcome with new Wings' bench boss Ned Harkness. As the legend goes, Stemkowski, always a practical joker, made a wisecrack about Harkness and his days at Cornell, as this job in Detroit was the head coach's first NHL gig.

(Of note, Harkness was so bad in Detroit, where even to this day, his time with the Red Wings is still known as the "Darkness with Harkness" era.)

Without knowing it at the time, Stemmer's affinity for comedy paid off. Harkness wanted the center out. What happened next splendidly worked out for both the Rangers and Stemkowski.

Following the trade, the new number 21 in blue would spend the next seven years of his life in New York, where he became part of the many deep Stanley Cup Playoff runs of the Francis era.

In fact, Stemmer grew to love New York so much (where he met his wife at the time and raised his family), that he remained on Long Island following his playing days. (To this day, Stemmer maintains a Nassau County residence and still works with the Rangers today - as both a member of the alumni and on radio broadcasts.)

As discussed in detail in my first book, Stemmer scored two overtime goals (including a triple-overtime game-winner) against the Blackhawks in the Rangers' 1971 semifinal series with the Blackhawks. Unfortunately, the Rangers lost the seventh and deciding game of the series.

And had the Rangers and Stemmer defeated the Blackhawks and won the Stanley Cup that year? Stemmer's place in Rangers' history would have dwarfed Stephane Matteau's eventual spot - and that's not a shot at, nor an indictment of Matteau. It's just that Stemmer was the better player.

Plus, and more importantly, when making this argument, if the Rangers won the Stanley Cup in 1971, there would be no 54-year-old "curse" either. But, alas, I'm dealing with "what if" questions again!

Along with Rod Gilbert and Walt Tkaczuk, Stemkowski survived the end of the Emile Francis era. Following the 1976-77 season, he would play one more NHL season in Los Angeles with the Kings before calling it a career after 24 games played with the AHL Springfield Indians, which took place during the 1978-79 season.

Again, this was an easy win for Francis.

**DATE OF TRADE: November 2nd, 1970**

**RANGERS ACQUIRE: Steve Andrascik**

**DETROIT RED WINGS ACQUIRE: Don Luce**

Don Luce, a center from London, Ontario, who was acquired by the Rangers with their third-round pick (14th overall) of the 1966 NHL Amateur Draft, had only 21 NHL games under his belt at the time of this trade - all with the Rangers.

Luce would then play in 873 more NHL games. After a one-and-done season in the Motor City, he spent the bulk of his career with the Sabres, becoming a Buffalo mainstay for a decade.

Following ten games with the Kings during the 1980-81 season, Luce played one more season with the Toronto Maple Leafs. Ironically, as of this 2022 writing, he's a scout for the Leafs, where prior to this gig, he also performed coaching and front office duties for both the Sabres and Flyers.

The native of Sherridon, Manitoba, right-wing Steve Andrascik, who was the eleventh-overall pick of the 1968 NHL Amateur Draft, never played in the NHL. After toiling in the minor leagues for most of his career, he'd get a chance to play professional hockey during the 1974-75 season - in the WHA.

In two WHA seasons, Andrascik played with three teams - the Indianapolis Racers, the Michigan Stags, and the Cincinnati Stingers. He played 97 WHA games in all, picking up 22 points.

In other words - this trade was a huge loss. I know you can't *"win 'em all,"* but this swap was particularly awful.

Speaking of awful, let's get into our next trade.

**DATE OF TRADE: January 26th, 1971**

**RANGERS ACQUIRE: Glen Sather**

**PITTSBURGH PENGUINS ACQUIRE: Syl Apps Jr. and Sheldon Kannegiesser**

Okay, okay, okay - I'm joking. Glen Sather wasn't awful when he played for the Rangers. I'm not a fan of his front office tenure with the franchise, a brutal experience that is now in its 22nd year at the time of this writing, and an experience that has produced no championships!

(Fun Fact: Glen Sather appears in both my "New York Rangers Rink of Honor" and "New York Rangers Stink of Dishonor" lists. I think I may have plugged my first book enough!)

Defenseman Sheldon Kannegiesser, from North Bay, Ontario, was the "player to be named later" following this deal. He finished the 1971-72 season with the Penguins and joined the Rangers the following season. Thirteen games into the 1972-73 season, he was traded again in a deal we'll soon discuss.

Kannegiesser, following his career (where most of his success came with the Kings), wrote a poetry book entitled, "Warrior of Winter." In promotion for the book, which was released in 2009, the blue liner said the following:

*"Sheldon did not always endear himself to his teammates by being an outspoken proponent of Christianity – one of the first Christians in the NHL to make his faith known.*

*"Some of Sheldon's poems speak to his faith in God and he is also writing a second book called "Cut to the Core" which deals with more spiritual issues."*

(Of note: I have not read either of Sheldon's books.)

Syl Apps Jr., from Toronto, Ontario, had played in 31 games for the Rangers at the time of this trade. The center, the son of a Hall of Famer, spent parts of eight seasons with the Penguins. Following a trade made in November 1977, he'd finish out his career with the Kings. He retired after the 1979-80 season.

Apps Jr. played in 727 NHL games, while Kannegiesser played 366 NHL games. And here's a fun fact: Both Apps Jr. and Kannegiesser spent their entire NHL careers with the Rangers, Penguins, and Kings.

Left-wing Glen Sather, known as "Slats," was part of the peak of the Francis era. Born in High River, Alberta, only to eventually become the pride of Banff, Alberta, Sather has spent his entire adult life in the NHL.

The Class of 1997 Hall of Famer (as a builder, due to his work in Edmonton - an experience that current Rangers' owner, James Dolan, has paid Sather millions of dollars for - and we'll soon get more into this observation once we hit the year 2000), played in the NHL for ten years. The prime of his playing career took place across parts of four seasons with the Rangers - including a trip to the 1972 Stanley Cup Final.

Just like the Ted Irvine trade, while Sather wasn't the best player of this lot, he did serve a purpose during his playing days on Broadway - as opposed to his days while behind a desk with the Rangers!

From a talent standpoint, the Penguins won this trade. However, from a "putting together a complete roster" perspective - Francis didn't lose either.

**DATE OF TRADE: February 1st, 1971**

**RANGERS ACQUIRE: Larry Brown and Bruce MacGregor**

**DETROIT RED WINGS ACQUIRE: Arnie Brown, Tom Miller, and Mike Robitaille**

This trade was another big win for Francis, as this deal completed the trifecta of the greatest third-line in franchise history.

Bruce MacGregor, the right-winger from Edmonton, Alberta, aside from Irvine and Stemkowski, had already logged 675 games of NHL experience during his near eleven-season tenure in Detroit.

Like other veteran acquisitions, while statistically, MacGregor had his best years in Detroit, he was more than serviceable, now in his new role on the Rangers' third line.

Worth mentioning: In Detroit, he finished his career with a plus/minus stat of negative 34. During parts of four seasons with the Rangers, he finished with a plus/minus stat of positive 53.

Also worth mentioning: After finishing with the Rangers, MacGregor jumped to the Edmonton Oilers of the WHA, where he finished his two seasons in Alberta with a plus/minus stat of negative 44.

(And, yes, I know the plus/minus stat doesn't mean as much as it used to, but needless to say, these numbers are telling. They illustrate how much success the right-winger had in New York.)

Like others previously mentioned in this book, MacGregor was also part of the best years of the Francis era. However, despite fourteen seasons in the NHL, he'd never win the Stanley Cup as a player. Instead, he won five Stanley Cups in Edmonton as the team's assistant general manager - while serving under Glen Sather.

Rearguard Larry Brown, previously dealt to Detroit in the Stemkowski trade, returned to Broadway three months later. However, following this 1970-71 season, he was sent to Philadelphia as a result of the NHL intra-league draft. He didn't last long in Philly, either, as at the mid-point of the 1971-72 season, he was traded to Los Angeles, where he would remain until the 1977-78 season was complete.

After two seasons in the minors, Brown retired in 1980. Ultimately, he finished his NHL career with 455 games played.

Going to Detroit was defenseman Mike Robitaille, who, of note, is of no relation to a one-time Ranger himself (and former Red Wing), Luc Robitaille.

Following the move to the Red Wings, the native of Midland, Ontario, spent parts of four seasons with the Buffalo Sabres and then crossed the border to Vancouver.

Unfortunately, at age 29, he suffered a career-ending injury due to a blind-sided, dirty hit from Dennis Owchar of the Pittsburgh Penguins. Robitaille would later sue the Canucks for mistreating his neck injury - a lawsuit he won.

Despite his time in the NHL being cut short, he still finished his career with 382 games played.

Southpaw center Tom Miller, from Kitchener, Ontario, wasn't long for the Wings, having played in only 29 games for Detroit in the 1971-72 season. Following his brief time with the spoked wheel, Miller became an "Original Islander," as selected by the trashy franchise (hey, I'm a Rangers fan - go with it!), during their 1972 expansion draft.

Miller played in 69 games for the orange and blue in their inaugural campaign. Following that season, he played in parts of two more seasons with the Isles, where during that time, he also split time in the minors. After one game played, he retired following the 1974-75 season.

The last player going to Detroit was a long-time Ranger, Arnie Brown, who spent parts of the previous seven seasons with the Rangers - the prime seasons of his career, where the defenseman manned the Blueshirts' blue line.

One of the pieces who came to New York following the Andy Bathgate trade, Brown set career highs in goals (15), assists (21) and points (36) during the 1969-70 season.

After finishing the 1970-71 season with Detroit, he remained with the Red Wings for the 1971-72 campaign - the season where the Rangers made it to the Stanley Cup Final. During the 1972 NHL Expansion draft, he, too, like Tom Miller, joined the Islanders for their first season of existence.

However, Brown, unlike Miller, was near the end of his career at this point in time. Brown wouldn't finish the season at the Nassau Coliseum. At the mid-mark of the season, he was dealt to the other expansion team, the Atlanta Flames, the team that he ended his NHL career with following the 1973-74 season.

After wrapping up in Atlanta, Brown would play in one more professional season, this time in the WHA, splitting time between the Vancouver Blazers and the Michigan Stags.

While losing Brown was tough for Ranger fans at the time, MacGregor's tenure in New York more than made up for it. Give a checkmark in the win column for "The Cat."

**DATE OF TRADE: March 2nd, 1971**

**RANGERS ACQUIRE: Dale Rolfe**

**DETROIT RED WINGS ACQUIRE: Jim Krulicki**

This trade was another "slam dunk" - I'm sorry, wrong sport - "hat trick" win for Francis.

Jim Krulicki, a right-winger out of Kitchener, Ontario, only played in the NHL for one season, where all of his games took place during this 1970-71 campaign. After 27 games with the Rangers, he played in 14 more NHL contests for the Red Wings.

Despite being only 23 years of age, and with better financial options for him elsewhere, Krulicki, who found the NHL to be much more difficult than the minor-league levels he was used to, retired and pursued a non-hockey career.

Dale Rolfe, a left-handed defenseman, like others mentioned in this period of the early 1970s, was an established NHL veteran who joined the Rangers at the height of the Francis era. He was also part of the deep Stanley Cup Playoff runs that the Rangers went on before Francis blew everything up in 1975.

Rolfe, who had previously spent time with the Bruins, Kings, and Red Wings, went on to have five great years in New York. Following the 1974-75 season, the veteran of 509 NHL games called it a career.

A native of Timmins, Ontario, Rolfe was a defensive defenseman, relying on his skills and long reach to deny his opponents. He finished his career with 25 goals and 125 assists, for a nice round number of 150 points.

With Krulicki finding the NHL to be above his head, and with Rolfe's success - Francis continued to build his team that would eventually challenge for the Stanley Cup in 1972.

**DATE OF TRADE: May 1st, 1971**

**RANGERS ACQUIRE: Mike McMahon Jr.**

**LOS ANGELES KINGS ACQUIRE: Wayne Rivers**

Mike McMahon Junior, whose father also played in the NHL (Senior won a Stanley Cup in 1944 with the Canadiens), and just like his dad, the son was also a defenseman.

While the native of Quebec City, Quebec, wouldn't win a Stanley Cup like his father, he was a two-time Ranger, playing for the Blueshirts during the 1963-64 season. On June 15th, 1966, McMahon, who had logged sixty games with the club at this point in time, was claimed by his father's former team, the Habs, during an intra-league draft. However, he would never play for Montreal.

After being traded by Montreal to Minnesota, McMahon bounced around the league and the minors a bit, playing for the North Stars, Blackhawks, Red Wings, Penguins, and the Sabres.

Now with the Kings at the time of this trade, he'd never suit up for the club. Following the trade, he played in one game for the Rangers in the 1971-72 season. The rest of his season was spent with the Providence Reds (AHL).

Following this 1971-72 campaign, he joined the WHA for four seasons, playing for the Minnesota Fighting Saints and the San Diego Mariners.

A veteran of 224 NHL contests, and 279 games in the WHA, he retired after the 1976-77 season as a member of the Springfield Indians (AHL).

As mentioned earlier, Wayne Rivers, a native of Hamilton, Ontario, was mainly a career minor leaguer.

The final four games of Rivers' NHL career took place in the 1968-69 season. Following this trade, he, too, jumped to the WHA, playing for five seasons, including two seasons for the New York Raiders and three seasons with McMahon's club, the San Diego Mariners.

Of note: While the WHA was a professional league, while also being much more inferior to the NHL, Rivers had the best seasons of his career in the second league, including a 54-goal and 107-point season for the Mariners during the 1974-75 campaign.

Rivers, following the 1978-79 season, now in the PHL for the San Francisco Shamrocks, retired. In the season prior to his retirement, Rivers, now in a dual player/head coach role, won the Pacific Hockey League championship with San Fran.

This was a long way of saying this trade was a wash. The next trade wouldn't be. Far from it.

**DATE OF TRADE: May 25th, 1971**

**RANGERS ACQUIRE: First-Round Pick of the 1971 NHL Amateur Draft (#10 - Steve Vickers)**

**ST. LOUIS BLUES ACQUIRE: Peter McDuffe**

Goaltender Peter McDuffe, a product out of Milton, Ontario (where he's part of that town's Hall of Fame, an induction in 2017), was hardly a goaltender of the NHL starter variety.

While he did play in 57 NHL games for parts of four seasons, he played in ten for the Blues. He'd later return to the Rangers, where once returning (he played in seven games for the club over two seasons), he mocked the St. Louis system, saying, *"in St. Louis, they don't tell you which end of the stick to hold."*

The majority of McDuffe's NHL experience took place with the expansion Kansas City Scouts. (A franchise that later became the Colorado Rockies, the now New Jersey Devils.) McDuffe would receive 36 games of action in the 1974-75 season with the Scouts and four more with the Red Wings during the 1975-76 season.

McDuff finished his career in the WHA, where he last played for the Indianapolis Racers in 1978.

St. Louis, in a state of peril, soon saw Scotty Bowman leave the organization following a disagreement with the Salomon family, the team's owners. He'd move on to Montreal. The rest was hockey history.

Temporarily replacing Bowman was the team's first general manager, ex-Ranger Lynn Patrick. For whatever reason, Patrick saw something in McDuffe, so much so that he gave up his tenth-overall pick in the 1971 NHL Amateur Draft - aka the Guy Lafleur and Marcel Dionne draft - two players we'll soon discuss.

Sixteen days following this trade, Emile Francis selected left-winger Steve Vickers out of Toronto, Ontario. The rest was history (and as extensively covered in my first book - but I'm sure you're sick of these reminders already!)

After the draft, Vickers, soon to be "The Sarge," played the 1971-72 season out in Omaha with the Knights (CHL). A season later, behind 30 goals and 23 assists, he'd win the Calder Trophy in 1973.

All in all, Vickers played in 698 games for the Rangers in his nine-season career. He also finished with 246 goals, 340 assists, and 586 points. To this day, just like he was in his prime - he remains a heavy fan favorite.

A two-time All-Star with the Rangers, this trade wasn't just a hat-trick of a win, it was a seven-point game, too, just like the seven points (still a franchise record) Vickers picked up in a February 18, 1976 game against the Washington Capitals.

What was Lynn Patrick thinking?

**DATE OF TRADE: May 25th, 1971**

**RANGERS ACQUIRE: Player To Be Named Later (Bobby Rousseau)**

**MINNESOTA NORTH STARS ACQUIRE: Bob Nevin**

Bob Nevin (and my obligatory statement of "someone else who was featured in 'The New York Rangers Rink of Honor and the Rafters of Madison Square Garden'") was hated through no fault of his own when he first came to the Rangers. After all, the right-winger was the key piece coming back to the Rangers in the Bathgate trade.

Over time, not only did Nevin eventually earn the respect and hearts of Ranger fans - but he also served the franchise as team captain spanning seven different seasons.

In a cruel irony, not only did Nevin (who won the Stanley Cup twice with the Leafs before the Bathgate trade) miss the Leafs' 1964 Stanley Cup victory - he'd miss the Rangers' run to the 1972 Stanley Cup Final.

Following this trade, Nevin spent two seasons with the North Stars and then three more seasons with the Kings before retiring at the conclusion of the 1976-77 campaign with the Oilers, then of the WHA, with thirteen games in all.

Bobby Rousseau, also a right-winger like Bathgate and Nevin before him, and also an NHL veteran at the time of this trade, won the Calder Trophy in 1962 with the Montreal Canadiens. He also won four Stanley Cups (1965, 1966, 1968, and 1969) with the Habs.

At the time of this trade, Rousseau, who was also previously a three-time NHL All-Star with over a decade's worth of NHL experience, had been floundering with the North Stars, so the trade to New York was a welcome one.

In the 1972 Stanley Cup Playoffs, Rousseau led all Rangers in assists (11) and points (17). He was a big reason for the team's run to the final round.

The native of Montreal, Quebec, remained with the Rangers for three more seasons but would play in only eight games during the 1974-75 season - his last. And as you may already know, things changed big-time for the franchise in 1975.

When it comes to this trade featuring talented right-wingers, due to how Rousseau performed in the 1972 Stanley Cup Playoffs (the season following this trade), this was a win - even if Minnesota and Nevin aren't losers here either. Francis went all in. The goal fell just two wins shy. And had Jean Ratelle been at 100% - who knows?

**DATE OF TRADE: June 10th, 1971**

**RANGERS ACQUIRE: Seventh-Round Pick of the 1971 NHL Amateur Draft (#96 - Doug Keeler)**

**CHICAGO BLACKHAWKS ACQUIRE: Cash**

Southpaw defenseman Doug Keeler never played in the NHL. Instead, following this draft, the native of Espanola, Ontario, spent the next five years of his life playing for inferior minor leagues, such as the OHA, NAHL, and IHL.

Francis spent a few bucks on a seventh-round long shot. It didn't work - no big deal.

**DATE OF TRADE: June 14th, 1971**

**RANGERS ACQUIRE: Cash**

**ST. LOUIS BLUES ACQUIRE: Glenn Patrick**

This trade was a weird one, not because defenseman Glenn Patrick had a great career or anything like that.

Patrick was a hometown kid born in New York, NY. He was also Lester Patrick's grandchild and Lynn Patrick's son - where yes, his father was the general manager of the Blues at the time.

When first brought to the Rangers by his father, Lester, Lynn Patrick often heard the word "nepotism" early in his career - especially when he struggled. (As you may know, he would soon overcome that talk.) Lynn's brother, Muzz, didn't have to hear such talk, as Lester's other son quickly excelled upon his arrival. So when trading for his own son, Lynn was hoping for a fate similar to Muzz's.

Francis threw Glenn's father a bone with this trade, but Lynn's son wasn't long for St. Louis nor the NHL.

Following one game played during the 1973-74 season (over two years following this trade), the defenseman then moved on to the Seals, playing in two games during the 1974-75 season.

Lester's grandkid would play in 35 more NHL games - his final games - with the lowly Cleveland Barons (the relocated Seals) in the 1976-77 season.

Released by the Barons on February 17th, 1977, he signed a contract with the WHA Edmonton Oilers a day later. That's where he would finish his professional career, logging only four points in twenty-three games with the Oil.

In short - this was a favor that did Francis no harm.

**DATE OF TRADE: November 15, 1971**

**RANGERS ACQUIRE: Gene Carr, Wayne Connelly, and Jim Lorentz**

**ST. LOUIS BLUES ACQUIRE: Andre Dupont, Jack Egers, and Mike Murphy**

Andre Dupont, who, as mentioned earlier in the failed Phil Goyette trade, was the Rangers' eighth-overall pick of the 1969 NHL Amateur Draft. He played seven games for the Rangers in the 1970-71 season before being dealt away. (At the time of this trade, the defenseman was toiling with the Rangers' AHL affiliate, the Providence Reds.)

After this trade, Dupont went on to log 810 games played in the NHL. (He also won two Stanley Cups along the way with the Flyers.)

Following his run in Philly, Dupont spent the final three years of his career with the Quebec Nordiques, where he retired after the 1982-83 season.

Right-winger Jack Egers, from Sudbury, Ontario, had played in 83 games across parts of three seasons with the Rangers. The Rangers' fourth-round pick of the 1966 NHL Amateur Draft (20th overall) then moved on to St. Louis, starting with this 1970-71 season - had the best years of his career with the Blues.

For comparison, Egers finished the 1972-73 season with 24 goals and 48 points - his career highs in these scoring categories. Prior to this trade, Egers' best numbers with the Rangers were seven goals and 17 points, which were recorded in the 1970-71 season.

Ironically, due to the success that Egers had in St. Louis, he'd later be back with the Blueshirts. More on that to come.

Mike Murphy, who, after retiring, would later become the head coach of both the Los Angeles Kings and Toronto Maple Leafs. As

207

of this writing, Murphy is currently a Senior Vice President of the NHL's hockey operations.

The right-winger out of Toronto, Ontario, was playing for the Omaha Knights (CHL) at the time of this trade. Like Egers, Murphy would also soon rejoin the Rangers.

Coming over from St. Louis to New York was center Jim Lorentz from Waterloo, Ontario. Lorentz had previously won a Stanley Cup in 1970 with the Boston Bruins.

Lorentz, who had played only twelve games for the Blues this 1971-72 season, would play five more games for the Rangers. So he'd soon find himself wearing his third different jersey of the season in less than two months following this trade. It would also be the last NHL jersey Lorentz would ever have to wear, but more on that in just a bit.

The native of Rouyn-Noranda, Quebec, right-winger Wayne Connelly, wouldn't last in New York as long as Lorentz did - despite Lorentz not even lasting two months with the organization. In fact, Connelly would be traded just twenty-four hours later after this deal. However, before getting into that, let's talk about the biggest name of this trade, Gene Carr.

Carr, a center, was the "centerpiece" of this transaction. At twenty years old, Emile Francis had previously (and unsuccessfully) tried to trade up for Carr, a native of Nanaimo, British Columbia, during the 1971 NHL Amateur Draft.

The 1971 NHL Amateur Draft, the biggest NHL draft at this point in time, saw Guy Lafleur go number one overall (Montreal), Jocelyn Guevremont second overall (Vancouver), and Marcel Dionne third overall (Detroit). Carr went fourth overall, as drafted by St. Louis.

Fun fact: Over time, all the top-four picks of the 1971 NHL Amateur Draft would play for the Rangers.

208

Despite Egers being at the hospital when news of this trade first broke (his wife just gave birth to his child), the allure of Carr was too great to pass up. Carr was thought of to be the future of the Rangers - or at least in the eyes of "The Cat."

However, despite early glimpses of hope - Carr never worked out. Twenty-seven months later, after a demotion to the AHL - he, too, would find himself in a different location. (But more on Bill Chadwick and Gene Carr once we get to 1974!)

Without question, this trade was another dud on Francis' ledger. While the Rangers had a decent defensemen core, giving up on Dupont was a huge mistake. It also didn't help that Carr, the big fish of the trade, and Connelly & Lorentz, the "guppies" of this trade, didn't pan out.

And as stated, both Connelly and Lorentz were involved in the following two trades Francis made.

**DATE OF TRADE: November 16th, 1971**

**RANGERS ACQUIRE: Gary Doak and Jim Wiste**

**VANCOUVER CANUCKS ACQUIRE: Dave Balon, Wayne Connelly, and Ron Stewart**

Francis, seemingly one to never turn down a multi-player deal, made another one here - after making a big deal the day prior.

Dave Balon, as mentioned earlier, was re-acquired by Francis just three seasons prior. However, the heart-and-soul left-winger, a fan favorite, was nearing the end of his career at the time of this trade.

Balon would finish this season out with the Canucks. He would then skate with the team for one more season, 1972-73, where he had the worst year of his career. He completed his professional career in the WHA, playing only nine games for the Quebec Nordiques in the 1973-74 season.

Ron Stewart, who Francis stuck with following the tragic death of Terry Sawchuk, was 39 years old at the time of this trade.

209

Ironically, after playing 42 games with the Canucks, he would soon return to the Rangers this same season. More on that in a bit.

Wayne Connelly, acquired a day prior to this trade, was flipped here. A twelve-season pro at the time, the right-winger would finish out his NHL career in Vancouver, playing 53 games for the Canucks (1971-72).

Beginning with the 1972-73 season, Connelly jumped to the WHA, where he finished out the final five seasons of his career. He had the best professional seasons of his career with the Minnesota Fighting Saints, which took place during his first three years in the WHA.

Connelly's final professional season (1976-77) saw him finish out with the Edmonton Oilers.

Defenseman Gary Doak, a native of Goderich, Ontario, was a six-season veteran of the NHL. In 1970, he won the Stanley Cup with the Bruins. Ironically, he would be competing against the Bruins during the 1972 Stanley Cup Final.

Acquired to help bolster the Rangers' playoff hopes, Doak would finish out the season in New York, playing fifty regular season games in all.

Following the Cup loss to the Bruins, Doak made his way to another Original Six team, the Detroit Red Wings. However, Boston was where Doak's heart was. After all, Boston never traded him away in the first place - Vancouver just happened to claim him during the 1970 NHL Expansion Draft.

During the season that followed Doak's one-and-done run with the Rangers, the 1972-73 campaign, Boston traded Ace Bailey in return for their familiar face. Doak would spend the final nine seasons of his career with the B's.

All in all, Doak skated in 789 games as a pro. In retirement, he later joined the Bruins as an assistant coach.

Jim Wiste, a center who once was thought of as a high-end Chicago Blackhawks prospect, the native of Moosejaw, Saskatchewan, never panned out. After three games played with the Hawks in the 1968-69 season, the Canucks claimed Wiste in their 1970 expansion draft.

Now in Vancouver, it didn't take long for one of the NHL's newest teams to give up on him. Wiste played in only 23 games for the British Columbian team - his final games as an NHLer.

The Rangers assigned Wiste to the AHL once acquiring him. Following this 1971-72 season, Wiste, like many guys who couldn't crack it in the NHL, jumped ship to the WHA, where he had the best four seasons of his professional career.

Formerly a Cleveland Crusader but now an Indianapolis Racer for the 1975-76 season, Wiste was demoted to the NAHL, the WHA's version of the AHL, never to be seen again. After five games played for the Mohawk Valley Comets (Utica, NY), Wiste called it a career.

This trade was a win, but not a big one. Doak was a huge help for the Rangers in their bid for the Stanley Cup in 1972. Balon was at the end. Stewart would be back. Everyone else was basically a WHAer.

**DATE OF TRADE: January 14th, 1972**

**RANGERS ACQUIRE: Seventh-Round Pick of the 1972 NHL Amateur Draft (#21 - Larry Sacharuk)**

**BUFFALO SABRES ACQUIRE: Jim Lorentz**

Jim Lorentz was pretty much a journeyman center at this point in time, with stops in Boston, St. Louis, and New York along the way. He would remain in Buffalo for the remainder of his career. Following his retirement, which took place after the 1977-78 season, Lorentz moved to the commentator's booth in 1981, and lasted for 26 years as the Sabres' color analyst.

In 2010, Lorentz was honored by the franchise when he was inducted into the Buffalo Sabres Hall of Fame.

Defenseman Larry Sacharuk, from Saskatoon, Saskatchewan, and just like Lorentz, had a long career in the sport following his days as a player. However, unlike Lorentz, Sacharuk didn't have as long a career in the NHL. He only played in 151 games compared to the 659 games that Lorentz played.

Sacharuk had two stints with the Rangers, playing 31 games for the club from 1972-1974. He would later move on to St. Louis, and following the 1974-75 season, was back on Broadway.

By the time he returned, the Rangers were now entering a "rebuild" (not the word that was used back then, but for historical purposes, that is what it was), and he was demoted to the AHL after two games played during the 1976-77 season.

After fifteen games played with the Indianapolis Racers (WHA) during the 1978-79 season, Sacharuk bounced around internationally, where most of his days were spent in Austria. Following his retirement, he continued to bounce around in hockey, where he coached an assortment of different teams all over the globe, including a stint in Serbia.

This trade was easily a loss - like many of these trades from 1972 and beyond would turn out to be.

It's also why just three years following the Stanley Cup run of 1972, the Rangers would be in rebuild mode - where Francis would soon be removed. Ironically, his later moves at the beginning of the rebuild would all pan out. He just wasn't there to reap the rewards.

**DATE OF TRADE: February 20th, 1972**

**RANGERS ACQUIRE: Jim Dorey**

**TORONTO MAPLE LEAFS ACQUIRE: Pierre Jarry**

Jim Dorey, a defenseman from Kingston, Ontario, was known for setting the league's single-game penalty minutes record when, on

212

October 16, 1968, he received a whopping 48 penalty minutes in a match against the Pittsburgh Penguins.

Over time, as of this writing, ten players would later surpass the 48 penalty-minutes record Dorey set. Randy Holt, a rearguard, currently holds the league record with 67 PIM in one game. (March 11, 1979, Holt's Kings played vs. the Flyers.)

Toronto's General Manager at this time, Jim Gregory, never wanted to make this trade. However, with the WHA making lucrative offers, Gregory suspected his defenseman would take the money and cross leagues. Gregory would soon be proven correct.

Dorey's Rangers' career lasted one game, as, in his first game as a Blueshirt, he suffered a separated shoulder, thus ending his season.

In the offseason, as Gregory predicted, Dorey was in the WHA at the start of the 1972-73 campaign - as a New England Whaler.

The WHA is where Dorey would finish his professional career. Once there, he remained in the WHA for the next seven seasons. During this time, where he played for the Whalers, the Toronto Toros, and the Quebec Nordiques, he won two Avco Cups - the top prize of the inferior league.

After 232 NHL games played, Dorey spent the next 431 professional games of his career as a WHAer.

Right-winger Pierre Jarry, the Rangers' first-round pick of the 1969 NHL Amateur Draft (12th overall), played in 34 games for the Rangers, with all 34 of these games taking place during this 1971-72 season.

After finishing the season with Toronto, Jarry, a native of Montreal, Quebec, spent two more seasons with the Leafs before moving on to Detroit. Statistically, his season and a half with the Red Wings would be the best time of his NHL career.

Following his run in Detroit, beginning with the 1975-76 season, Jarry spent the final three seasons of his NHL career with the

Minnesota North Stars. However, at the tail-end of the 1977-78 season, he, too, would jump to the WHA, where he finished out his career with the Edmonton Oilers after twenty-three games - five of those games were in the playoffs.

While you can never predict injuries, it was rumored that Dorey was bound for the WHA. Francis traded for him anyway, hoping to win the Stanley Cup in 1972.

That said, Dorey played in only one game for the Rangers - his last in the NHL. Jarry, following this trade, would play in 310 more. This is another way of saying this trade was a loss.

**DATE OF TRADE: March 5th, 1972**

**RANGERS ACQUIRE: Phil Goyette**

**BUFFALO SABRES ACQUIRE: Cash**

Phil Goyette, now approaching the age of 39, was a great Ranger, and as mentioned earlier, was traded away nearly three years prior to this deal. Once this trade was made, Goyette was now back in the city where he had the most individual success of his career.

This was a great trade for Francis, who had to cough up only a few bucks to get his center back for one last playoff run.

In the 1972 Stanley Cup Playoffs, Goyette played in thirteen games, picking up a goal and three assists along the way. After the loss to Boston, Goyette retired.

In the summer following the 1972 Stanley Cup Final, Goyette became the first coach of the New York Islanders. Perhaps in one last send off to Ranger fans, Goyette was canned 48 games in, due to the team's poor record of 6–38–4.

This trade was a win for Francis, as he tried to beef up his roster for a playoff run with veterans. Plus, "The Cat" didn't have to part with any assets besides cash, which is just what he did in his next trade - another trade that took place on March 5th, 1972.

**DATE OF TRADE: March 5th, 1972**

**RANGERS ACQUIRE: Ron Stewart**

**VANCOUVER CANUCKS ACQUIRE: Cash**

After his 42 games in Vancouver, Ron Stewart was back with the Rangers to help finish what he started. He played in eight games in the 1972 Stanley Cup Playoffs. He'd also remain with the club for the start of the 1972-73 campaign, where he would soon become an answer to a trivia question, *"Who was the first Ranger ever traded to the Islanders?"*

Spoiler alert: We'll soon discuss that trade in just a few pages.

This trade was a win, not a big one, but a win either way.

**DATE OF TRADE: May 24th, 1972**

**RANGERS ACQUIRE: Joe Zanussi and First-Round Pick of the 1972 NHL Amateur Draft (#10 - Al Blanchard)**

**DETROIT RED WINGS ACQUIRE: Gary Doak and Rick Newell**

Following the 1972 Stanley Cup Final loss (and as mentioned earlier), the Rangers moved on from Gary Doak in the offseason. Francis also said "toodles" to defenseman Rick Newell, who split the 1971-72 season with the Omaha Knights (CHL) and Providence Reds (AHL).

Newell, born in Winnipeg, Manitoba, would play in only seven more NHL games following this trade - all with the Wings. Aside from a brief stint (25 games) with the Phoenix Roadrunners (WHA) in the 1974-75 season, he returned to the minor-league level, having last played in 1978 for the PHL.

Fellow defenseman Joe Zanussi, from Rossland, British Columbia, fared a little bit better than Newell, but not by much. However, Zanussi, a star in the WHA prior to Detroit acquiring his rights, would soon become a huge part of Rangers' history as the fifth player involved in "THE TRADE" of 1975.

Overall, Zanussi played in eight games for the Rangers during the 1974-75 season.

That said, he also had a career year in the AHL for the Providence Reds, where, following the season, he won the Eddie Shore Award (Best AHL Defenseman), finished second place for the league's MVP, and was named a first-team all-star. He was also named the Reds' team MVP. This is why Boston would later trade for him, which became part of the biggest trade in NHL history.

Southpaw right-winger Al Blanchard never made it to the NHL. During the 1972 NHL Amateur Draft, the Rangers/Francis selected the native of Sudbury, Ontario, with their first-round pick (10th overall). And just to think, the Rangers could have drafted fellow right-winger Bobby Nystrom in this same draft. Imagine how the course of hockey history would have been different had that happened! Ugh!

Blanchard spent his short professional career at the AHL level, with one game played with the Springfield Indians during the 1975-76 being his last.

With the success of Gary Doak, and Zanussi later becoming the "afterthought" of "The Trade," this was another loss for Francis.

**DATE OF TRADE: May 24th, 1972**

**RANGERS ACQUIRE: Curt Bennett and Future Considerations (Peter McDuffe)**

**ST. LOUIS BLUES ACQUIRE: Steve Durbano**

Defenseman Steve Durbano, from Toronto, Ontario, was Francis' first-round pick of the 1971 NHL Amateur Draft (13th overall). However, the enforcer never played one game for the Rangers. Instead, he spent his entire 220-game NHL career with the Blues, Penguins, and Scouts/Rockies.

Durbano also played in 45 games for the WHA's Birmingham Bulls in the 1977-78 season. He'd jump back to the NHL in the season that followed, where after thirteen games, he retired with the Blues - the first NHL team he ever played for.

Durbano, a tough guy on the ice, finished his professional career with 1,411 penalty minutes, including an NHL league-leading 370 penalty minutes in the 1975-76 season, as both a Penguin and a Scout.

In retirement, Durbano's life was crazier than one of his fights on the ice.

On February 7th, 1981, Durbano was arrested at Toronto International Airport when the Royal Canadian Mounted Police (RCMP) seized 474 grams of cocaine in his possession - a street value estimated to be worth at least $71,000 ($231,415 in 2022 money). Before the arrest, Durbano was boarding a flight from Toronto destined to Miami at the height of the cocaine era in southern Florida.

After a lengthy legal process, in 1984, Durbano was sentenced to seven years in prison. During this time, he also admitted to being a regular cocaine user as a player in the NHL - and he strongly suggested that he was not the only one.

Following his release from prison he was arrested again, this time for a lesser offense - shoplifting. (He was nabbed while attempting to steal five shirts from a men's clothing store.)

In 1995, the rugged bruiser returned to prison after trying to recruit an undercover police officer for his latest venture - a prostitution ring.

On November 16th, 2002, now out of jail and having relocated to the remote lands that make up Canada's Northwest Territories, he passed away at the age of fifty years old following a bout with liver cancer.

Peter McDuffe, as mentioned earlier, never panned out as NHL goaltender.

Center Curt Bennett, from Regina, Saskatchewan, would later become a two-time all-star as an Atlanta Flame.

Bennett would play in only sixteen games for the Rangers before moving on to Atlanta, where he spent the next nine seasons of his career. We'll get into that soon enough.

This trade was another failure on behalf of Francis, as Durbano had good years in St. Louis. In addition, and in hindsight, this trade was also a loss because of what Bennett would turn out to be - after Francis soon flipped him for Ron Harris.

**DATE OF TRADE: June 8th, 1972**

**RANGERS ACQUIRE: Ninth-Round Pick of the 1972 NHL Amateur Draft (#137 - Pierre Archambault)**

**ST. LOUIS BLUES ACQUIRE: Cash**

Emile Francis, who must have seen something special in his 137th overall pick of the 1972 NHL Amateur Draft, ponied up a few bucks to make this selection.

Prior to this selection, defenseman Pierre Archambault, from Laval, Quebec, had four so-so seasons at the QMJHL level. He would never play professional, or for that matter, minor-league hockey, either. And it cost Francis only a few shekels to see this all play out.

While we don't know what Francis paid for this pick, this is a loss, for as minuscule as it may be.

**DATE OF TRADE: June 8th, 1972**

**RANGERS ACQUIRE: New York Islanders promise not to draft certain players in the 1972 NHL Expansion Draft**

**NEW YORK ISLANDERS ACQUIRE: Seventh-Round Pick of the 1973 NHL Amateur Draft (#110 - Denis Anderson) and**

218

## Eighth-Round Pick of the 1973 NHL Amateur Draft (#126 - Denis Desgagnes)

Like the Vegas expansion draft of 2017, Francis took some preventive measures here. "The Cat" dealt two late-round picks of the 1973 NHL Amateur Draft to his new geographical opponent in exchange for the Rangers' soon-to-be heated rival's promise of not touching certain Blueshirts during the Isles' 1972 NHL expansion draft.

With the two Ranger picks now in tow, Bill Torrey, who later became known as "The Architect" (and his new position on Long Island, was the end result of butting heads with California/Oakland Seals' owner Chuck Finley just a year prior. Had the duo had a better relationship, who knows who the Isles would have tasked to run their show?), Torrey drafted defenseman Denis Anderson and center Denis Desgagnes.

Neither player would make it to the NHL. So much for that "Architect" nickname, am I right? (Then again, Torrey did select Denis Potvin with his first-overall pick of the 1973 NHL Draft. You may have heard about Potvin before. You may have even heard that he "sucks" too!)

Denis Anderson, from Sardis, British Columbia, never moved past the CHL level. He was out of hockey by 1976. Denis Desgagnes, from Tracy, Quebec, never made it past the CHL level, either. Aside from one comeback game in the IHL during the 1978-79 season, Degagnes was out of hockey by 1975.

Without knowing exactly who Francis asked Torrey to protect, either way, this trade was a win. The two Denis' (or is it Deni, like fungi?) never made it to the show.

**DATE OF TRADE: June 16th, 1972**

**RANGERS ACQUIRE: Bill Heindl**

**ATLANTA FLAMES ACQUIRE: Bill Hogaboam**

Center Bill Hogaboam,from Swift Current, Saskatchewan, later known as "Hogi" (and also later known as the captain of the Minnesota North Stars), never played for the Rangers. Instead, he spent the season prior to this trade in the CHL, with the Omaha Knights.

Following this trade, Hogi spent the next ten years of his life with both the Detroit Red Wings and Minnesota North Stars organizations. In total, he amassed 332 NHL games throughout his career, while also playing in 248 AHL contests in an era where the AHL was no longer as prestigious as it once was due to both NHL expansion and the WHA.

Left-wing Bill Heindl, from Sherbrooke, Quebec, played in four more games for the Rangers than Hogi ever did, where he received limited action with the Blueshirts in the 1972-73 season. During this season, he primarily was an AHLer, where he played 66 games for the Reds.

A year later, he jumped to the WHA and then played 67 games for the Cleveland Crusaders. This turned out to be Heindl's final season.

After his playing days, Heindl got into coaching. It wouldn't last long.

Between his father's death, a divorce, and a brutal car accident that led to a severe back injury, Heindl soon fell into a deep state of depression. Then, in 1980, he jumped off a Winnipeg bridge in what turned out to be a failed suicide attempt. While he survived, the incident left him a paraplegic for life.

Now at 34 years old and confined to a wheelchair for life, Heindl lived to 45 years of age. He passed away in 1995 from complications of his injuries.

While not trying to make light of Heindl's serious situation, this trade was another loss for Francis.

**DATE OF TRADE: November 14th, 1972**

**RANGERS ACQUIRE: Cash**

**NEW YORK ISLANDERS ACQUIRE: Ron Stewart**

Unless you count the trade that Francis made prior to the Isles' expansion draft - this is the first trade on record between the Rangers and the Islanders - or at the very least - a trade where a player was involved.

Ron Stewart had an impressive career, where at the end of it, he played in 1,353 NHL games.

After 838 games played in Toronto, Stewart also played 126 games for the Bruins, 42 games for the Canucks, and 19 games for the Blues. He also played 306 games for the Rangers at the peak of the Francis era and then finished his career with the Islanders, where he played for the "little brother" for 22 games.

At the time of this trade, Stewart was forty years old and pretty much done. He picked up two more goals and two more career assists with the former residents of the Nassau Coliseum - career lows.

Following a successful and lengthy career, at the start of the 1975-76 season, and with Francis embracing a rebuild (but not using that word verbatim), "The Cat" hired his former center to coach the team.

However, once John Ferguson took over the general manager gig from Francis on January 7th, 1976, the new Rangers' head honcho promptly fired Stewart, citing that he wanted to see his new team from behind the bench. (And, yes, I have a lot on Ferguson for you in this title too!)

With Stewart not lasting long with the Islanders, especially since he retired as a member of the much-later-coined "Fishsticks," whatever money Francis got out of Torrey was a win.

**DATE OF TRADE: November 28th, 1972**

**RANGERS ACQUIRE: Ron Harris**

## ATLANTA FLAMES ACQUIRE: Curt Bennett

Ron Harris, a defenseman, was most infamously known for a tragic incident at the time of his trade (an accident that still haunts him to this day despite recently hitting the age of eighty in 2022.)

On January 13, 1968, in a game where Harris' Seals were playing Bill Masterton's Minnesota North Stars, Harris had a collision with Masterton, which saw Masterton fall on the back of his head. (Masterton benefitted from NHL expansion, as he was a career minor leaguer before the NHL doubled in size.)

In an era where players didn't wear helmets (helmets, and goalie masks, for that matter, were frowned upon, the main reason being that NHL owners wanted their paying customers, the fans, to be able to see the faces of the players), Masterton, following the clean hit, fell on his head and started bleeding out of his nose, ears, and mouth.

Masterton, thirty hours later, passed away on January 15, 1968. He was only 29 years old.

Again, I should stress the hit Harris levied on Masterton was 100% clean. There was never an issue about this play being dirty at all - not then, not now, not ever.

However, following Masterton's tragic and accidental passing, the incident never left Harris - at least not mentally.

In a 2003 interview with the St. Paul Pioneer Press (Harris' only interview on the subject), he said the following:

*"It bothers you for the rest of your life. It wasn't dirty and it wasn't meant to happen that way. Still, it's very hard because I made the play. It's always in the back of my mind."*

It should also be stated in these pages that at the time of the hit, after the hit, and in the years that followed Masterton's death, his family held no animosity or ill-will towards Harris. They agreed that the play was a "fluke" and unavoidable. Masterton's family

222

would also advocate NHL players use helmets in an era where safety precautions were thrown out the window.

While Masterton's death is the biggest and saddest thing to take place here, his tragic ending is not forgotten. Starting with the 1967-68 season, when this event took place, the NHL founded the "Bill Masterton Memorial Trophy," an honor that *"best exemplifies the qualities of perseverance, sportsmanship, and dedication to ice hockey."*

Claude Provost, a nine-time Stanley Cup champion, and for whatever reason isn't in the Hall of Fame to this day, was the first recipient of the "Bill Masterton Memorial Trophy." (Many historians, for lack of a better term, are "pissed off" over Provost's omission.)

Over time, five Rangers have won the now prestigious trophy - Jean Ratelle (1971), Rod Gilbert (1976), Anders Hedberg (1985), Adam Graves (2001), and Dominic Moore (2014).

RIP Bill Masteron.

Let's now try to get back into this trade, where I'm not attempting to overlook Masteron's death - but I did have to mention it, especially whenever one talks about Ron Harris, for as messed up as that is.

Following this trade with the Flames, Harris was already a ten-season veteran, having also played with the Wings and Seals.

Harris finished his NHL career with the Rangers, where he retired after three games played during the 1975-76 season.

Harris was a serviceable Ranger and part of the deep playoff runs of 1973 and 1974. However, as you probably assumed or knew, he was also at the end of the line. It was often thought that Harris was never the same after Masterton's death.

After sixteen games with the Rangers before this trade, where he only picked up one assist, center Curt Bennett became a stalwart of the Flames organization and played for the new club for six seasons.

Following parts of two seasons with the Blues, Bennett returned to the Flames, where he finished his career after 21 games played with the club for the 1979-80 season.

Funny enough, Bennett could have extended his career with the Flames, but once the Flames relocated to Calgary, the native of Regina, Saskatchewan, decided not to make the move with them. Instead, he moved to the other side of the world, where he spent the next two seasons of his life as a player/coach of the Furukawa Denko franchise - a hockey team that once played in Japan.

Once finished in the land of the rising sun, Bennett moved back to Atlanta. He didn't stay there for long, as in 2000, he moved to Hawaii, where he opened up a landscape architecture company.

At the end of the day, following his brief stint on Broadway, Bennett went on to play in 564 games with the Flames. This trade was another black mark for Francis, even if Harris wasn't a bust.

**DATE OF TRADE: March 2nd, 1973**

**RANGERS ACQUIRE: Mike Murphy**

**ST. LOUIS BLUES ACQUIRE: Ab Demarco Jr.**

Ab Demarco Jr., who, like his father, also played for the Rangers (as mentioned earlier, Ab Demarco Sr. played for the club during the horrendous post-World War II era), began his NHL career with the Rangers. The younger Demarco, a defenseman (daddy was a center), received his first action in the 1969-70 season, where he played in three games in all.

Over time, Demarco Jr. became a reliable defenseman but was limited to only four games in the 1972 Stanley Cup playoffs.

Only 24 years old at the time of this trade, Demarco Jr. moved on to St. Louis, where it didn't pan out for him, either. Just under a year following this trade, he was moved to the Pittsburgh Penguins. He would not last a season there, either, as in November 1974, he would then be traded to Vancouver, where he had the best season - at least offensively - of his career.

After another quick trade, this time to the Kings, he would spend the 1977-78 season with the Edmonton Oilers. A season later, he'd return to the NHL, where he finished his North American professional career with three games played with the Bruins during the 1979-80 campaign.

Born in Cleveland, Ohio, in 1949 (his father was playing for the Barons at the time), Demarco Jr. spent the 1979-80 season with the HC Ambrì–Piotta of the Switzerland league. He retired once and for all following the campaign.

Mike Murphy, as mentioned earlier, still has a prominent job in the NHL as of this 2022 writing. The forward was traded again in the season following this deal after 31 games played with the Blueshirts.

Murphy, as we'll get into again, then spent ten seasons in Los Angeles, all with the Kings.

Francis got the better player here, so this trade was a win - but as was often the case, he would soon lose out in just a few months.

**DATE OF TRADE: March 4th, 1973**

**RANGERS ACQUIRE: Bert Marshall and Cash**

**CALIFORNIA GOLDEN SEALS ACQUIRE: Gary Coalter and Future Considerations (Dave Hrechkosy)**

Center Gary Coalter, the Rangers' fifth-round pick (67th overall) of the 1970 NHL Amateur Draft, never played for the franchise. The selection out of Toronto, Ontario, would log only 34 NHL games in his short professional career, with lowly teams such as the Seals and the Scouts. His final NHL game took place during the 1974-75 season while in Kansas City.

Left-winger Dave Hrechkosy, from Winnipeg, Manitoba, had more NHL success than Coalter, where he played in 140 NHL games - all with the Seals and Blues. After fifteen games played in St. Louis during the 1976-77 season, he, too, would be finished as an NHLer.

Bert Marshall, a defenseman out of Kamloops, British Columbia, who played in parts of eight seasons with both the Red Wings and the Seals at the time of this trade, would play eight games for the Rangers. Following the season, the Islanders claimed the rearguard, where Marshall remained for the next six seasons.

Then, at 36 years old, Marshall finished his NHL career with the Isles following the 1979-80 season. In other words, he missed out on four Stanley Cups, four Cups the much-hated Isles would go on to win after his retirement.

Marshall, who played in 868 NHL games, was the best player in this trade. Again, as usual, the Rangers missed out on his prime years.

Yes, Francis won this trade, but the win wasn't long-lasting.

**DATE OF TRADE: May 15th, 1973**

**RANGERS ACQUIRE: Cash**

**CHICAGO BLACKHAWKS ACQUIRE: Ninth-Round Pick of the 1973 NHL Amateur Draft (#141 - Steve Alley)**

We're now at a period of time where players who were NHL draft picks were also being selected during WHA drafts - and where these players were now signing with WHA clubs instead of signing with the NHL teams who drafted them.

Later (as in six years following this trade), some of these players became NHLers solely because the NHL added four WHA teams into their fold following the WHA's folding in 1979. (As we'll soon get into, some people may prefer the word "merger" instead of "folding.")

Starting with the 1979-80 season, the WHA, now defunct, saw the NHL acquire four teams into their league - Edmonton, Hartford, Quebec City, and Winnipeg. (And yes, this also helped the eye-popping numbers that Gordie Howe, then of the Whalers, added to his legendary NHL totals.)

Steve Alley, a left-winger from Anoka, Minnesota, never played for the Blackhawks.

In addition to being drafted by the Blackhawks, Alley was also drafted by the New England Whalers during the WHA's 1973 draft.

Rather than trying to break into the NHL, he soon found success in the WHA. Once Hartford became an NHL team in 1979, he logged fifteen NHL games under his belt.

Alley, who was exposed a bit when WHA games became NHL games, played eight games for the Whalers during the 1980-81 season. He spent most of this season in the AHL, playing 69 games for the Binghamton Whalers.

A 1977 graduate of the University of Wisconsin, Alley retired from hockey in 1981. He opened up an investment management firm based in Lake Forest, Illinois. As of this 2022 writing, he currently remains president of "Alley Company LLC."

All in all, Francis won this trade, even if it only added a couple of bucks to the Rangers' bank account.

**DATE OF TRADE: May 15th, 1973**

**RANGERS ACQUIRE: Thirteen Round Pick of the 1973 NHL Amateur Draft (No selection taken)**

**MONTREAL CANADIENS ACQUIRE: Thirteen Round Pick of the 1973 NHL Amateur Draft (#168 - Louis Chiasson)**

In a trade and a draft both exclusive to this era, the Montreal Canadiens had the last two picks of the 1973 NHL Amateur Draft - and the only picks of both the twelfth round (goaltender, Cap

Raeder, 167th overall) and a thirteenth round selection, too, Louis Chaisson.

And yes, this isn't a typo or a misprint - the Habs had a one-player round in both the 12th and 13th rounds of this 1973 Amateur Draft.

Francis, who previously had this draft pick, let Montreal select center Louis Chaisson out of Trois-Rivieres, Quebec - a Chaisson who promptly gave up on hockey after being selected.

Whether Francis received Canadian "loonies" or "toonies," or American "quarters" or "half-dollar" coins in this trade - it doesn't matter. He won this trade, for as insignificant as it was.

**DATE OF TRADE: October 28th, 1973**

**RANGERS ACQUIRE: Jack Egers**

**ST. LOUIS BLUES ACQUIRE: Glen Sather and Rene Villemure**

Rene Villemure, not to be confused with Gilles, was Francis' second-round (31st overall) draft pick of the 1972 NHL Amateur Draft. After 72 games played with the Providence Reds (AHL) during the 1972-73 season, the twenty-year-old left-wing from Shawinigan Falls, Quebec, would never play at a high level of hockey again.

A career minor leaguer, Villemure called it a career after 41 games with the Maine Nordiques of the inferior NAHL, contests during the 1976-77 season.

Glen Sather, well known to Ranger fans (and just wait until we get into the year 2000), would play the 1973-74 season with the Blues.

After one season in Montreal and another in Minnesota thereafter, the worst general manager in New York Rangers history (an opinion, but maybe a fact, too!) would play one more professional season with the Edmonton Oilers (and we all know how that turned out), for the 1976-77 season - before moving on up within the Edmonton organization.

228

Jack Egers, now back in New York, would finish out this 1973-74 season with the Rangers, where he also played in eight playoff games in the 1974 postseason.

Come the 1974 expansion draft, Francis opted not to protect the right-winger. The Washington Capitals selected him.

During the 1974-75 season, now as a Capital, Egers scored the first game-winning goal in their history in a game against the Chicago Blackhawks on October 17, 1974.

A season later, and after twelve games played, Egers retired.

This trade was a loss, albeit a small one, as Sather had the best career of the three players involved in this trade, both during and after. However, this trade was also a huge win for Sather himself, as he'd soon go on to have a twenty-year tenure as general manager of the Oilers.

**DATE OF TRADE: November 30th, 1973**

**RANGERS ACQUIRE: Real Lemieux and Gilles Marotte**

**LOS ANGELES KINGS ACQUIRE: Sheldon Kannegiesser, Mike Murphy, and Tom Williams**

Sheldon Kannegiesser, who Francis ironically traded to Pittsburgh three years prior for Sather (in the lovely "player to be named to be later" transaction), was sent to sunny Los Angeles, where he remained until 1977. The defenseman would then move on to the Canucks, where following the 1977-78 season, and after 42 games played, he retired.

A right-winger, Mike Murphy, as mentioned earlier, had a hell of a run in Los Angeles, spending nearly a decade in the "city of angels."

Tom Williams, a left-winger from Windsor, Ontario, played in only 25 games with the Rangers at the time of this trade, with the 1971-72 season being his first. (He played in three games that season.)

Willams would play in 372 games with the Kings, where he retired at the start of the new decade, 1980, following the 1979-80 season.

Real Lemieux, who Francis must have liked, at least temporarily, re-acquired the right-winger again after dealing him away over three years prior. Francis would trade him away again just under two months later. More on Lemieux in our next Francis trade.

Defenseman Gilles Marotte, a veteran of over eight NHL seasons at the time of this trade, was already a name in NHL trading history. In 1967, the native of Montreal, Quebec, was part of a Phil Esposito trade, where following the deal, the future Rangers' general manager (and boy, does Esposito's tenure take up a lot of space in this book) became a legend in Boston after being traded away by the Chicago Blackhawks. Oops!

Marotte spent three seasons manning the Rangers' blue line and also played twelve games during the Rangers' playoff run of 1974. Two sour seasons in Rangers' history then followed. After playing the 1976-77 season in St. Louis, he jumped to the WHA, playing for both the Cincinnati Stingers and, as mentioned earlier, Indianapolis Racers.

After his lone season in the inferior professional league, Marotte finished his career with 808 NHL games and 73 WHA games under his belt.

This trade was another loss for Francis as we approach the end of his era as ruler of the Rangers.

**DATE OF TRADE: January 21st, 1974**

**RANGERS ACQUIRE: Paul Curtis**

**BUFFALO SABRES ACQUIRE: Real Lemieux**

This wasn't much of a loss, as Real Lemieux went on to play eleven more games of his NHL career with the Sabres.

Paul Curtis, a journeyman defenseman from Peterborough, Ontario, and who also had stints with the Canadiens, Kings, and Blues -

never played for the Rangers. Instead, Francis sent his newest rearguard to Providence, where Curtis finished out the season with the Reds.

Come the start of the 1974-75 season, both men would never play in the NHL again.

Curtis jumped to the WHA, where he played for the Michigan Stags/Baltimore Blades. (Michigan moved to Baltimore in the middle of the season.) Following his one year in the WHA, Curtis remained in Baltimore, where he played for the AHL Clippers during the 1975-76 season. He retired.

Real Lemieux, a two-time Ranger, was cut by the Sabres at the start of the 1974-75 season. A veteran of 457 NHL games, rather than jumping to the WHA or accepting an AHL club assignment - and now at 29 years old - he opted to retire. A year later, he passed away.

Sadly, on October 24th, 1975, Lemieux died after developing a blood clot in his brain. The man known as "Frenchy" was only 30 years old.

This trade was pretty much a wash, but if you look at who remained in the NHL following the trade, despite Lemieux playing in only eleven more games than Curtis - this was a slight loss on Francis' record.

**DATE OF TRADE: February 14th, 1974**

**RANGERS ACQUIRE: First-Round Pick of the 1977 NHL Amateur Draft (#13 - Ron Duguay)**

**LOS ANGELES KINGS ACQUIRE: Gene Carr**

Gene Carr, who Francis was high on from day one (and as previously mentioned - Francis gave up a lot to acquire Carr), never truly worked out in New York. For a player whose potential was once thought to be the equivalent of Bobby Hull, Carr never came close to reaching it.

Carr was serviceable and played in all sixteen games in the 1972 Stanley Cup Playoffs (one of his duties was to shut down Montreal's Yvan Cournoyer, which Carr succeeded in doing). However, the following season, 1972-73, he broke his collarbone in a December 20th, 1972 game against the St. Louis Blues.

The injury occurred when ex-Ranger Bob Plager crushed the current Ranger with a clean yet vicious hit. Carr would finish the season with nineteen points in fifty games played. He was never the same again.

What didn't help Carr's case at this time was the ascension of rookie Steve Vickers - especially when Francis tried flipping Carr to the left wing. Carr never felt comfortable at the position, and with Vickers rolling, it would soon make Carr even more expendable.

Carr had a rough start to the 1973-74 season. Not helping matters was Rangers' color analyst, Bill "The Big Whistle" Chadwick, who was riding the center about all of his scoring woes - which became apparent. Carr's troubles grew with time, so much so that the former fourth-overall pick of the 1971 draft was sent down to Providence.

Chadwick, known to say anything that came to his mind (and without worrying about offending anyone), pretty much put the final nail in the coffin of Carr's tenure with the Rangers.

(And, yes, Bill Chadwick is covered extensively in my first book too!)

At the time, Chadwick was already a Hockey Hall of Famer member of the Class of 1964. He was also the first true color analyst the Rangers ever had on their broadcasts, as before Chadwick, every announcer walked a straight line and called what they saw rather than throwing in their two cents as Chadwick was known for.

Chadwick's most famous quote as a broadcaster (some might say that "SHOOT THE PUCK, BARRY!" was more memorable) and a quote that haunts Carr to this very day: During a game from the 1973-74 season where Carr couldn't get anything going offensively, Chadwick dropped this bomb:

"He [Carr] couldn't put the puck in the ocean off a pier!"

At the time of this book's publication, Chadwick's assessment of Carr is now nearly fifty years old. Just imagine if social media and/or the internet were around when Chadwick blurted this out. Such a clip would've been shared throughout every social media platform. It also would've been something the ravenous beat reporters would make as their top story.

As talked about earlier, George Grimm, author of *"We Did Everything But Win,"* and a fellow Rangers' historian (and also a Stan Fischler confidante), interviewed Carr for his 2017 book.

In an interview that originally appeared in *"We Did Everything But Win,"* and then later appeared on Grimm's website, https://insidehockey.com, Carr, who was 66 years old at the time, talked about Chadwick's comments.

Here was what Carr told Grimm:

*"Chadwick used to jump on me about putting the puck in the ocean and I don't know why he attacked me. He had no idea how that affected me mentally. I used to just cringe when I heard them say something or they would bring up my name. I wish I could've talked to Bill before he passed away. I would have asked him why did you attack me like that? I didn't do anything to you. That's a lot of years ago but people still talk to me about Chadwick. Anytime he would come into the dressing room or whatever I would just walk by him because I just couldn't bring myself to even say hello to the guy."*

Of note, if you ever read Grimm's entire interview with Carr, the former Ranger does sound a bit "whiny" and seems to have a lot of excuses too. Just this author's opinion - not a fact.

During the same season when Chadwick first made his scathing comments, Carr was involved in a car accident with teammate Mike Murphy.

After a night out on the town, Carr and Murphy hailed a cab back to the team's hotel. While heading back, a police car, chasing a thief who had just stolen a car, ran a red light and t-boned the cab.

Here is how Carr recalled the incident, and its aftermath, as told to George Grimm for *"We Did Everything But Win"*:

*"I never thought about how severe it was and how close I was to being killed in that car accident. I was with Mike Murphy and we were headed back to the hotel for curfew. We had gone out to have something to eat, and then we were headed back to the hotel, and this cabbie, he wasn't exactly going very slowly, it was winter and there was snow on the ground, but we had a green light and apparently this black-and-white was in pursuit of a stolen car, and he went through a red light and T-boned us.*

*"The cabbie was injured really badly, and of course, so were Murphy and me. I mean our heads hit that Plexiglas probably at Mach One speed. We hit that Plexiglas and it knocked us silly. All I remember was I was helping Murphy in the cab and there was his blood like everywhere it was spurting out of his head, and I had blood all over me too. I remember Murph and me trying to get to the hospital. We were walking from the accident. We were just so out of it, I didn't even know my own name, and I was holding Mike and I knew I needed to get him to the hospital. We got picked up by Derek Sanderson who recognized us and stopped and drove us to Boston General and tried to explain what happened.*

*"I didn't realize how severe that was on my body. I don't think I ever recuperated from that body trauma because it seems like I had nothing but physical problems after that. My back, I mean to this day I've had multiple back and neck surgeries. I can't walk without my crutches, that's how bad I am now. I can walk maybe five or ten feet with difficulty but anything more than that I need crutches to*

*get around. That accident in the cab was the beginning of a lot of physical problems that I developed over the years."*

It should be noted that before the accident, Carr wasn't exactly lighting the league on fire. So, while no one can second guess or question Carr about how this automobile accident impacted his life, at the same time, he wasn't living up to his potential on the ice before it.

Since this trade was big news when it happened, let's go to George Grimm one more time, as he asked Carr for his thoughts on it in "We Did Everything But Win":

*"My situation when I left there didn't have anything to do with Emile. I just wanted to go somewhere where I could play 15 – 20 minutes a game like I should have, but after I got hurt and each player on the team was so great it was tough as hell to break into the lineup.*

*"I remember approaching him a couple of times and saying, hey you have to play me. You can't play me for a couple of shifts in the third period. I can't do that. I'm not Glen Sather. Glen Sather could sit on the bench and go out there in the third period and look like he never missed a shift but I couldn't do that. I didn't have the confidence.*

*"I told him, you've got to play me. But he couldn't do it because the guys who were making half a million a year and were scoring fifty goals, they had to play. He was in a tough situation.*

*"Finally, I remember talking to Emile one night after a game in Philly. My contract was up at the end of the year and I said, 'hey, I'm done, you either trade me now or I'll sit for the next few months or I'll sign with the World Hockey Association and you won't get anything for me.'*

*"I didn't even let my attorney handle that. I just told him after the game I need to go somewhere where I can play all the time because*

*I'm too good to be sitting here and I'm losing my confidence and I've got to get it back."*

The above quote is why I thought Carr was a bit "whiny." It's also why I felt that he had a sense of self-entitlement about himself. Then again, every player should be their own best promoter - especially at contract time.

Again, granted, all players should have egos and should want to play. It's what drives them to be successful. However, with Carr struggling and not being the player that many expected him to be, he did seem out of line with the ultimatum that he once laid upon Francis.

Carr would have the best seasons of his career in Los Angeles, but he never sniffed the lofty expectations that were first bestowed upon him during the 1971 NHL Amateur Draft.

Ironically, his best offensive season took place during the 1977-78 season, where he was dealt to the Pittsburgh Penguins just five games in.

In Pittsburgh, although the team had a horrid season in 1977-78, Carr finished with 17 goals, 37 assists, and 54 points - all career highs - as he did well on a bad team.

Still clinging to his perceived self-entitlement issues, he bolted out of town in the offseason that followed and accepted a free-agent contract with the Atlanta Flames. Carr would play only thirty games for the Flames during the 1978-79 season. Due to back issues he suffered after the car accident, he was forced to retire.

At the time of his last game, the once promising prospect was only 28 years old.

To sum up this particular trade, Emile Francis was able to receive a first-round draft pick in exchange for a former first-round draft pick. However, Francis wouldn't reap the rewards of this trade, as the first-round pick he received was for the 1977 NHL Amateur Draft - which was over three years away at the time of this deal.

By the time the 1977 NHL Amateur Draft rolled around, Francis was there making picks - but as the general manager of the St. Louis Blues.

Ironically, Francis would soon make another trade toward the end of his run on Broadway, a trade that gave the Rangers another first-round pick for this 1977 NHL Amateur Draft - and with the Blues nonetheless!

We will discuss both Ron Duguay and that 1977 NHL Amateur Draft later in this book.

For now, this trade was an easy win for Francis.

And if it were he and not John Ferguson at the helm during this 1977 NHL Draft, spoiler alert: Perhaps the Rangers would have selected Mike Bossy.

Talk about one of the biggest "what if" questions in Rangers' history - *"what if Mike Bossy, and not Lucien DeBlois or Ron Duguay, were taken by the Rangers during the 1977 NHL Amateur Draft?"*

It's painful to think about but had that event taken place, perhaps the Rangers wouldn't have had a 54-year curse. And for a cherry on top - it's highly likely that the Islanders wouldn't have won four, if any, straight Stanley Cups in the early 1980s.

**DATE OF TRADE: February 28th, 1974**

**RANGERS ACQUIRE: Brian Lavender**

**DETROIT RED WINGS ACQUIRE: Claude Houde**

Defenseman Claude Houde, from Drummondville, Quebec, was pretty much a career minor leaguer. At the time of this trade, he was in the Rangers' system, where he split time between the Reds and Clippers (AHL).

Houde wouldn't last long in Detroit, either. After 25 games with the Virginia Wings, one of Detroit's AHL affiliates, he was shipped off to the down-and-out Kansas City Scouts.

Houde would remain with the Scouts through the 1975-76 season, where he played 59 games in total - the extent of his NHL career.

Following the 1975-76 season, Houde played in 22 games for the Beauce Jaros (NAHL) and soon retired.

Brian Lavender, a left-winger from Edmonton, Alberta, had a little more success than Houde. He had previously been bounced throughout the NHL at this point in time, where he had runs with the Blues, Islanders, and Red Wings. In Detroit, like Houde, he played at the AHL level.

Lavender would never play for the Rangers. Instead, he was sent to Providence, where, following the season, he'd soon be traded again - to the California Seals.

No general manager lost here in a trade that boiled down to one AHLer for another. Of course, neither general manager won either, but, hey, the former sounds better!

**DATE OF TRADE: May 27th, 1974**

**RANGERS ACQUIRE: Nick Beverley**

**PITTSBURGH PENGUINS ACQUIRE: Vic Hadfield**

(... Deep breath ...)

Without question, this trade was a complete and utter failure.

Similar to the trades of Andy Bathgate and Harry Howell - this trade signaled the end of an era. And like the trades of Bathgate and Howell - Francis didn't come out looking good here when he traded #11, the native of Oakville, Ontario.

Why would Emile Francis trade away Vic Hadfield, the left-winger of the "Goal A Game" line (GAG line) and who at the time not only

238

was the forward with the most games played in franchise history (841) - but was also the team's captain?

Compounding matters to the confusion was that just two years prior to this trade, Emile Francis had signed one of his most favorite players to a five-year deal.

As the story goes, after eight-consecutive seasons of qualifying for the playoffs, including one Stanley Cup Final appearance, Francis was getting pressure from his bosses to win - and win *now*.

Like Ranger fans, the people who signed "The Cat's" paychecks wanted a Stanley Cup - especially after losing a semi-final playoff round to that year's (1974) Stanley Cup Champions - the Philadelphia Flyers.

And as a reminder, the Flyers were just in their seventh season of existence at the time of their first Stanley Cup championship. (They'd win it a year later, too, in 1975.)

At the time, and later confirmed throughout it, Francis was forced to do something big to shake his team up. The GAG line was one of the best lines in NHL history, but they had no Stanley Cup to show for it. (We can talk about Jean Ratelle's injury once we get to "The Trade.")

In his first comment following the trade, Hadfield remarked to the media, *"You don't win a Stanley Cup with a trade like that."*

He would be proven correct. Not only would it take the Rangers twenty years and a few weeks from the time of this trade to win the Stanley Cup again - but during the next three seasons when Hadfield was in Pittsburgh, the Rangers suffered an embarrassing 1975 first-round playoff loss to the Islanders. They missed the playoffs the next two seasons that followed, the 1976 and 1977 campaigns.

Due to the many failed playoff runs, their opponents and the media frequently mocked Francis and his team during this era. Emile's

"FAT CATS" was the negative moniker; a dig at the team for the bloated salaries that Francis' Rangers earned. (Often the biggest salaries of any non-Stanley Cup winner).

Hadfield was one of the "FAT CATS."

Despite being a leader and featured on one of the best lines in Rangers' history (I would put the "Bread Line" of Frank Boucher and the Cook brothers above Gilbert, Ratelle, and Hadfield, while others may champion for the GAG line instead), Hadfield was the first big-salaried player to be singled out for the team not winning the Stanley Cup.

As mentioned, two years prior, Hadfield had signed a five-year deal with Francis and the Rangers, where he would earn $175,000 per season. This was a huge figure at the time. It should also be mentioned that while Hadfield deserved to be paid well (he just came off a 50-goal, 56-assist season - good for a whopping total of 106 points), the WHA was also very active in luring top NHL names to their league. In turn, NHL salaries went up.

After his remark suggesting that this was a bad trade, Hadfield also said:

*"I believe it was pressure from above. You make a deal you figure will help the club. But I figure there was pressure to get rid of the older guys, the high salaried players."*

When Hadfield was dealt to Pittsburgh, he finished his thirteen seasons on Broadway with 262 goals and 310 assists, good for a point total of 572. He also was involved in eight playoff runs with the Rangers, where in 62 games, he scored 22 goals and picked up 19 assists.

A beloved teammate and a leader, losing Hadfield was a crushing blow to the Rangers' locker room, including for both Rod Gilbert and Jean Ratelle - two players who not only played with Hadfield in New York but knew him from their days in the minors.

240

When this trade was first announced, Bob Woolf, Hadfield's agent and lawyer at the time was asked for a comment. He only had two words: *"Nick who?"*

"Nick Who" was Nick Beverley, a right-handed defenseman and a native of Toronto, Ontario. He made his NHL debut during the 1966-67 season for the Boston Bruins but wouldn't become an NHL regular until the 1972-73 season.

It should also be noted that while Beverley was in Boston during the two Stanley Cup wins in 1970 and 1972, he was a minor leaguer at the time. While he did play in two games during the 1969-70 season, and in one more game during the 1971-72 season, he didn't play during the playoffs, and as a result, like Hadfield - never won the Stanley Cup.

On October 25th, 1973, the Bruins gave up on Beverley when they sent the defenseman to Pittsburgh. And when Jack Button, then general manager of the Penguins, had the opportunity to land Hadfield - off Beverley went again, this time to New York.

One talking point at the time was that Hadfield was six years older than Beverley, as the Rangers' left-winger was 33 years old when this trade was executed. In addition, the 27-year-old Beverley was also relatively healthy when compared to Hadfield, a Hadfield who had thumb injuries at this stage of his career.

Now in New York, Beverley never panned out. While he was never going to be able to replace Hadfield (especially since they played different positions), he also wasn't like Bob Nevin - a Nevin who was able to escape Bathgate's shadow following that epic trade.

Beverley played in two complete seasons with the Rangers. Then, nine games into the 1976-77 season, and with Francis no longer with the club, Beverley was traded again and headed north to Minnesota.

However, Beverley's suitcases didn't get any rest. He'd eventually finish out his career by playing in Los Angeles and Colorado before retiring from his days as an active NHL player following the conclusion of the 1979-80 season.

Of note, Beverley's three games played in the crushing three-game series loss to the Islanders in 1975 would be the final playoff games of his career too.

While it was Francis succumbing to pressure, it was very easy for Ranger fans to paint Beverley as the enemy. Also not helping matters was that Vic Hadfield, now in the steel city, had two career seasons with the Penguins.

For comparison, let's now take a look at Hadfield's last two seasons with the Rangers (which were also the first two years of his new five-year deal), and then the final three seasons of his career with Pittsburgh (the end of the contract).

1972-73 Season: 28 goals and 34 assists (62 points) in 63 games with the Rangers.

1973-74 Season: 27 goals and 28 assists (55 points) in 77 games with the Rangers.

1974-75 Season: 31 goals and 42 assists (73 points) in 78 games with the Penguins.

1975-76 Season: 30 goals and 35 assists (65 points) in 76 games with the Penguins.

1976-77 Season: 0 goals and 2 assists (2 points) in nine games with the Penguins - Hadfield's final season as a pro.

Towards the end of the 1975-76 season, Hadfield suffered a knee injury and tried to play through it. He couldn't, and he retired.

Obviously, when healthy, Hadfield continued to play like the star he was.

And while the GAG Line could never win the Stanley Cup, despite having Brad Park, Eddie Giacomin, and the best third line in franchise history along with them for the ride, at the very least, if Hadfield was on the Rangers' roster during the 1974-75 season - it's not out of line to think that they at least would have beaten the Islanders in the first round of the 1975 Stanley Cup Playoffs.

While a lot of Francis' moves didn't work out following the 1972 Stanley Cup Final loss, and while there were other bad moves made before this trade - this transaction was truly the first one that ushered in the end of an era.

This was just the first move of the offseason - and a fruitless season ahead. Come the start of the 1975-76 season, the era would be over.

**DATE OF TRADE: June 12th, 1974**

**RANGERS ACQUIRE: Derek Sanderson**

**BOSTON BRUINS ACQUIRE: Walt McKechnie**

Two days prior to this trade, the Rangers claimed California Seals' center Walt McKechnie during an intra-league draft. At the time, McKechnie was a seven-season NHL veteran, where he had logged games with two expansion franchises - the Minnesota North Stars and the Seals themselves.

The native of London, Ontario, was also the Leafs' first-round pick (6th overall) of the 1963 NHL Amateur Draft.

Following this trade for Sanderson, McKechnie wouldn't stay in Boston for long. On February 1st, 1975, he was sent to Detroit, where he remained for the next three years.

McKechnie, who played for nine teams throughout his NHL career after his stint in Detroit, would later play for the Washington Capitals, Cleveland Barons, Toronto Maple Leafs, and the Colorado Rockies.

Prior to the 1981-82 season, the center returned to Detroit, where he finished out his career. He retired following the 1982-83 season.

All in all, McKechnie played in 955 career NHL games. During his fifteen seasons in the big leagues, he scored 214 goals and picked up 392 assists for a total of 606 points. However, none of these numbers came with the Rangers. Instead, he was traded for the somewhat controversial Derek Sanderson, a native of Niagara Falls, Ontario.

Derek Sanderson, whose life can fill a book (he wrote two autobiographies), was brought in with the hopes of replacing the production Francis gave up when he traded away Hadfield. It almost worked out according to plan.

At the time of this trade, Sanderson, another center, was just four days shy of his 28th birthday. More importantly, he was one of the biggest names in hockey - for both his on-ice accomplishments and off-ice activities.

Originally starting out his career with the Boston Bruins, Sanderson played two games for the B's during the 1965-66 season and then played in two more games in the season that followed. Come the 1967-68 season, the season when the NHL doubled in size - he was a full-time NHLer.

Known for his offensive prowess, his role in Boston soon changed due to the Bruins possessing two of the greatest offensive powerhouses of the era - Phil Esposito and Bobby Orr. Adapting to the situation, Sanderson won the Calder Trophy in 1968. Two years later, he was a Stanley Cup champion. And as you're probably aware, two years after winning his first Stanley Cup - he won it again in 1972.

Sanderson, now in the prime of his career and a proven winner, had options. He could return to the Bruins for the 1972-73 campaign and try to defend the Stanley Cup victory or desert the team that made him a star by joining the new fledgling World Hockey Association. He chose the latter.

(And needless to say, the WHA is a whole topic in itself. For a great book about the league, check out *"Rebel League"* by Ed Willes.

I've read most of the books about the WHA. It's my opinion that Willes' tale is the best.)

At its inception, while looking to establish credibility, the WHA routinely overspent on talent - especially during Year One. Sanderson would soon become one of these names - the highest-paid player at that.

A total of 67 NHLers would jump to the new league, where Bobby Hull became the most prominent player to change sides. The now former Blackhawk received a ten-year deal from the WHA - a contract worth $2.75M overall - an unheard of amount of money at the time.

Although Hull would play for the Winnipeg Jets, all of the WHA owners pooled in their money to help soften the financial blow. For the league, having someone of Hull's caliber was necessary - as it not only made the new league legit - it would also entice other big-name talents to jump ship. Sanderson was one of these players.

In the offseason following the 1972 Stanley Cup victory, Sanderson became a household name for fans of all professional sports.

The Philadelphia Blazers and Sanderson agreed to a five-year deal worth $2.65M overall, making Sanderson the highest-paid professional athlete - not just in the world of hockey but the entire sports world. In other words, Sanderson had earned a contract that guaranteed him $100,000 less than Hull, but in half the time.

While Hull would earn $275,000 a season, Sanderson would earn $530,000 per season - a salary that completely shattered previous contracts from this era and numbers that did not sit well with NHL owners and general managers. However, the NHL owners and general managers would not only have the last laugh - they would have the first laugh too.

Sanderson received $600,000 up front, with the rest of his money paid out to him over ten years. In turn, he only played in eight games for the Blazers.

After scoring only three goals in eight games, Sanderson was injured on November 1st, 1972, after a freak accident when he slipped on a piece of paper on the ice. With Sanderson already not living up to potential, the Blazers had buyer's remorse and hoped Sanderson would void his contract by not returning. Fat chance.

Sanderson was too clever for that. With already bad feelings in Philadelphia, Sanderson did what was required of him. Eventually, the Blazers and the highest-paid athlete in sports agreed - a $1,000,000 buyout. Sanderson took the money and ran back home to the Bruins.

After a rich trial-run in the WHA, Sanderson played 29 games for the Bruins during the 1972-73 season, which was supposed to be the first of five with the Blazers. He also played in all five of the Bruins' 1973 playoff games.

While not under the same circumstances in Philly, Sanderson wasn't exactly a hero in Boston. He'd soon wear out his welcome with Boston's front office and head coach, Bep Guidolin. Also making matters worse was that Sanderson was no longer the same person he once was in his first run with Boston.

After 29 games played during the 1973-74 campaign, Boston made it known that they wanted to deal Sanderson. Despite the risk - the potential for Sanderson's offensive abilities was appealing to Emile - especially after being coerced into trading Hadfield.

Sanderson's first season in New York was solid. In 75 games played, he scored 25 goals and racked up 25 assists for a nice, clean, round number of 50 points. However, this would be his lone complete season with the Rangers.

After eight pointless (as in no points recorded, not "pointless," as an adjective) games with the Rangers during the 1975-76 season, he was sent off to St. Louis. Ironically, Emile Francis would soon join him there.

Of course, now in a new home, Sanderson finished out the 1975-76 season with 24 goals, and 43 assists - a grand total of 67 points.

Once Francis took over the general manager job in St. Louis, he would trade Sanderson again, where the once highest-paid athlete in sports played sixteen games for the Canucks during the 1976-77 season.

A season later, after thirteen games with the Penguins, Sanders retired at the age of 32.

While this is a book about the trading history of the New York Rangers and not a biography about Sanderson, it should be mentioned that during his first season in New York, Sanderson's substance abuse issues, with alcohol being the biggest culprit, continued to grow. (Sanderson, as he's admitted himself, also had issues with cocaine.) This is also why Sanderson never stayed in one place for too long following his prime years in Boston.

And for all the money he was paid throughout his career, he would eventually go broke and become practically homeless. But, as #4 has done so many times, both before and after his playing days, Bobby Orr raised money for his ex-teammate and helped turn Sanderson's life around.

Sanderson, who was at rock bottom after retiring, eventually became a success story because of the assist that Orr gave him, this time off the ice.

While Sanderson did have one good season in New York, this trade was a loss. Despite never being a Ranger, McKechnie went on to have a longer career and didn't bring any baggage along with him.

And yep - the Rangers would have been better off with Hadfield than Sanderson too.

**DATE OF TRADE: July 29th, 1974**

**RANGERS ACQUIRE: Cash**

**WASHINGTON CAPITALS ACQUIRE: Andre Peloffy**

Andre Peloffy, a center out of Sete, France, was the Rangers' ninth-round pick (111th overall) of the 1971 NHL Amateur Draft. However, he'd never play for the big club, as following the draft, he spent his days with the Providence Reds (AHL).

Peloffy would play in only nine NHL games - all with the Capitals during the 1974-75 season. Due to his limited number of games, Peloffy also has a unique distinction in NHL history; he's the first-ever French-born player to play in the NHL.

After his brief stint as an NHLer, Peloffy remained at the AHL level. He would later jump to the WHA during the 1977-78 season, playing ten games for the New England Whalers. That would be it for his North American professional hockey career.

Following his time with the Whalers, Peloffy returned home, where he would continue to play hockey in France until 1990. To this day, he's still considered as one of France's greatest hockey players.

However, when it comes to this deal, where the Rangers said *"au revoir"* to the Frenchman - this trade was a win, even if it was a tiny one.

**DATE OF TRADE: August 29th, 1974**

**RANGERS ACQUIRE: Greg Polis**

**ST. LOUIS BLUES ACQUIRE: Larry Sacharuk and First-Round Pick of the 1977 NHL Amateur Draft (#8 - Lucien DeBlois)**

Defenseman Larry Sacharuk, as discussed earlier, was dealt to the Blues in this trade. Now in St. Louis, Missouri, Sacharuk would have the best pro season of his career when the rearguard scored 20 goals and picked up 22 assists. Along with his 42 points, these would be Sacharuk's career highs. It's also why the Rangers would soon trade back for him.

Francis also dealt his first-round pick of the 1977 NHL Amateur Draft here, but like Sacharuk - that, too, would return. More on Lucien DeBlois in just a bit.

The Penguins' seventh-overall pick of the 1970 NHL Amateur Draft, left wing Greg Polis out of Westlock, Alberta, had the best seasons of his career in Pittsburgh, where he was also named to three All-Star games (1971-1973 - he was also named MVP of the 1973 All-Star Game).

After being traded by the Penguins to the Blues on January 17, 1974, Polis traded in a Blues jersey for a Blueshirts jersey. Starting with the 1974-75 season, he'd remain with the Rangers until January 15,1979, when the Washington Capitals claimed him off waivers.

In New York, Polis played respectably, but joined the team during some down years, as he played through the end of the Francis era into the Ferguson era. Once Fred Shero took over, Polis was no longer needed.

Polis' best season in the Big Apple was his first season, where he scored 26 goals and picked up 15 assists for 41 points. However, during the 1977-78 season, his numbers dropped off, where he only scored seven goals and had 16 assists for a grand total of 23 points.

Since the Rangers kept Polis, and then regained the two pieces they gave up to acquire him - this trade was a win, even if it's somewhat a hollow victory.

**DATE OF TRADE: September 23rd, 1974**

**RANGERS ACQUIRE: Hartland Monahan**

**CALIFORNIA GOLDEN SEALS ACQUIRE: Brian Lavender**

As mentioned before, Brian Lavender, a left-winger, never played for the Rangers. He was primarily a minor leaguer who only played for bad NHL teams in the early years of expansion, including the

"Darkness with Harkness" Red Wings, the Islanders, and the Seals themselves.

Forward Hartland Monahan, a native of Montreal, Quebec, not only played in the NHL, but he also married the daughter of Hall of Famer Bernie "Boom Boom" Geoffrion. And wouldn't you know it, just like "dad," Monahan played for the Rangers too.

That said, Monahan wasn't long for Rangerstown. During the 1974-75 season, he only played in six games for the Rangers, as he primarily spent the season in Providence with the Reds.

Following the season, the Washington Capitals would claim Monahan, where "Boom Boom's" son-in-law first became a true NHLer. Prior to joining the Capitals, Monahan had only seven games worth of NHL experience, six with the Rangers and one with the Seals.

After his days with the Capitals, Monahan later played for the Penguins, Kings, and Blues.

Monahan retired at the conclusion of the 1980-81 season, finishing his career with 334 games played.

This trade was another win for the Rangers. While Monahan most likely wouldn't have fit into their long-term plans, it's a win nonetheless - despite "The Cat" quickly moving on from him.

**DATE OF TRADE: June 3rd, 1975**

**RANGERS ACQUIRE: Thirteenth-Round Pick of the 1975 NHL Amateur Draft (#200 - Steve Roberts)**

**ST. LOUIS BLUES ACQUIRE: Cash**

Who knew what Francis saw in Steve Roberts when he paid the Blues some dough for the right to draft the defenseman from Edina, Minnesota?

Following the draft, Roberts remained at Providence College, graduating in 1978 and to never play hockey again.

Fun Fact Part I: A Rangers' nemesis, Lou Lamoriello, coached Roberts at Providence. The more you know!

This was an insignificant loss for Francis. It was also one of the last draft picks that Francis would make in New York.

Fun Fact Part II: Emile's last draft pick as general manager of the Rangers also took place during this 1975 NHL Amateur Draft. Francis opted for left-wing Tom Funke, who Francis took in the 16th round with his 212th overall selection. Like Roberts, once Funke graduated college, he, too, moved on from hockey. Maybe this fact wasn't so fun after all.

**DATE OF TRADE: June 18th, 1975**

**RANGERS ACQUIRE: Bill Collins and John Davidson**

**ST. LOUIS BLUES ACQUIRE: Jerry Butler, Teddy Irvine, and Bert Wilson**

In a trade where Francis kept moving pieces from the height of his era, Teddy Irvine, part of the best third line in Rangers' history, was moved. However, what no one knew then, and we know now, is that Francis set up the next era of Rangers' hockey with the next franchise goalie of their future (and for as limited as it was) with his acquisition of John Davidson.

When you look at the five names involved in this trade, bringing John Davidson to New York gives Francis an automatic win. However, before getting into "JD," let's take a look at everyone else.

Teddy Irvine, after a great run on Broadway, was never a fan of playing in St. Louis. While he would play the last two seasons of his career with the Blues (and like others previously mentioned, under Francis), he felt a part of him was gone following this trade.

That said, Irvine was also a professional, and posted decent numbers for the Blues - even if they were lower numbers than what he was used to.

251

After the 1976-77 season, Irvine, a veteran of 724 games in the NHL, retired. To this day, he tells interviewers that the best years of his career were under Francis in New York.

Left-winger Bert Wilson, from Orangeville, Ontario, was drafted by Francis in the second round of the 1969 NHL Amateur Draft (23rd overall). Many years after being drafted, Wilson then played in five games for the club during the 1973-74 season. He was then promoted full-time during the 1974-75 season, where he played 61 games.

After a poor outing with the Blues, Wilson would be on the move again when he was dealt to the Kings - just a month before Francis' arrival in St. Louis.

Wilson had his best career years while in LA. His final NHL action would be with the Calgary Flames during the 1980-81 season. Now with 478 games under his belt, Wilson played two more seasons with the Salt Lake Golden Eagles (CHL). Come the spring of 1983, Wilson retired once and for all.

Right-winger Jerry Butler, like Irvine and Wilson, also had a long NHL career.

Francis' fourth-round pick (55th overall) of the 1971 NHL Amateur Draft, the native of Sarnia, Ontario, went on to play in 643 NHL games.

During the 1972-73 season, Butler played in eight games of call-up duty. However, a season later, he'd cement himself as a regular player, where after 26 games played at the end of the 1973-74 season, he'd play in 78 games in the 1974-75 campaign.

Butler spent parts of three seasons with the Blues, having the best statistical season in his first year in St. Louis, with 17 goals and 24 assists.

At the end of the 1977-78 season, Butler moved on to Toronto. He spent parts of three seasons there before moving to the other side of the country, where in 1980, he became a Vancouver Canuck.

After the 1982-83 season, where he played 43 games with the Winnipeg Jets, the penalty-killing specialist chose to retire rather than accept a minor-league assignment.

At the time of this trade, center Bill Collins, from Ottawa, Ontario, had a lot of mileage on him. Now approaching the age of 32, he was previously a beneficiary of the league's 1967 expansion. Prior to expansion, Collins had bounced in and out of every minor-league level possible, including the AHL, WHL, CPHL, and EPHL.

Once the league grew twofold, the Minnesota North Stars claimed Collins, playing for the Baltimore Clippers (AHL), from the Rangers.

Now in Minnesota, this is where Collins became an NHLer, where over time, he amassed 768 games played. Both expansion, and the WHA threat, were good for him.

Ultimately, Collins played in fifty games for the Rangers during the 1975-76 season, scoring four goals and adding four assists - the worst numbers of his career when it comes to points-per-game production.

After nine games with the Flyers in the season that followed, Collins finished out his NHL career with the Washington Capitals, where he then retired after the 1977-78 season.

That said, while Collins had better years in Washington than he did in New York, he was always the "throw in" of this deal. This trade was always about getting someone to succeed Eddie Giacomin - we just didn't know how fast this would all go down.

Goaltender John Davidson, born in Ottawa, Ontario, and again, as covered in detail in my first book, the man known as "JD" would eventually become one of the faces of the Rangers' return as a perennial playoff contender. Only crippling knee and back injuries would do him in.

Behind JD, the Rangers would make it to the Stanley Cup Final in 1979 - a five-game series loss to the Montreal Canadiens.

JD, who not only played for the Rangers, but spent two decades in the broadcast booth, would later serve the franchise as their team president. (More on this to come.)

To this day, JD remains one of the most beloved men to have ever been associated with the franchise.

We'll get more into John Davidson in just a few pages - and then again in 2021.

**DATE OF TRADE: September 9th, 1975**

**RANGERS ACQUIRE: Jerry Byers**

**ATLANTA FLAMES ACQUIRE: Curt Ridley**

Left-winger Jerry Byers, from Kentville, Nova Scotia, had 36 games of NHL experience before this trade. Once acquired, he was sent straight to the AHL. Sans a seven-game stint during the 1977-78 season, where he'd remain for the rest of his career.

He retired after the 1979-80 season, where he played for the AHL Nova Scotia Voyageurs.

Francis, who now had four goaltenders on his roster (JD, Eddie Giacomin, Dunc Wilson, and Doug Soetaert), had to move on from the native of Winnipeg, Manitoba, goaltender Curt Ridley. Prior to this trade, Ridley had only played in two games in the 1974-75 season, as he spent the bulk of that season with the Providence Reds (AHL).

Ridley, primarily a backup goalie for the majority of his career, would later go on to become the starting goalie in Vancouver. He was traded to Toronto during the 1979-80 season.

After three games with the Leafs during the 1980-81 season, Ridley chose to play the 1981-82 season in the CHL, where he last played for the Cincinnati Tigers. This was when he retired, where he played in 104 NHL games with a win-loss-tie record of 27-47-16.

This trade wasn't much of anything, as Francis had to make room for JD. Ridley didn't go on to become a Vezina Trophy winner, which means that this trade didn't backfire.

**DATE OF TRADE: September 20th, 1975**

**RANGERS ACQUIRE: Larry Sacharuk**

**ST. LOUIS BLUES ACQUIRE: Cash and Bob MacMillan**

As mentioned numerous times already, defenseman Larry Sacharuk rejoined the Rangers, where after 42 games played in the 1975-76 season, he'd play in two more games in the season that followed (his final two NHL games). Sacharuk spent most of the 1976-77 season with the New Haven Nighthawks (AHL). After fifteen games played in the WHA for the Indianapolis Racers during the 1978-79 campaign, his days as a pro were over.

Center Bob MacMillian, from Charlottetown, Prince Edward Island, was Francis' first-round pick from the 1972 NHL Amateur Draft (15th overall). He began his professional career in the WHA instead of joining the Rangers, where he logged two seasons with the Minnesota Fighting Saints.

Come the 1974-75 season, he accepted a Rangers contract offer, splitting the season between Providence and New York. During this season, he played in a total of 22 games for the Rangers.

Following this trade, MacMillan, who would later enter politics once his hockey days were over, would go on to play in 731 NHL games. Oops.

Of course, like others from this time, MacMillan also spent parts of three seasons playing under Francis elsewhere - in St. Louis.

On December 12th, 1977, Francis, now with the Blues, would trade MacMillan again. Just as he did once leaving the Rangers, MacMillan went on to burn Francis again, where the center then spent parts of five seasons with the Flames organization - both in Atlanta and in Calgary.

MacMillan, who was part of one organization's relocation, would soon go on another ride in another relocation. After 57 games with the Colorado Rockies in the 1981-82 season, he made the move from Colorado to New Jersey, where once in the Garden State - he became an "Original Devil."

At the end of the 1984-85 season, and now with the Blackhawks, the man of 577 total points called it a career.

Towards the end of the Francis era, he was criticized for not winning and sticking with his "FAT CATS" for too long. Once removed from the gig, and as time ran its course, he was criticized for giving up on young player after young player. MacMillan was no exception - in fact, he was part of the rule.

**DATE OF TRADE: October 28th, 1975**

**RANGERS ACQUIRE: Doug Jarrett**

**CHICAGO BLACKHAWKS ACQUIRE: Gilles Villemure**

Gilles Villemure (who is also extensively covered in my first book - and I'm sure you're already tired of all of these mentions), was a victim of his own era.

Born on May 30th, 1940, in Trois-Rivieres, Quebec, had Villemure been born ten years later, he would have been an NHL starting goaltender for many years. Instead, despite some limited work (thirteen games in emergency work from 1963-1969), he wouldn't become an NHL full-timer until the 1970-71 season - at the age of 30.

And wouldn't you know it, in his first season as a true NHLer, Villemure won the Vezina Trophy in 1971, along with his good friend and brother of the barrel, Eddie Giacomin.

Villemure was there for the height of the Francis era, where the soon-to-become greatest backup goaltender in Rangers' history played for the club for five complete seasons. Aside from the Vezina Trophy win, Villemure was also named to the All-Star game in 1971, 1972, and 1973.

Villemure, who was known for his love of the horses (where he even spent time as a jockey in the offseason), embraced his time in New York. While all players wanted to play in every game, Villemure was happy to share time with Giacomin. As the story goes, whenever Giacomin was starting, Villemure would be checking out "The Daily Racing Form," and was eyeing his next bet.

As mentioned in the Terry Sawchuk profile, it was always Francis' goal to get Villemure up to New York. Making things easier for the general manager was that Villemure never complained about playing time - or lack thereof - one less headache for "The Cat."

(That said, while Villemure played plenty during these five years, even when he was out-performing Giacomin, especially during the pair's last season with the Rangers, it was always #1's net.)

With Francis accepting that his old core did everything they could, like others, Villemure was shipped out of New York for a younger player, albeit only younger than Villemure by four years.

Defenseman Doug Jarrett, from London, Ontario, began his NHL career during the 1964-65 season with the Chicago Blackhawks. He'd remain in Chicago until the time of this trade, logging 721 games in all for the Indian head jersey.

Following this trade, Jarrett played in only 45 games for the Blueshirts during the much-maligned 1975-76 season. A season later - his last - he played in nine games for the Rangers. Following a demotion to the New Haven Nighthawks (AHL), he retired at the end of the 1976-77 season.

In retirement, Jarrett became a prominent member of the Chicago Blackhawks Alumni Association, a role he enjoyed until his passing on February 10th, 2014. At the time of his death, the 69-year-old was battling cancer.

Like Jarrett, Villemure would spend only two seasons in his new Original Six home, where he backed up Tony Esposito. And just like Jarrett, Villemure became a prominent member of his original team's alumni association.

All in all, the 1971 Vezina Trophy winner only played in 21 games as a Blackhawk.

Following the 1976-77 season, Villemure returned to New York, where as of this writing, he maintains a home in Nassau County, Long Island.

This trade wasn't a win. It wasn't a loss unless you consider sentimental losses as actual losses. Plus, with John Davidson's ascension soon to come, it made sense for Francis to move on.

**DATE OF TRADE: October 30th, 1975**

**RANGERS ACQUIRE: First-Round Pick of the 1977 NHL Entry Draft (#8 - Lucien DeBlois)**

**ST. LOUIS BLUES ACQUIRE: Derek Sanderson**

At the time of this trade, Sanderson's substance abuse issues were widely known (and where you can throw the phrase "chain-smoker" into the mix). You even had media members of this era asking the two-time Stanley Cup champion flat-out if he was an alcoholic.

Despite Sanderson having a great first season in St. Louis, this trade was a win. After all, in Lucien DeBlois' first season, the 1977-78 season, the right-winger from Joliette, Quebec, scored 30 points in 71 games. Conversely, in this same season, Sanderson, after thirteen games with the Penguins, retired/could no longer play.

258

And, of course, Part I: as we'll later discuss - this draft pick could have been much bigger than DeBlois.

And, of course, Part II: we'll soon get more into DeBlois once we get to the Fred Shero era and Barry Beck.

And, of course, Part III: this was the last true win that Francis had as Boss of the Blueshirts.

**DATE OF TRANSACTION: October 31st, 1975**

**RANGERS ACQUIRE: Heartbreak**

**DETROIT RED WINGS ACQUIRE: Eddie Giacomin**

While this wasn't a trade, I'd feel remiss if I didn't mention this transaction. Plus, I promised to write about this when I first brought up Giacomin's arrival in New York!

Following the extremely embarrassing first-round playoff series loss to the Islanders in 1975, the Rangers opened up the 1975-76 season at 4-5-1 after ten games played. Knowing that the end was near, Francis continued to rebuild - sentimentality be damned.

With John Davidson thought to be the goalie of the future (and Francis would be right about this, even if fans at this point weren't having any of that), on October 29th, 1975, Francis waived his franchise goaltender of ten seasons. If you were a fan and/or living at this time, you'll never forget where you were when you first heard the news, and you haven't forgotten Giacomin's return game at Madison Square Garden either.

Keep in mind, Part I: Francis was a day-one fan of Giacomin. After all, in May 1965, Francis gave up four NHLers to the Providence Reds in order to get the rights to Giacomin, a native of Sudbury, Ontario, in the first place. (As discussed earlier, those players were Aldo Guidolin, Jim Mikol, Marcel Paille, and Sandy McGregor.)

Keep in mind, Part II: When Giacomin first began his career with the Rangers (which took place after the failed Jacques Plante experiment that also saw former franchise goalie Gump Worsley shine in Montreal), the man soon to be known by his first name didn't start out so hot. In fact, Giacomin's rookie season was the worst of his career.

The Worsley trade and the lack of success from Plante (and the team in general) meant that Ranger fans had no patience. And who can blame them?

When Giacomin (who, again, was traded for four NHLers - don't lose sight of that - as this practice wasn't commonplace then) finished the 1965-66 season with a win-loss-tie record of 8-19-7 and a goals-allowed average of 3.66 (both career lows). Fans weren't shouting "EDDIE! EDDIE! EDDIE!" as they would in the years/seasons to come. Instead, these fans were throwing batteries and vegetables at him. (By the way, who sneaks a tomato into Madison Square Garden?)

Fast-forward ten years following his rookie season - the fans weren't throwing items at Giacomin anymore. Instead, they showered him with adulation and praise.

At the time of this trade, Giacomin held pretty much every single positive goaltending record in franchise history, except for one - Stanley Cup wins. (These records would later be broken in time by Mike Richter, and after Richter, Henrik Lundqvist.)

A six-time All-Star with the Rangers, and the co-winner of the Vezina Trophy with teammate Gilles Villemure, Giacomin was the most beloved Ranger of this era that includes Rod Gilbert, Jean Ratelle, Vic Hadfield, and Brad Park.

For many fans, not only was Giacomin their favorite player - they personally loved him.

This is why it was so crushing when "The Cat" not only moved on from Giacomin - he got nothing in return. Perhaps a player, any player at that, would have softened the blow. Then again, maybe not.

It should be said (and I'll duck as I write this), that while Giacomin was a legend in New York, he wasn't in the same class, nor had the hardware like other goalies from his era had, including Worsley, Plante, Hall, Esposito, Bower, Cheevers, and Sawchuk. And even with Giacomin being inducted into the Hall of Fame (Class of 1987), he's arguably one of the least accomplished goalies to do so - and I know that sounds sacrilegious. (You can send all the hate mail to BULLSMC@aol.com!)

Furthermore, you can't say that Giacomin, unlike Worsley, Plante, and Chuck Rayner before him, didn't have deep Ranger teams in front of him either. In fact, Giacomin had the deepest Ranger teams since the days of "The Bread Line," and perhaps to be superseded only by the eventual 1994 Stanley Cup champion Ranger club.

I know this somewhat sounds like a hit-piece right now, but that's not my intent. It's just to explain why Francis felt that he had to move on - especially as someone who saw talent in Giacomin from day one - and as a general manager-head coach who stuck by his goalie through #1's early struggles as an NHLer.

To boil it all down - Giacomin had his run. He didn't win. Francis had to move on to the future, and the future was with John Davidson.

However, giving away Giacomin for free wasn't easy, either, especially when Giacomin, in his first game with his new team, the Detroit Red Wings, stepped on the ice at Madison Square Garden on November 2nd, 1975 - as a visitor - just two days after being waived.

Truth be told, while I could write a whole book on just the Rangers vs. Red Wings game from November 2nd, 1975 alone, and how that game, to this day, is the most emotional Rangers' regular season game of all time - moving on from Giacomin didn't hurt the Rangers in the short-term, nor the long-term, either.

Sure there were bad feelings once Detroit claimed Giacomin for nothing, but for the man simply known by his first name of "Eddie" - he was already on the downswing of his career.

Aside from Giacomin's rookie season, his final three years in Detroit (where over time, just like his last days in New York, was phased out in another youth movement) were the worst of his career. On the other side, John Davidson helped to lead the Rangers to the Stanley Cup Final in 1979.

In pro sports, fans are often reminded to root for the front of the jersey, not the nameplate on the back of it.

However, Giacomin was one of those rare players where fans wanted to see him succeed more than the team. Need proof? Just go back and watch that game from November 2nd, 1975, where for sixty minutes, Ranger fans shouted "EDDIE! EDDIE! EDDIE!" (They also chanted "KILL THE CAT" too!)

If there was something even sadder than watching Giacomin cry on the ice as fans shouted his name on that November 1975 night, it was how his relationship with the organization, and the fan base he so adored, became fractured. Needless to say, he didn't have the same relationship that Rod Gilbert would later have with the franchise.

While the Rangers would eventually retire Giacomin's number 1 jersey in March 1989, Eddie never moved back to New York like others of his era did. Instead, he maintained a residence outside of Detroit, Michigan, where he still lives today.

Over time, many stories of Giacomin's relationship with the Rangers and the alumni became publicized. Unlike Gilbert and others who would make appearances on their own time and dime (that's not to say Gilbert and others didn't receive paid appearances, too, this is to say that they'd show up to Ranger-related events for free, whenever needed) - Giacomin always held out for money.

As one story has it, when the Rangers were within one game from winning the Stanley Cup in 1994, the organization wanted every prominent member of the alumni in the building, including Giacomin. When asked to show up at Madison Square Garden, Giacomin agreed - only after he was paid a hefty sum.

Despite Francis being long gone from the organization, Giacomin never forgot about being waived. Like Ranger fans themselves, he was crushed when he changed jerseys.

While Giacomin still makes rare appearances for the organization to this day, he never became the ambassador the Rangers would have liked, a role Gilbert thrived in during his retirement and into his final days.

Ironically, John Davidson, Giacomin's replacement, would soon become just as beloved, if not more. (Due to JD's longer tenure with the franchise as a result of his broadcasting work. To be fair, there is a recency bias in this opinion.)

Perhaps even more ironic? In May of 2021, Rangers' owner James Dolan fired John Davidson after only two years on the job, where JD served the Rangers as their Team President. Just like Giacomin, he, too, was cast away for nothing and relocated to middle America, where the former Rangers' netminder now serves the Columbus Blue Jackets as team president.

I know this is tough to say, but this transaction was a win for Francis. It got Giacomin's money off the books (even during a non-salary-cap era) and it allowed Davidson to become fully installed as the team's starting goalie.

Tougher to assess? Our next trade, a trade that over time, has been simply known as just that - "The Trade."

**DATE OF TRADE: November 7th, 1975**

**RANGERS ACQUIRE: Phil Esposito and Carol Vadnais**

## BOSTON BRUINS ACQUIRE: Brad Park, Jean Ratelle, and Joe Zanussi

Yep, this is the trade that you've all been waiting for. So let me crack my knuckles!

To this day, this is still considered one of the biggest trades in not only Rangers' history - but in all of NHL history.

Some may argue that the August 9th, 1988 trade of Wayne Gretzky from Edmonton to Los Angeles was bigger than this one. They'd be wrong. That said, the Gretzky trade is the second-biggest trade in NHL history. This one, featuring three Hall of Famers, is the biggest.

And, yes - since Phil Esposito (and Carol Vadnais) were such a big part of my first book - I have already discussed this trade in detail. However, I'll give you a new spin here, as there is no way I can breeze through this deal - the most profound transaction in 95 years of Rangers' history.

Unlike the Gretzky trade, which was made 100% because of financial reasons - this trade between the Rangers' Emile Francis, and his counterpart in Boston, Harry Sinden, was purely a hockey trade. This trade wasn't about contracts, salary caps, padding bank accounts, or anything like that. This was a trade made by both general managers in an attempt to improve their hockey teams.

And lastly, when speaking of the Gretzky trade, everyone knows what that trade was. Then-Oilers' owner, Peter Pocklington, got cheap and could no longer afford his star. While the Edmonton Oilers would go on to win one more Stanley Cup without "The Great One," the Oilers definitely lost that trade.

As both Mark Messier, the captain of the 1990 Oilers' Stanley Cup winning team, and Wayne Gretzky himself, would later go on to say - had Gretzky (who never really wanted to leave Edmonton in the first place) stayed - the Oilers may have gone on to win two or more Stanley Cups. (Gretzky, in some interviews, has stated that he thought they could've won at least four more - and he may be correct with that opinion.)

And just think about that for a second; had Gretzky stayed in Edmonton, that Mark Messier fellow most likely never goes to New York, either. And if Messier doesn't go to New York, well, we can talk about that once we get to the year 1991!

Over 45 years later, this trade between these two Original Six teams remains highly discussed.

Some fans, media members, "experts," and others consider this the worst trade in all of New York Rangers' history. I would not be in that camp. In fact, as you'll soon see, I think John Ferguson Sr., the man who followed Francis as general manager of the Rangers, made the worst trade in Rangers' history!

Other people consider this trade as a no-doubt-about-it loss for the Rangers. Again, I'm not so sure about that, either, which is why this trade is the most debated in franchise history.

Conversely, some consider this trade as a slight win - because, after all, if it wasn't for the Ulf Nilsson injury (POTVIN SUCKS) in 1979, who knows? Maybe the Rangers win the Stanley Cup with Phil Esposito as the driving force.

Let's now take a look at all five of these players. Since I covered both Esposito and Vadnais in my first book, I'll add a few more words about them here.

Carol Vadnais, a southpaw defenseman out of Montreal, Quebec, won a Stanley Cup with his hometown team in 1968. However, following the championship, the California Seals claimed him from the Montreal Canadiens in that summer's intra-league draft.

In both a different country and time zone, Vadnais, now with more playing time, quickly became one of the Seals' best players. He was named the franchise's captain when the 1971-72 season came along. However, he wouldn't wear the "C" for long in California, as before the 1972 trade deadline, the Boston Bruins picked up the reliable rearguard.

Vadnais, who once again was making a 3,000-mile trek to play hockey, played admirably behind Bobby Orr, where with Phil Esposito, the Bruins won the Stanley Cup in 1972. (I don't think I have to tell you who they beat to win it!)

Already a three-time All-Star with the Seals (1969, 1970, and 1972), Vadnais was named to the All-Star Game one more time with the Bruins (1975). Later on, with the Rangers, he reached the All-Star Game twice more, in 1976 and 1978.

At the time of this trade, Vadnais didn't want to report to New York. In fact, he flat-out refused to join the Rangers, as he had a "no-trade clause" in his contract. (Esposito didn't want to report to New York, either, but we'll get to that in just a moment!)

In a 2008 NHL.com interview with John McGourty (which was conducted six years prior to Vadnais passing away in 2014 at the age of 68), Vadnais said:

*"I was a little shocked at the time because I had a no-trade contract which I asked for because I felt I played better when I had security, and because my wife was very sick. She had an operation three days after the trade. Emile was very good to me and told me to relax and he would take care of everything.*

*"I didn't know Emile, but he was a tremendous gentleman. The main guy was Esposito. New York wanted Esposito for Park. Then, one needed a center and one needed a defenseman. I was definitely the throw-in, I thought. I didn't know they were really after me, but Emile said he wanted me when I was in Oakland and said he had offered more than Boston. Hey, you're just a player, in those days you didn't ask questions."*

In the same 2008 story about this trade, Emile Francis told McGourty:

*"I saw Vadnais in the Central League. The Rangers had the Omaha Knights, and Montreal had the Houston team. He [Vadnais] and Serge Savard played together for Houston, two big, tall, rangy defensemen. The kind of guys you like playing defense. I liked him from the first and tried to get him from the Oakland Seals. I thought I had a deal, but their GM sent him off to Boston. He could carry the puck, handle the puck, had a good shot and skated with his head up. That first pass out of your own end is so important and he did that really well."*

In other words, Vadnais was never a "throw in" player. That would be Joe Zanussi!

Once in New York, Vadnais spent seven seasons with the Rangers, where he was one of the key contributors to the team's success.

Vadnais, who was always reliable, had the best individual seasons of his career with the Rangers - although he never won the Stanley Cup with the franchise as he previously did while in Montreal and in Boston.

Following the 1981-82 season, Vadnais played one more season with the New Jersey Devils and then retired in 1983. In retirement, Vadnais rejoined the Rangers, serving as an assistant coach during the 1983-84 and 1984-85 seasons.

All in all, Vadnais finished his NHL career with 1,087 games played, 169 goals, 418 assists, and 587 points.

With the Rangers, where Vadnais spent the majority of his career, he finished with 485 games played, 56 goals, 190 assists, and 246 points.

So, yes, acquiring Vadnais did work out, although at the same time - he wasn't Brad Park. Then again, outside of Bobby Orr from this era - who was?

Center Phil Esposito, famously of Sault Ste. Marie, Ontario, and the key piece going to the Rangers, absolutely despised this trade. In fact, he even threatened suicide once hearing of the trade, threatening to jump out of a hotel window.

As Emile Francis said in 2008, he felt he had to make a major splash. Ditto Sinden in Boston. Neither general manager felt trading second- and third-liners would have made a difference. So this trade had to be an epic one. Here's how Francis put it to McGourty:

*"So, I made the initial call and we were discussing this guy and that guy and I said; 'Harry, there's no point talking twos and threes. If we're going to shake these teams up, let's talk about the better players.'*

*"I said I'd talk about Brad Park. He asked who I wanted to talk about and I said Orr. This went on for about a month and I flew in there a couple of times.*

*"Then, about a week before the trade, we looked really bad in Philly and I put the whole team on waivers. I did. I told them I was going to do it. Then Harry asked about Ratelle and I said I needed Espo, but those names didn't come up the first three weeks.*

*"I said again, 'Harry, there's no point talking twos and threes. If we're going to shake these teams up, let's talk about the better players.'"*

And that's what happened.

As mentioned in "The New York Rangers Rink of Honor and the Rafters of Madison Square Garden," Phil Esposito, in his 2003 tell-all book, *"Thunder and Lightning,"* hated this trade at the time. While he'd eventually warm up to playing in New York, he always thought the Rangers were inferior to the Bruins.

Even in his 2008 interview with McGourty, Esposito said:

*"The last place I wanted to be traded to was the Rangers because they were our enemies. But they treated me really well in New York, and I played hard for them.*

268

*"I loved Boston, and I loved the Bruins. We were really a team. We played hard, and we hung out together, and we won Stanley Cups together. I think if I had stayed, we would have won a couple more.*

*"In Boston, if we lost a game, everybody was angry. Especially if we lost to a team that we never should have lost to, like California. Our philosophy was to always beat the teams you're supposed to beat. Especially the teams that are worse than you -- you have to beat them."*

In *"Thunder and Lightning"* and in other interviews conducted since that book's release, Esposito singled out Rod Gilbert, the leader of the Rangers at the time, for his partying ways. He felt that Gilbert put partying over winning.

Esposito also felt there was no winning culture in New York, especially after a loss, when Gilbert told him, *"you can't win 'em all."* It was at that moment that Esposito knew that he was no longer in Boston.

While Esposito was no stranger to partying/drinking, he knew that these blowing-off-steam activities were a reward for winning. In New York, he felt the Rangers didn't care about wins and losses.

Running down all of Esposto's accolades is a whole book for another time. Plus, we still have to get to his tenure as Rangers' general manager!

However, at the time of this trade, he already was a year-in and year-out All-Star, a two-time Stanley Cup champion, and a multiple-time recipient of both the Art Ross (five times) and Hart (two times) trophies. He was also considered as either the best or second-best player in the game, where only teammate Bobby Orr was in the conversation with him.

In his career, which first began in Chicago (and if you're looking for a bad Esposito trade, look no further to May 17th, 1965, when the Hawks shipped him to Boston), number 77 of the Rangers finished his NHL career with 1,282 games played, 717 goals, 873 assists, and 1,590 points.

With the Rangers, where Esposito spent the final six years of his career, he finished with 422 games, 184 goals, 220 assists, and 404 points. He'd also later become the first man in franchise history to play, coach, and serve the team as both a color analyst and general manager. If this trade never happens - most likely - Ranger fans would never have experienced the "Trader Phil Era" - but more on that to come.

Going to Boston was the previously discussed Joe Zanussi, a former WHAer (Winnipeg Jets) who never got much time with the Rangers. In fact, he played in only eight games with the Rangers prior to this trade.

The defenseman out of Rossland, British Columbia (and just like he did in New York), split time between the Bruins and their AHL team, the Rochester Americans.

Zanussi spent parts of only two seasons with the Bruins, 68 games in all, before being dealt to St. Louis during the 1976-77 season, where, ironically, it was Emile Francis acquiring Zanussi for a second time.

However, with the Blues, Zanussi played in only eleven games, his final eleven NHL games of his career. He'd spend the final seasons of his career mainly with the Blues' CHL affiliate, the Salt Lake Golden Eagles, where he retired at the end of the 1977-78 season.

This is a nice way of saying that Zanussi was the extra part of this trade, where despite his limited success, perhaps Francis didn't need to include him in this deal.

Brad Park, another player covered in depth in my first book, was the second-best defenseman in the league at the time of this trade. Now in Boston, the native of Toronto, Ontario, joined the best defenseman in the league, the one who robbed him of multiple Norris Trophies, Bobby Orr.

However, Orr and Park wouldn't last together for long. After just ten games, Orr, whose knee injuries were crippling his play at the time, these chronic injuries would cut into his 1975-76 season.

After a dispute with the Bruins, spearheaded by the evil Alan Eagleson, Orr moved on to Chicago for the 1976-77 campaign. (Eagleson could be another topic for a different book. There are many books out there that cover Eagleson, who never presented contract details that the Bruins were offering their Hall of Famer.)

However, once with the Blackhawks, Orr was never the same, as his injured knees nagged him. He'd later miss the 1977-78 season, and after six games played during the 1978-79 season (and over a dozen knee surgeries later), he retired.

Silver lining? At least Francis received Vadnais, and not Orr, in this deal. Once leaving Boston, Orr played in only 26 games over the course of the next three seasons.

It must be mentioned that Brad Park, who made a career out of being number two, is the all-time leader in most second-place votes for the Norris Trophy. He also wore #2. Brian Leetch later wore that same number and shattered all of Park's defenseman records; because of Orr, Park was the second-best, and not the best defenseman of his era, as Park has repeatedly said himself.

During his career, Park finished in second place for the Norris Trophy six times. Eight-time winner Bobby Orr, Park's teammate for ten games, took the award away from Park on five occasions while Park was with the Rangers. In Boston, Park finished second place in 1978, where Denis Potvin (ugh) beat him out for the hardware.

For what it's worth, Park has said the following multiple times about his failure to win the Norris:

*"I saw no reason to be upset because I was rated second to Bobby Orr. After all, Orr not only was the top defenceman in the game but he was considered the best player ever to put on a pair of skates. There was nothing insulting about being rated number two to such a super superstar."*

One question you might be asking is this one; *"why wasn't this trade just a straight swap of Ratelle for Esposito?"*

At the time of this trade, Park was 27 years old. Also prior to the trade, Ranger newspaper reporters said that Park was *"overweight, overpaid and over the hill, and is no Denis Potvin."*

It was also thought that, like Orr, Park's knees were starting to betray him. Here's Sinden in his 2008 interview with McGourty:

*"We checked it [Park's knees] out, and we watched him [Park] play. I had my chief scout watch him play in four-straight games, one in Montreal, one in Vancouver, and one in New York -- and another I can't remember -- and he was the No. 1 star in each game.*

*"I had the same concern about Orr's knees, so we wanted Park because of that concern. I knew I couldn't give up Orr, I valued my life. (Sinden laughed when he said this.)*

*"So, I guess I got around to Esposito somehow. Ratelle had that broken ankle a few years earlier, but he was OK. We weren't concerned about his injury. He had played in all their games for them that year.*

*"The key from our standpoint was Park. The reason we went on with Ratelle and Vadnais was because they needed a defenseman, and I needed a center to replace Esposito. We did that so each wouldn't have a big hole in the lineup.*

*"Emile ended up with one of the great centers of all time and I wound up with one of the great defensemen of all time.*

272

*"Park was one of the top-six defensemen to ever play in the NHL. Both Phil and Park went to the Hall of Fame, as did Ratelle. This was a trade of really top players. Providing injuries didn't get in the way, the deal should have worked for both teams.*

*"My only concern [at the time] was losing Orr to his injury.*

*"In Boston, we were able to see the value of a top defenseman. Orr was the top defenseman in the history of the NHL at that time and, in my opinion, still is. We were in danger of losing him. If we could get the defenseman who was second to Orr, which Park was, we could afford to give up the best scorer in the League. Emile may have had concerns about Brad's knees as I had about Orr."*

This Sinden interview also tells you that it was Brad Park, not Jean Ratelle, who was the apple of his eye.

Funny enough, and in another "what if" of NHL history, it was the Rangers under Francis who selected Brad Park with their second-overall pick of the 1966 NHL Amateur Draft. Guess who had the first pick of that draft? Yep, you guessed it - the Boston Bruins.

While the irony would've been stronger if Sinden was the general manager of the Bruins at this time, it was B's general manager, Hap Emms, who selected Park's fellow defenseman, Barry Gibbs, with his first-overall pick.

While Gibbs carved out a nice career for himself (797 NHL games in all), only eight of them came with the Bruins.

Barry Gibbs, not to be confused with Barry Gibb of "The Bee Gees," "stayed alive" following his trade from Boston to Minnesota, where he spent many years with the North Stars and Flames. He would round out his career with the Blues and Kings before retiring in 1981.

And can you imagine if the Bruins had Park and Orr together in the prime of their careers rather than for just ten games at the end of Orr's career? Egads!

Back to Park.

Here are Park's numbers:

Overall, in a sixteen-season career that included eight campaigns with the Rangers, eight with the Bruins, and his final two seasons with the Red Wings, Park finished with 1,113 games played, 213 goals, 683 assists, and 896 points.

In his eight seasons with the Rangers, Park logged 465 games, 95 goals, 283 assists, and 378 points.

In his eight seasons with the Bruins following this trade, Park logged 501 games, 100 goals, 317 assists, and 417 points.

In other words, despite the criticism, the Rangers beat reporters of the time they were giving him - Park wasn't *"overweight, overpaid and over the hill."*

Instead, Park had the best seasons of his career in Boston.

And while this is no shot at Vadnais - Park was much better than the defenseman he was traded for, as is evident by Park's Class of 1988 Hall of Fame induction.

The final piece of this trade "Gentleman" Jean Ratelle, the southpaw center out of Lac St. Jean, Quebec.

Here's Sinden, again from 2008, on his acquiring Ratelle:

*"Jean Ratelle got almost 100 points in both his first two years with us.*

*"You know, I've often used his name as players have come along since and pointed out what a great defensive player he was without*

274

*being an aggressive type of forward. He was a terrific checker. A lot of players who don't have an aggressive nature think you're talking body-checking, but Ratelle is a great example of how you can check so well without necessarily being a body-checker.*

*"He brought a lot to this team. He was an excellent faceoff man and more of a creative playmaker than a shooter. He'd get 35 goals while Espo would get around 60, but Jean was able to put a lot of points up there with his playmaking."*

At the time of this trade, depending on how you see it, Ratelle was either the first or second-best center in all of Rangers' history. (Frank Boucher would be my first pick, and in later years, some may give the nod to Mark Messier. This is all a difference of opinion, where the only thing to take away from this is that Ratelle was one of the best.)

A veteran of sixteen seasons with the Rangers, the center of the "Goal a Game" line, number 19 was one of the greatest to do it. It's just too bad that the Rangers retired his jersey on February 25, 2018, and only after Rod Gilbert politicked for it to happen.

This ceremony should have taken place right after Ratelle's 1981 retirement when Ranger fans who saw the peak of his career would have appreciated it more rather than the polite golf claps Ratelle received in 2018 in front of fans who never saw him play.

Alas, I digress again.

A two-time winner of the Lady Byng Trophy (once with the Rangers in 1972 and once with Boston in 1976), Ratelle is considered to be one of the classiest players to ever lace up a pair of hockey skates.

In his 22 seasons as an NHLer, which earned him Hall of Fame status in 1985, Ratelle spent sixteen of them with the Rangers and then played in six seasons with the Bruins.

Here are Ratelle's career numbers: 1,280 games played, 491 goals, 776 assists, and 1,267 points.

In New York, Ratelle's numbers were: 861 games played, 336 goals, 481 assists, and 817 points.

In Boston, Ratelle's numbers were: 419 games played, 155 goals, 295 assists, and 450 points.

Ratelle, like Park, flourished in Boston. However, unlike Park, Ratelle's best years took place in New York.

Just like the center he was traded for, Ratelle continued his association with the Bruins once retiring as a player, where he served the black and gold for four-consecutive seasons as an assistant coach, where his days behind the bench reached an end following the 1984-85 season.

Both Ratelle and Esposito, the two "center-pieces" of this trade, retired after the 1980-81 season. Offensively, Esposito was much more efficient than Ratelle. Plus, unlike Ratelle in Boston - Esposito was a leader in New York and often carried the team in scoring.

What hurt Esposito was, as he said, the winning culture wasn't there in New York.

That said, the Rangers, with Esposito doing the heavy lifting, did make it to Game Five of the 1979 Stanley Cup Final - where Esposito's suggestions to head coach Fred Shero were often ignored.

In Boston, both Park and Ratelle, ironically on the wrong end of the 1972 Stanley Cup Final to these same Beantown Bruins, would play in two more Stanley Cup Finals - and in back-to-back years at that.

However, Scotty Bowman and his Montreal Canadiens' dynasty team, just as they'd later defeat Esposito's Rangers in 1979 - swept the Bruins in 1977 and then beat them in six games in 1978.

If you're going tit-for-tat here, the Bruins reached two Stanley Cup Finals with Park and Ratelle. The Rangers reached one with Esposito and Vadnais.

That said, if Ulf Nilsson doesn't get injured in 1979, and as mentioned earlier - maybe Esposito's Rangers win the Stanley Cup in 1979, had that happened - we could proudly say that Emile Francis won this trade.

However, Nilsson did get injured, Shero did ignore Esposito's suggestions, and the Rangers fell in five games to the Habs.

So, as we get to the end of this trade here - who won, who lost, and how bad was this decision?

Prior to that answer, I should tell you that before writing this book, I always thought this trade was somewhat "Even-Steven." I have said as much prior to authoring this book.

However, when you look at all the facts presented, and if you don't deal in the "what if" game - this trade was a loss. Plus, this trade was the end of Emile's tenure in New York, too, as Rangers management had seen enough.

Even if you cancel out Ratelle and Esposito as equals, and for as much as I liked Vadnais - he wasn't Brad Park. Adding Zanussi to this trade, for as little as that may be - there's no way I can say this trade was a win - even if I want to.

And while Francis wasn't behind what Ferguson would later do - who knows if he would've traded Rick Middleton for Kenny Hodge?

Yep, I'm reversing a previously stated opinion from my BlueCollarBlueShirts.com website - this trade was a bonafide loss. However, is this the worst loss or a top-five loss? I wouldn't agree with that.

Francis would make one more trade before receiving his walking papers.

**DATE OF TRADE: November 14th, 1975**

**RANGERS ACQUIRE: Al Simmons**

**BOSTON BRUINS ACQUIRE: Cash**

After many big trades and roster decisions, Emile Francis ended his tenure as Rangers general manager with all of the power of a quiet "excuse me" poof fart.

Al Simmons, drafted in the seventh round by the California Seals in the 1971 NHL Amateur Draft (85th overall), the defenseman from Winnipeg, Manitoba, played in only one game for the rotten franchise during the 1971-72 season.

In the 1975-76 season, Simmons played in seven more games for the Bruins - the final matches of his NHL career.

Now under Rangers' control, Simmons played in 56 games for the Providence Reds (AHL). He'd never play for the Rangers, or in the NHL again, as he retired after this season.

Whatever Francis paid Sinden was too much. This was a loss, albeit not a major one.

Furthermore, whatever Francis had planned next would never be revealed. Enter John Ferguson.

John Ferguson (right), pictured here with his player and a future general manager of the Rangers himself, Phil Esposito. Ferguson's redesign of the Rangers' iconic sweater is what he's most known for - outside of his horrific trades.

## <u>JOHN FERGUSON SR.</u>

Tenure as Rangers General Manager: January 7, 1976 – June 2, 1978

Depending on how you assess short tenures, John Ferguson Sr. is arguably the worst general manager in Rangers' history.

While his run at the top of the Rangers' food chain was only thirty months long (and he made only five trades during this time), Ferguson made the worst trade in franchise history when he traded Rick Middleton to Boston for Ken Hodge Sr.

There was also that whole 1977 NHL Amateur Draft, too, but we'll soon explore Lucien DeBlois, Ron Duguay, and Mike Bossy in due time.

If there's anything nice to say about Ferguson's tenure, it's the fact that he was able to lure a pair of superstar Swedes away from the Winnipeg Jets, then of the WHA, Anders Hedberg and Ulf Nilsson, via free agency. That said, it should be noted that Ferguson signed the pair of Swedes in March 1978 - less than three months prior to being fired.

Ferguson has the unique distinction of being the first Rangers' general manager (and head coach) never to have played for the Rangers. And if you care about such things, he's also the first general manager profiled in this book that's NOT included in "The New York Rangers Rink of Honor and the Rafters of Madison Square Garden!"

Before trading in his sticks and skates for pens and pencils, Ferguson had played in 500 games (eight seasons) with the Montreal Canadiens. During that time, and while playing the left-wing position on some stacked Habitant teams, Ferguson won the Stanley Cup five times as the team's take-no-prisoners enforcer. In total, the man known as "Fergy" accumulated a whopping 1,214 penalty minutes throughout his career.

When Francis was fired, it signaled the end of an era. It also meant that Francis wouldn't see his rebuild through.

When then Rangers' Team President Bill Jennings fired Francis, he hired Ferguson with the sole intent of "Fergy" replacing "The Cat" as general manager. Ironically, before Jennings' decision, Francis had previously offered Ferguson the Rangers' head coach gig, as Francis wanted to focus on his general manager duties. As would often be the case - Francis could never find a head coach as successful as himself, and he would repeatedly be lured back behind the Rangers' bench.

Following the 1974-75 season, Ferguson rebuffed Francis' initial offer. Once turned down by the NHL tough man, Francis then hired his former player, Ron Stewart. A few months later, and in a twist of events, Ferguson, like everyone before him, was now serving the Rangers in the dual role of head coach and general manager.

Once hired by Jennings, Ferguson, who previously had no NHL head coaching or general manager experience, fired Stewart.

Stewart had coached only 39 games for the Rangers, where the rebuilding team went 15-20-4.

When Ferguson decided to make himself the head coach, Jennings, on January 9th, 1976 (two days after firing Francis/hiring Ferguson), said, *"Fergy wasn't hired for both jobs. I hired him to be the general manager. He chose to take over as coach for the remainder of the season to evaluate his players. After this season, he'll look for a new coach."*

On the same day, Ferguson, when asked if he would stay on as head coach for the 1976-77 season, in the event that his 1975-76 Rangers turned it around (and qualified for the playoffs), said, *"no, no. I'll be looking for a coach in or out of the organization."*

The Rangers ultimately finished in fourth-place (last place) in their division (the Patrick Division) at the end of the 1975-76 season. Come the 1976-77 season, Ferguson remained in his dual role. The team finished in fourth place again.

In 121 games in a season and a half with the Rangers, Ferguson compiled a record of 43-59-19.

Once the 1977-78 season rolled around, Ferguson hired his friend and fellow Stanley Cup champion teammate, Mr. Tracksuit himself, Jean-Guy Talbot, to coach the Rangers. Both men were fired after the season (where Ferguson's club finished last place for the third-consecutive season) for another tough-as-nails character, Fred Shero, the brains behind the brawn of the "Broad Street Bullies" - the Philadelphia Flyers teams of the mid-1970s.

While there weren't that many positive moments during Ferguson's tenure, "Fergy" did try to change the Rangers' reputation.

At the time, the Rangers were known as Francis' "Fat Cats," which led to a joke among NHL circles - *"they collected more paycheques than threw checks."*

The Rangers, also accused of being more "blue blood" than "blue collar," saw a change when Ferguson brought a pair of young players, Don Murdoch and Nick Fotiu, into the mix.

While Ferguson had respect for Francis (despite turning down Francis' head coach offer), he also wasn't shy when talking about his predecessor.

In a January 10th, 1977 interview with Peter Gammons of *Sports Illustrated*, Ferguson reflected on his one-year anniversary:

*"First of all, I had to give the Rangers something they always lacked - a mean streak. To be a winner, a team, like an individual, must have some killer instinct. Second, we had to get in condition. When I helped coach Team Canada against the Soviet Union in 1972, I saw for the first time what conditioning really means. The Soviet players were in fantastic shape.*

*"There were too many guys on the Rangers who had proved they could never play for a winner, so I made up my mind to go with the kids. If we're going to lose, I'd rather lose with kids."*

Ferguson, by June of 1978, got his wish - the Rangers got tougher, and he did lose with his kids. Fred Shero would soon help turn those kids into men - albeit temporarily.

Let's now take a look at a general manager tenure that, at best, can only be described as disastrous.

Rick Middleton, from November 17th, 1974, following his four-goal game in a 10-0 Rangers' win over the California Seals. Emile Francis was high on "Nifty." Despite Ferguson saying that he wanted to get younger, he traded Francis' first-round pick (14th overall) of the 1973 NHL Amateur Draft for an end-of-the-line Ken Hodge in the worst trade in Rangers' history that Ferguson will always be infamously remembered for.

Photo Credit: NHL Archives and https://www.nifty16.com/ - the official website of Rick Middleton. This photo is reprinted under Common Creative Usage laws.

---

**DATE OF TRADE: May 26th, 1976**

**RANGERS ACQUIRE: Ken Hodge Sr.**

**BOSTON BRUINS ACQUIRE: Rick Middleton**

My friends, this trade, Ferguson's first, was the **ABSOLUTE WORST TRADE IN ALL OF NEW YORK RANGERS' FRANCHISE HISTORY!**

While we can debate many trades discussed in this book, this one is not up for debate. This is a fact and not an opinion - NO TRADE WAS WORSE THAN THIS ONE.

How about I give you the black-and-white numbers first, and then the analysis afterward?

Ken Hodge, the right-winger, born in Birmingham, England, but raised in Toronto, Ontario, was one month shy of his 32nd birthday at the time of this trade.

Here are his career numbers with the Rangers:

In 96 games and parts of two seasons, Hodge finished with 23 goals and 45 assists, for a grand total of 68 points. He also finished with a lovely plus-minus stat of negative -26.

Rick Middleton, also a right-winger from Toronto, Ontario, at the time of this trade, was ten years younger than Hodge. He was also a Francis first-round pick of the 1973 NHL Amateur Draft when he was selected fourteenth overall.

As a Ranger, Middleton only played in two seasons with the club prior to this upcoming 1976-77 season. During his tenure with the Blueshirts, he finished with 46 goals, 44 assists, and 90 points in 124 games played.

And, oh, did I mention that Hodge's 96 games and the stats he accrued were the final numbers of his NHL career? Have I failed to mention that the Rangers weren't chasing a Stanley Cup at this time, so going "all-in" at the expense of youth wasn't the right strategy?

With Hodge soon-to-be retired, here are Middleton's final stats from his days in Boston:

Twelve seasons, 881 games played, 402 goals, 496 assists, and 898 points. Oh, yeah, as opposed to Hodge's Rangers career plus/minus number of negative 26 - Middleton finished his Bruins career with a plus/minus stat of positive 220 - as in 246 points better than Hodge.

As the great Candace Cameron Bure would say (sister-in-law of Pavel Bure, who we'll get into later on in this book) - "OH, MYLANTA!"

I could say here - *"what was John Ferguson thinking?"*

However, we know what he was thinking.

Hodge, a three-time All-Star and a two-time Stanley Cup champion in Boston, was brought in solely to help Phil Esposito.

Hodge, who previously had two seasons of 105 points each in Boston while serving Esposito on the right wing, was thought of as someone who could help get Esposito going, while also replicating his past success. Needless to say, this didn't go according to plan. Far from it.

While it's not my intention to take a monstrous diaper-sized dump on Hodge, because, after all, he was a great Bruin and had many tremendous years in Boston prior to this trade - he was just an absolute BUST in New York, where, really, his run in New York is the definition of that capitalized word.

Making matters worse was how great Middleton would go on to be. While not in the Hall of Fame as of this writing - there are many people, including fans, media members, and others alike, all politicking for Toronto to do the right thing.

I hate to use this word in this book because I really do have a deep respect for anyone who has ever played this game - but I can't stress this enough - when trying to tell you how bad this trade was, Hodge just *"sucked"* as a Ranger. Just eighteen games into the 1977-78 season, he was demoted to the New Haven Nighthawks (AHL).

Rick Middleton, "the one who got away," was an absolute stud in Boston.

In a career that amassed 1,005 NHL games and 988 points, he was named to three All-Star teams (1981, 1982, and 1984), won a Lady Byng Trophy (1982), and as a cherry on top - won a gold medal for Canada in 1984.

A perennial playoff beast and a former captain of the Bruins, too, on November 29, 2018, Boston retired Middleton's number 16 jersey before a game against the Islanders. Of course, if Boston wanted to troll, they could have held this ceremony when the other team from New York was the opponent.

This trade alone is partly why Ferguson only lasted one month shy of eighteen months as general manager of the New York Rangers. This was a bad trade at the time, and it only got worse as time moved on.

One last time - THIS WAS THE WORST TRADE IN ALL OF NEW YORK RANGER HISTORY.

**DATE OF TRADE: May 28th, 1976**

**RANGERS ACQUIRE: Mark Heaslip**

**LOS ANGELES KINGS ACQUIRE: John Campbell**

Mark Heaslip, an American right-winger out of Duluth, Minnesota, played in nineteen games for the Rangers during the 1976-77 season. He would play in 29 more games in the season that followed.

Come the 1978-79 season, he was back in Los Angeles, where he played 69 games in the final season of his NHL career.

John Campbell, from Sault Ste. Marie, Ontario, was also a right-winger. In addition, Campbell was a Francis third-round draft pick (46th overall) of the 1973 NHL Amateur Draft. However, he'd never make it to the NHL. Instead, he spent the bulk of his career in the Southern Hockey League, where he played for the Winston-Salem Polar Twins - where prior to writing this book - was a team that I never heard of before!

This trade was a small win for Ferguson, but obviously, not a trade to brag about - especially when you think of the trade that he made two days before!

**DATE OF TRADE: October 8th, 1976**

**RANGERS ACQUIRE: Fourth-Round Pick of the 1978 NHL Amateur Draft (#59 - Dave Silk)**

## PITTSBURGH PENGUINS ACQUIRE: Dunc Wilson

Dunc Wilson, a goaltender out of Toronto, Ontario (and perhaps most famously known for his mask that depicted a Confederate flag on it), had spent parts of five seasons with the Flyers, Canucks, and the Leafs, prior to Francis acquiring him off waivers on February 15th, 1975.

As a Ranger, Wilson wasn't exactly the best backup goaltender in the league. During his time in New York, he served as John Davidson's number two and finished the 1975-76 season with a goals-allowed average of 4.22 and a save percentage of .863. Wilson was also demoted during this season, where he then spent time with the Baltimore Clippers (AHL).

Now in Pittsburgh, Wilson turned it around a bit, and spent two seasons there, playing in 66 games in total.

In the 1978-79 season, Wilson was back in Vancouver, where he played from 1970-1973.

Now back with the Canucks (in what would be his last season), Wilson won only two games in his seventeen starts.

At 41 years old, after retiring in Vancouver, he'd later sue the organization for misdiagnosing a mole that wound up being cancerous.

All in all, he finished his NHL career with a record of 80-153-33 in 287 NHL games played.

Following this trade, the Rangers relied on "Gratoony the Loony," real name Gilles Gratton, as their backup goaltender.

As Gratton would later admit in his 2015 autobiography, also entitled *"Gratoony the Loony,"* he hated playing hockey, always thought of it as a job, and his 41 games from this 1976-77 season would be the final games of his NHL career. However, he'll always be remembered for his sweet tiger mask.

As you may be aware, Dave Silk, a right-winger out of Scituate, Massachusetts, was not only a fourth-round draft pick of the Rangers during the 1978 NHL Amateur Draft (59th overall) - but more important for his career - he was part of "The Miracle on Ice" team, where he won a gold medal in the 1980 Olympics.

Silk never played under Ferguson. Heck, he barely played under Ferguson's successor, Fred Shero, either.

Instead, while playing on Broadway, Silk played under Rangers' General Manager Craig Patrick (a lot more on him in this book to come), the same Patrick. He served as Silk's assistant general manager and assistant head coach during USA Hockey's gold medal run in Lake Placid, NY. (Again, you may have heard about this before!)

As a professional hockey player, Silk had a so-so tenure with the Rangers, 141 games in all, where, ironically, his buddy Craig Patrick would then trade him in 1983.

However, this was another minor win on Ferguson's record, as the Rangers were fine without Wilson, and Silk was somewhat reliable during his Ranger years - the best seasons of his career.

**DATE OF TRADE: November 11th, 1976**

**RANGERS ACQUIRE: Bill Goldsworthy**

**MINNESOTA NORTH STARS ACQUIRE: Nick Beverley and Bill Fairbairn**

Right-winger Bill Goldsworthy, from Waterloo, Ontario, was 32 years old at the time of this trade. He was originally a product of the Boston Bruins, where he received his first taste of NHL action in the 1964-65 season. However, due to the NHL's status as a six-team league at the time - the promising player had trouble breaking into the B's lineup.

Just like other players discussed in this book from that era, once the league doubled in size for the 1967-68 season, Goldsworthy headed out west, where he was drafted in the eleventh round (62nd overall) by the Minnesota North Stars.

Now in Minnesota, Goldsworthy had the best years of his career with his new club, where he spent a decade of his life representing the North Stars. Over these ten years, he was named to the All-Star Game four times and set multiple franchise records. (Following his retirement in 1979, he was still the franchise's top scorer of all time.)

At the time of the trade, Goldsworthy (whose #8 jersey would later be retired by the club in 1992), was the captain of the North Stars. The team, just like the Rangers, was undergoing a rebuild of their own. Somewhat similar to Derek Sanderson, Goldsworthy also had a problem with alcohol, which made it easier for Minnesota to say goodbye to their captain.

The man known for the "Goldy Shuffle," his post-goal celebration dance with the Stars, the right-winger finished the 1976-77 season with the Rangers with only ten goals to his name - the lowest total of his career as a full-time NHLer.

A season later, following seven goalless games, he was demoted to the New Haven Nighthawks (AHL). He lasted four games before becoming involved in the first-ever trade between an NHL and WHA franchise.

On December 5th, 1977, Ferguson came to terms with the Indianapolis Racers of the WHA, where Goldsworthy would switch leagues. Even better for the Racers, Ferguson's Rangers would eat the bulk of Goldsworthy's salary, worth $180,000 annually - and a contract that still had three years remaining.

The NHL would never have allowed such a trade to happen in 1972 when the WHA first opened for business. And heck, before this trade, they still hadn't!

However, the WHA was practically on its last legs by this time. There were already talks about a "merger," where in reality, the

NHL would "absorb" four WHA franchises (Oilers, Jets, Nordiques, and Whalers) at the start of the 1979-80 season.

With the WHA no longer a threat to NHL business, this trade was approved.

While paying a player not to play for you never sits well with anyone, at the time, both Eddie Johnstone and Lucien DeBlois, both right-wingers themselves, were significantly better than both Goldsworthy and Ken Hodge. In other words, this deal was an "addition by subtraction" transaction, as it allowed Johnstone and DeBlois to receive more playing time. This would work out for the Rangers but not for the Racers.

In Indianapolis, Goldsworthy served the club not only as a player but as their head coach. However, his alcoholism, combined with his regression and the team's status as a bottom-feeder, led him to the Edmonton Oilers during the 1978-79 season. He played in seventeen games for the Oil and then retired at the end of the season.

The veteran of 771 NHL games, and 49 contests in the WHA, passed away at a young age.

While becoming the first NHLer ever to be traded to a WHA team is a "fun fact," his status as the first NHL player (at least publicly) to contract HIV and die of AIDS wasn't.

On March 29th, 1996, Goldsworthy died at the age of 51 as a result of AIDS. Prior to his death, he had publicly spoken about his HIV-positive status - only after Magic Johnson (NBA) had done so first.

At the time of both Goldsworthy's announcement (and at the time of his death), HIV and AIDS were considered a disease/illness/affliction that only homosexuals could contract. Even during the 1980s, HIV and AIDS, to the majority of the American public, was simply known as "the gay disease."

Magic Johnson eventually helped change that erroneous line of thinking, but it would take years for HIV and AIDS to shed the false notion that they were "homosexual exclusive."

Only as time passed did the American public (and the rest of the world, too) learn that anyone could get the virus in several different ways. For example, not only could one contract the virus through sexual activity (no matter who your partner was) but the virus could also be spread by sharing needles and receiving blood transfusions.

While we know everything about how one can contract the virus today, in every obituary posted at the time of Goldsworthy's death, the word "heterosexual" appeared in all of them. And several times at that. The word "promiscuous" also appeared concerning Goldsworthy's affinity for females, which had previously led to his divorce.

One other word also appeared in every single one of Goldsworthy's death notices - the word "alcoholic." His own children told media members that once their father tested positive for HIV, his drinking, which was already out of control, even going back to his days as a player, just got worse.

This was my long-winded way of telling you that Goldsworthy never worked out for the Rangers.

As discussed during the Vic Hadfield trade, Nick "Who?" Beverley never worked out for the Rangers, which is why he was sent off to Minnesota.

"Bulldog" Bill Fairbairn, from Brandon, Manitoba, began his career with the Rangers in 1969. And like many other names that I have discussed in this book, he is another featured member of "The New York Rangers Rink of Honor."

A right-winger, Fairbairn was a great Ranger. He was there for the height of the Emile Francis Era - and the lows that came after.

Following Francis' dismissal, Fairbairn only played in nine games in the 1976-77 season, the campaign prior to this trade.

Known as a masterful penalty killer, Fairbairn finished the season in Minnesota. Then, six games into the 1977-78 season, the North Stars put him on waivers. Who was there to claim him? Yep, his old buddy Emile Francis - now the St. Louis Blues' general manager.

Now in St. Louis, Fairbairn finished the season with the Blues. He would play in five more games for Francis during the 1978-79 season, but chronic back injuries soon forced the then-32-year-old into retirement.

In a 2015 interview with George Grimm, Fairbairn said the following:

*"I still love New York and I love the team I played with. It was very disappointing all the years I was there that we were contenders but we just couldn't come up with the Stanley Cup. That was the only bad part about being there. But my life wouldn't be as it is now if I hadn't gone to New York and played with the players that I was with. I couldn't have played for a better coach than Emile Francis, I can't say enough about him. I made a lot of friends and still have a lot of friends from the game. I love New York and still love the Rangers. They are my only team."*

While this trade never came back to haunt Ferguson (especially since he'd soon be gone himself), this trade was a loss.

Yes, Fairbairn was at the end of the line, and Beverley wasn't much better, but Goldsworthy never worked out.

It also didn't work out when the Rangers had to spend a ton of money for Goldsworthy to play elsewhere.

Suffice to say, this trade was a hands-down loss.

**DATE OF TRADE: August 31st, 1977**

**RANGERS ACQUIRE: Future Considerations (Third-Round Pick of the 1978 NHL Amateur Draft) (#44 - Dean Turner)**

**LOS ANGELES KINGS ACQUIRE: Pete Stemkowski**

We have already discussed Pete Stemkowski, but following this trade, he'd finish his NHL career in Los Angeles, where he scored 13 goals and picked up 18 assists in his final season, 1977-78.

The 1978 NHL Amateur Draft took place on June 15th, 1978, thirteen days after Ferguson was removed from the general manager position.

(Of note, this was the last time that the NHL Draft had the word "Amateur" between the words "NHL" and "Draft." From this point forward, starting in 1979, the draft became known as the "NHL Entry Draft.")

We have no clue what Ferguson would've done at the draft had he not been fired. It's why we can't say this trade was a win or a loss. Furthermore, with Stemmer retiring after his one season in LA - it's not like he was the "missing piece" of a potential 1978 Stanley Cup victory.

What we do know is that defenseman Dean Turner, from Dearborn, Michigan, played in one game in the 1978-79 season for the Rangers. He spent the rest of the season with the New Haven Nighthawks (AHL).

Turner, a Michigan Wolverine prior to being drafted, was mainly a career minor leaguer. However, his name will pop up later in this book once we get to our next general manager - Fred Shero who - wouldn't you know it - was part of the following trade in Rangers' history.

The hiring of Fred Shero, aka "The Fog," marked the return of a former Ranger now serving the club in the dual role of the head coach and general manager. Mainly a minor leaguer during his playing days, Shero first played with the Rangers during the 1947-48 season and remained with the team throughout the Stanley Cup Playoff run of 1950. This picture was taken sometime in 1948.

## FRED SHERO

Tenure as Rangers General Manager: June 2, 1978 – November 21, 1980

The hiring of Fred Shero was the result of a trade - the first of its kind by the Rangers - and a trade made by then Team President Sonny Werblin.

During the middle of the 1977-78 season, at the turn of a New Year, Werblin, who made his name in professional football (AFL and NFL), was named as the President of Madison Square Garden, where among his numerous duties, he oversaw the Rangers.

Following the Rangers' three-consecutive last-place finishes, Werblin, in his first major move as the boss, cleaned house. He, and just like Ranger fans, was sick and tired of hearing all of the criticism, where Ferguson's Rangers became known as *"The New York Strangers"* and *"the worst team that money can buy."*

There were other reasons why Werblin canned Ferguson, outside of the fact that Fred Shero (who was nicknamed "The Fog" long before taking over in New York) was now available.

During the transition period following Francis' departure, Madison Square Garden, which was always loud and sold out for Ranger home games, remained noisy for the wrong reasons.

MSG, which didn't sell out in the Ferguson era, often heard boos and jeers rather than cheers. And those new jerseys that Ferguson designed weren't exactly a smashing success, even if today, these sweaters, now considered "retro" and "old school," are appreciated. At the very least, today, these jerseys are now considered collector items rather than collecting dust as they did back then.

While you can understand why Francis made his rebuild trades, which featured many beloved Ranger fan favorites, what wasn't acceptable was how Ferguson and Talbot treated the last Rangers' legend of that era, #7, Rod Gilbert. It was Ferguson who humiliated and degraded the iconic Gilbert (who was also a box office draw) into retirement during the 1977-78 season - something that no one was a fan of, including Werblin himself.

After Werblin fired the pair of former Montrealers, he said, *"the Rangers were even more undisciplined than the Titans were in the early years. Ferguson and Talbot didn't seem to know what the problem was. That's because I think they were the problem."*

When Shero's reunion with the Rangers became official, the coach, often accused of "having his head in the clouds" (hence "The Fog" nickname), and while looking at his two Flyer Stanley Cup rings said, *"this is the last day for these rings."* Shero then added, *"I want a Ranger ring on that hand."*

While Shero saw his Rangers reach the 1979 Stanley Cup Final, that ring never came.

Not even two years after first signing his five-year contract worth $250,000 overall, Shero stepped down from his positions as the team's head coach and general manager. This was a "quit before you get fired" situation, as Werblin allowed his hand-picked successor to Ferguson to "gracefully" bow out.

Let's now look at Werblin's acquisition of Shero and the trades that "The Fog" made himself.

Sonny Werblin (left) with Fred Shero, after the hiring of "The Fog."

Photo Credit: This is an 8x10 picture from my Rangers' memorabilia collection. The original photo appears in the NHL archives and is deemed for public use under Creative Common Usage laws.

**DATE OF TRADE: June 2nd, 1978**

**RANGERS ACQUIRE: The right to hire Head Coach Fred Shero**

**PHILADELPHIA FLYERS ACQUIRE: First-Round Pick of the 1978 NHL Amateur Draft (#7 - Ken Linseman) and $200,000**

Shero himself didn't make the first trade of the Fred Shero era, and in a first - the Rangers traded a first-round draft pick to acquire the man known as "Freddy The Fog," in a trade where the Rangers gave up a draft pick for their next head coach and general manager in franchise history.

David Werblin, known as "Sonny," was one of the original men behind the construction of the Meadowlands in East Rutherford, NJ.

Prior to building the football stadium, in 1963, along with his business partners, he bought the New York Titans, then of the AFL.

With the Titans now under his leadership, Werblin rebranded the team as the New York Jets, a miserable football franchise that still plays games today. (Sorry, I'm a Giants fan - I had to get that in!)

In a "fun fact," and perhaps some irony, Werblin, who was also responsible for bringing Joe Namath to town, was bought out/fired before the NFL's 1968 season. At the end of the season, the New York Jets won the Superbowl with Namath himself.

The Jets haven't won a Superbowl since, which has led many to believe in a "Curse of Sonny Werblin."

Now out of the NFL, in 1978, Werblin was named President of Madison Square Garden, where outside of the arena itself, he was also the top name on the ladder of both the New York Rangers and the New York Knicks.

After firing John Ferguson, Werblin bought two-time Stanley Cup champion Fred Shero back to New York.

Prior to Shero leaving the Philadelphia Flyers, "The Fog" once played with the Rangers during the post-World War II seasons, 1947-48 through 1949-50. Had the Rangers won the Stanley Cup in 1950, Shero would have first won a Stanley Cup some twenty-five years earlier in his life as a player.

During Shero's playing days, Frank Boucher was high on him. Shero, despite amassing only 145 NHL games in his professional career (all with the Rangers), "The Fog" always appreciated the way Boucher and the Rangers treated him. That's why he always wanted to return to New York - even if he had spent most of his playing days in the minor leagues and become a legend in the "city of brotherly love."

At the time of this trade, Shero had already won two Stanley Cups with the Flyers (1974 and 1975) and made it to another Stanley Cup Final in 1976. In both 1977 and 1978, the Flyers reached the penultimate round of the playoffs before being ousted.

With the thinking that he accomplished all he could in Philly while believing that the franchise needed a new voice for the greater good (just like head coach Paul Maurice's resignation from the Winnipeg Jets in 2021) - Shero resigned from his post. However, he still had one year left on his contract.

The Flyers were wise to Shero and knew his heart was in New York. Officially, they refused his resignation. (And this was in an era where contracts weren't as strictly enforced as they are today.)

Shero, with the thinking that his resignation meant he was legally through with the orange and black, "The Fog" then accepted a five-year contract worth $250,000 with the Rangers, as presented by Werblin.

As part of the contract, Shero would serve the Rangers as both a general manager and head coach, where it was also thought that he'd only coach the team for one or two seasons and finish out the deal solely in the front office.

Ed Snider, the boss in Philadelphia, wasn't having any of it.

Rather than taking this up with the league's office, or even worse - the courts, Werblin and Snider struck a deal.

To avoid tampering charges, Werblin agreed to give Snider $200,000 and the Rangers' first-round pick (seventh overall) of the 1978 NHL Entry Draft - a draft which was scheduled thirteen days after this deal.

With the pick, Shero's former boss, Flyers' General Manager Keith Allen, selected Ken Linseman, a southpaw center out of Kingston, Ontario. It should also be noted that Linseman, long before Brad Marchand ever came around, first had "The Rat" nickname - and for the same reasons why #63 in Boston has that nickname today.

Linseman's early days in Philadelphia weren't exactly a success. However, he'd soon become successful, but prior to that, he was known as "The Million Dollar Mistake" and "Moneybags." Once shedding these negative nicknames, many in Philadelphia referred to him as "Yes We Ken!"

Once being drafted by Allen, the Flyers' general manager had to entice the nineteen-year-old to leave the Birmingham Bulls (WHA), where Linseman had just logged 38 goals and 38 assists during the 1977-78 season. Allen offered Linseman a contract worth $500,000 and paid the Bulls $500,000 (using $200,000 of the money given to him by the Rangers) to acquire Linseman.

In turn, Linseman had an impressive career. During his days in the NHL, he scored 256 goals and picked up 551 assists for a grand total of 807 points in 860 games. In other words, he averaged nearly a point per game throughout his nearly fourteen full seasons as an NHLer.

His final NHL games took place in the 1991-1992 season, where he played in only two games for the Leafs. Outside of the Flyers and Leafs, Linseman also played for the Bruins and Oilers, where in Edmonton, he won the Stanley Cup in 1984.

Statistically, Linseman had the best seasons of his career in Philly, including 92 points in 1981-82.

As mentioned, Linseman remained in the NHL for a long while, with his final game taking place in October 1991.

After a 4–13–3 start to the 1980-81 season, Shero, as he did before in Philadelphia, resigned from his positions. He would never coach or serve as an NHL general manager again.

Had the Rangers won the Stanley Cup in 1979, you wouldn't care about Ken Linseman nor the $200,000 Werblin paid.

However, they didn't. That's why this trade was a loss; with hindsight being 20/20 - the Rangers probably should never have fired Francis in the first place.

That said, the Rangers did, and it would be "The Fog," and not "The Cat," behind the Rangers' bench (and desk) during the 1979 Stanley Cup Final.

In addition, with the way Shero's tenure went in New York, where many believed he also had a problem with alcohol (read Larry Sloman's *"Thin Ice"* book for a detailed explanation, where it's suggested that "The Fog" nickname was a result of Shero nipping the bottle) - you can't call this trade a win.

Lastly, while Shero's job title was as the head coach and general manager of the Rangers, Shero's assistant coaches primarily dealt with the players.

It was also suggested, especially with Werblin new to the role, that Shero was just a figurehead. While that wasn't 100% accurate - there was something to it. If there weren't anything to it - this suggestion would have never been made in the first place.

Let's now take a look at the trades that Shero made.

Barry Beck was the biggest name Fred Shero traded for during his tenure as general manager. Here's the Rangers' captain prior to a game from the 1984-85 season.

## DATE OF TRADE: November 1st, 1978

## RANGERS ACQUIRE: Cash

## COLORADO ROCKIES ACQUIRE: Don Awrey

A defenseman by trade, Don Awrey, from Kitchener, Ontario, was 35 years old during the time of this transaction.

A two-time Stanley Cup winner with the Bruins teams of the early 1970s, it was in Boston where Awrey spent the first ten seasons of his NHL career.

Following an impressive decade in Beantown, Awrey later logged time with the Blues, Canadiens, and Penguins, becoming a journeyman in the second half of his career.

Prior to this trade, Awrey, as a free agent, played with the Rangers for one season, the 1977-78 season. He finished the season with a career low in points (ten) and a career-worst plus/minus stat of negative fourteen.

His next season, the 1978-79 season with the Rockies, he recorded worse numbers than in New York, where he finished with only five points and a plus/minus stat of a whopping -33. This would be the last season of his career, a sixteen-season career that saw him play in 969 games.

The Rangers, while not recouping the $200,000 they paid the Flyers for Shero, at least got back a few bucks here for a player in his twilight years.

This was a small victory for Shero (and maybe Werblin too!)

**DATE OF TRADE: March 12th, 1979**

**RANGERS ACQUIRE: Jocelyn Guevremont**

**BUFFALO SABRES ACQUIRE: Third-Round Pick of the 1979 NHL Entry Draft (#55 - Jacques Cloutier) and Third-Round Pick of the 1980 NHL Entry Draft (#56 - Sean McKenna)**

Jocelyn Guevremont, a defenseman drafted third overall during the 1971 NHL Amateur Draft (and as mentioned before, where Guy Lafleur went first overall, Marcel Dionne went second overall and Gene Carr, as selected by Francis, went fourth overall), became the second player of the top four picks of that draft to play for the Rangers. (Lafleur and Dionne would later wear the familiar blue jersey on Broadway - more on them to come.)

Once arriving in New York, Guevremont would play in only twenty games for the Rangers during the 1979-80 season. More on that in just a bit.

The native of Montreal, Quebec, spent the first three seasons of his career with the Vancouver Canucks. Two games into the 1974-75 season, he left one new franchise for another, playing for the Buffalo Sabres for five seasons.

Guevremont, whose days in the NHL were impacted by playing on some bad teams for most of his career, didn't have the finish he would've desired.

Now with "The Fog," the former third-overall pick of the 1971 NHL Amateur Draft, butted heads with Shero over playing time. In fact, Guevremont got so fed up that he asked to go down to the Rangers AHL affiliate, the New Haven Nighthawks. In New Haven, the French-Canadian played in 36 games.

Guevremont, who was also battling chronic shoulder injuries, told the Rangers that, come next season, if he wasn't going to get ice time, they should consider him as injured long term. In response, Shero essentially "blackballed" Guevremont and spread the word throughout the NHL that his defenseman was damaged goods.

With teams now scared off, a bad situation in New York, coupled with his real shoulder issues - Guevremont opted to retire at the young age of 29 rather than pursue his career elsewhere. Had the WHA still been around, it could have been an option for him.

So without even telling you the futures of the two draft picks that Buffalo acquired in this trade - you already know that this deal was a loss.

Jacques Cloutier, a goaltender, chosen by the Sabres with their 55th-overall pick of the 1979 NHL Entry Draft, the native of Rouyn-Noranda, Quebec, was primarily an NHL backup goaltender. After seven years in Buffalo, he would later play in parts of two seasons for the Blackhawks, where statistically, he had the best years of his career in Chicago.

In January of 1991, Cloutier was moved to his home province of Quebec where he then played with the Nordiques through the 1993-94 season. Once the season reached its end, he retired.

In retirement, Cloutier hung around the Nordiques and then made the move to Colorado with the franchise when they rebranded as the Avalanche for the 1995-96 season. He would remain with the Avalanche as an assistant coach until 2009, where during his run in the mile-high city, he won two Stanley Cups (1996 and 2001).

In all, Cloutier played in 255 NHL games, compiling a win-loss-tie record of 82-102-24. However, with the Rangers having Mike Richter and John Vanbiesbrouck in the prime of Cloutier's career - they didn't miss out on this goaltender.

Right-winger Sean McKenna, from the lovely named town of Asbestos, Quebec, played with the Sabres for parts of five seasons. He would also play for the Kings and Leafs, where after the 1989-90 season, and now in Toronto, he called it a career that saw him finish with 162 points in 414 games played.

While McKenna, nor Cloutier, never were game changers, the Rangers got only twenty games out of Guevremont, so this trade was an epic fail.

**DATE OF TRADE: May 12th, 1979**

**RANGERS ACQUIRE: Dennis Owchar and Larry Skinner**

**COLORADO ROCKIES ACQUIRE: Future Considerations (Bobby Sheehan)**

At the time of this trade, center Bobby Sheehan, from Weymouth, Massachusetts, was a 30-year-old veteran of ten seasons. Sheehan, like Shero and the rest of the Rangers, were coming off the Stanley Cup Final run of 1979.

Initially beginning his career during the 1969-70 season with the Canadiens, he was in California playing for the lowly Seals by the time the 1971-72 season rolled around. However, a season later, Sheehan jumped to the WHA, where he played for four seasons.

Come the 1975-76 season, Sheehan returned to the NHL, where he spent one season in Chicago and the season after that in Detroit.

After his stint with the Wings and some time in the AHL, Sheehan returned to the WHA, playing 29 games for the Indianapolis Racers in 1977-78. He jumped back to the AHL for the 1978-79 season, playing the entire regular season for the Nighthawks.

However, come the 1979 Stanley Cup Playoffs semifinals against the Flyers after a game-one loss, Shero called him up. The center then played in every remaining playoff game, centering a line featuring Ron Duguay and Pat Hickey as his flanks.

Following this trade, he spent the next two seasons of his career with the Rockies. At the start of the 1981-82 season, he then found himself with the Los Angeles Kings. He played the final four games of his professional career in LA. He retired a season later after a 48-game stint with the Binghamton Whalers (AHL).

Sheehan played in 310 NHL games and 241 WHA games in a professional career, eclipsing a dozen seasons. However, aside from his important fifteen playoff games from 1979 - he never played a regular season game with the Rangers.

Defenseman Dennis Owchar, a native of Dryden, Ontario, never played for the Rangers. Larry Skinner, a center from Vancouver, British Columbia, never played for the Rangers either. In fact, the 1979-80 season was the last time either man would ever play in the NHL, and each player then finished out their careers in the minor leagues.

If there's another "fun fact" to present to you here, it's that Larry Skinner scored the first-ever goal in Colorado Rockies' history when he did so on October 5th, 1976, in a 4-2 win over the Maple Leafs.

This trade was another loss on Shero's ledger.

**DATE OF TRADE: July 2nd, 1979**

**RANGERS ACQUIRE: Bill Lochead**

**COLORADO ROCKIES ACQUIRE: Hardy Astrom**

Fred Shero, who must've loved trading with Colorado Rockies General Manager Ray Miron (we're getting to the big trade between these two teams shortly), made another deal with him here when

306

"The Fog" sent Swedish goaltender Hardy Astrom, born in Skelleftea, to Denver.

Prior to the trade, Astrom had only played in four games for the Rangers during the 1977-78 season, finishing with a record of 2-2.

However, one of those victories took place on February 25th, 1968 - a Rangers' 6-3 win over the Canadiens. This win halted the Habs' unbeaten streak that reached twenty-eight consecutive games prior to Astrom's rare night out in net.

In addition, Astrom became not only the first European Ranger, but the first European NHLer to ever start a game in net. However, after two shaky seasons in Colorado, he'd soon be back in Sweden.

In Astrom's first season with the Rockies, he finished with a win-loss-tie record of 9-27-6. In his second season in Colorado, the last of his NHL career (1980-81), he finished with a win-loss-tie record of 6-15-6.

Things got so bad in Colorado that head coach Don Cherry nicknamed Astrom as *"The Swedish Sieve."* Astrom didn't last long after those remarks. In Sweden, he continued his career, eventually retiring in 1986.

Bill Lochead, a left-winger out of Forest, Ontario, entered the NHL with great promise. After all, not only was he the ninth-overall pick of the 1974 NHL Amateur Draft (Detroit Red Wings), he was also the second-overall pick of the WHA's 1974 NHL Amateur Draft (Indianapolis Racers).

Despite totaling 131 points in 330 NHL games, Lochead could never reach his potential as a high-end draft pick. Knee injuries contributed to that.

Following the trade, he began the 1979-80 season out in New Haven and would eventually play in seven games for the Rangers - the final seven contests of his NHL career.

Like Astrom, he, too, would continue his career in Europe, playing mainly in Germany for the next seven years; once there - he bounced around for an assortment of teams.

Lochead grew to love Germany, so following his 1987 retirement, he remained in the country and tried out his hand at coaching. Lochead still maintains a home in Germany to this day, where he is now an agent living in Frankfurt.

This trade was a wash, a deal between two players who were pretty much done in the NHL then but would go on to extend their careers in inferior leagues overseas.

At this point, you'd soon start to see NHLers extend their careers in Europe - which wasn't an option for players from previous generations. This trend is commonplace today (2022), as many hockey players, no longer NHL caliber,  seek (and earn) roster spots in Europe and Russia.

**DATE OF TRADE: July 25th, 1979**

**RANGERS ACQUIRE: Future Considerations**

**WINNIPEG JETS ACQUIRE: Wayne Dillon**

Left-handed center Wayne Dillon, from Toronto, Ontario, was an Emile Francis draft pick, where "The Cat" selected Dillon with his first-round pick (twelfth overall) of the 1975 NHL Amateur Draft. At the time of the selection, Dillon (underaged for the NHL at the time) had already played two seasons in the WHA with the Toronto Toros.

Come the start of the rebuilding 1975-76 season, Dillon began his NHL career with the Rangers, where he remained through the 1977-78 season. During these three seasons, Dillon played in 216 games, picking up 109 points.

However, following the season, he jumped back to the WHA, where he played for the Birmingham Bulls during the 1978-79 campaign. As a result, he missed his chance to play in a Stanley Cup Final.

At the time of this trade, Dillon had already suffered numerous injuries that plagued him, and he could never fully recover.

Now back in the NHL with the Winnipeg Jets, Dillon played in thirteen games, where he didn't record a point.

In the 1981-82 season, Dillon attempted a comeback in the AHL, but it was short-lived. He then retired in 1982.

Based on my research, the Rangers never received anything in return from Winnipeg, although they traded for "future considerations" in this transaction.

Due to Dillon's early retirement (he was only 25 years old at the time), and because of his injuries - Shero and company never pressed the issue.

This trade amounted to nothing - just like the return the Rangers received!

**DATE OF TRADE: October 12th, 1979**

**RANGERS ACQUIRE: Cash and Future Considerations**

**WINNIPEG JETS ACQUIRE: Bud Stefanski**

A southpaw center, Bud Stefanski, a native of Timmins, Ontario, is among the eclectic list of players to have played only one game in the NHL. Stefanski's one game took place during the 1977-78 season.

With the Jets, Stefanski was assigned to the Tulsa Oilers (CHL).

All in all, Stefanski was a decent enough player but not good enough for the NHL. The center had a career that spanned thirteen seasons, including stops at the AHL, CHL, and IHL levels.

He last played for the Maine Mariners (AHL) during the 1986-87 season, retiring at the end of the campaign.

And how about another "fun fact?"

Stefanksi's son-in-law is former NHLer Cory Stillman, who, needless to say, had a better NHL career than dear old "dad." Stillman, during his NHL career that featured 1,024 more games than Stefanski, also saw the left-winger win two Stanley Cups. (Tampa in 2004, Carolina in 2006.)

Stillman, who married Stefanski's daughter Mara, also produced two hockey players of his own.

Bud Stefanksi's grandson, Riley Stillman, debuted with the Chicago Blackhawks during the 2020-21 season. He's already surpassed the amount of NHL games that his grandpa played in.

Stefanski's other grandson, Chase Stillman, five years younger than big brother Riley, was drafted in the first round of the 2021 NHL Entry Draft (29th overall) by the New Jersey Devils.

The more you know!

As far as this trade goes, Shero helped reclaim some of the $200,000 the Rangers paid to get him in order to make such a blockbuster trade of Stefanksi!

All jokes aside, Shero's next trade was a true blockbuster.

**DATE OF TRADE: November 2nd, 1979**

**RANGERS ACQUIRE: Barry Beck**

**COLORADO ROCKIES ACQUIRE: Lucien DeBlois, Pat Hickey, Mike McEwen, Dean Turner, Cash, and Future Considerations (Bob Crawford)**

This one was the big one, as following the 1979 Stanley Cup Final loss - Shero thought the Rangers needed a big-boy defenseman to bring his team to the promised land. The 6'3" and 215-pound man known as "Bubba" was Shero's answer.

I know you're sick of hearing it, but yeah - Barry Beck is covered in detail in my first book. In other words, I'll give you information I didn't include when talking about Beck's "Rink of Honor" status.

After his first season in New York, Beck was then named captain of the Rangers - a title he held for the next six seasons. However, Beck's Rangers would never make it to a Stanley Cup Final, as the Ranger team did before his arrival.

Before entering the NHL, the entire hockey world knew that Beck was the real deal. It's why during two separate amateur drafts of 1977 (the NHL's and the WHA's), the native of Vancouver, British Columbia, was the second-overall pick of each draft.

And if you're wondering, center Dale McCourt was the first pick (Red Wings) of the 1977 NHL Draft. He was also the 35th-overall pick (fourth round) of the WHA Draft (Racers). Conversely, defenseman Scott Campbell was the first-overall pick of the 1977 WHA Draft (Aeros) and the ninth-overall pick of the NHL Draft (Blues).

Beck, who was also the second-overall pick of the WHA's Calgary Cowboys, never played for the second league. Instead, as the second-overall pick of the Colorado Rockies, the defenseman chose to turn pro with that club.

Beck had a fantastic rookie year with the Rockies. And if it weren't for Mike Bossy, Beck would have won the Calder Trophy that season. (Bossy won 47.93% of the vote, with Beck finishing as first runner-up with 23.35% of the vote.)

While not truly a "sophomore slump," Beck's numbers from his second year weren't as good as the numbers from his first season. Still, he was one of the best players on a struggling team.

This is now the point of this profile where you have to ask yourself - *"why would Colorado trade Beck?"*

Prior to the start of his third season, Beck asked to renegotiate his contract, since he was underpaid for the production that he was putting out. That didn't help his case, no matter what his status was.

However, Beck, in an NHL.com interview conducted after his playing days in the NHL, believes it wasn't his contract that led to his exit. Instead, he believes his departure from Colorado was because of an incident with Don Cherry's dog. Here's Beck:

*"One time, in Colorado, [head coach] Don Cherry's dog Blue came waddling into our locker room. He came in and, you know how those dogs do it, he rubbed his butt on the floor - right in front of my locker, in the area where I used to do push-ups. So I gave Blue a little whack with my stick and he ran yelping down the hall back to Don's office. Don then came in and asked who did it? We kind of looked around, and said we didn't know. The next day I got traded to New York."*

Whatever the case, just ten games into his third season, Beck was off to New York.

Going to Colorado as a "future consideration" in this five-for-one trade was right-winger Bobby Crawford. (The one from New York, NY, not to be confused with the other Bob Crawford who we'll later talk about during Esposito's tenure as general manager.)

A career minor leaguer, Crawford played in fifteen games in the 1980-81 season with the Rockies and then would play in one more NHL game during the 1981-82 season with the Red Wings. He would finish his career in Europe, where he last played in Germany for the 1988-89 season.

Immediately after the trade, Fred Shero said, *"this is one of the biggest trades in Ranger history."*

Shero also said the following about the players involved in an interview with the New York Times:

*"They gave us a list of who they were interested in and who they wouldn't take under any circumstances. They wanted a defenseman and two forwards."*

On Beck, Shero said:

312

*"Some guys are just big. I think he's got more than that going for him. He's big and strong enough to play a regular shift and play on the power play and kill penalties."*

On Mike McEwen, a defenseman going the other way, Shero added:

*"He's a great offensive defenseman, but that's also a weakness."*

Ray Miron, Shero's counterpart added:

*McEwen is gifted offensively. And they weren't going to give up Greschner."*

Regarding Pat Hickey, Miron said:

*"He plays left wing and can score goals and that's one of the areas we are weak."*

Miron also added that trade talks began a week prior to the deal, where he stated that Arthur Imperatore, then the Rockies' chairman of the board, and Sonny Werblin, Imperatore's peer, had a business lunch together when the two dined in New York.

(This is also another reason why many believe that Werblin was pulling a lot of the strings during Shero's tenure as general manager.)

Since I have already teased the following in this book, in addition to having already mentioned Mike Bossy's name, too (for what it's worth, Beck was also involved in this very same draft), I guess it's time to mention that Lucien DeBlois, from Joliette, Quebec, was John Ferguson's eighth-overall pick of the 1977 NHL Amateur Draft. Ron Duguay was Ferguson's thirteenth-overall pick of that same draft.

Class of 1991 Hall of Famer Mike Bossy went fifteenth overall to the Islanders.

Needless to say, neither DeBlois nor Duguay, both good Rangers, were Mike Bossy, so I'll spare you from repeating my "what if" question from earlier. However, I should mention that when asked why he chose DeBlois over Bossy, Ferguson once said, "Bossy doesn't check enough for the NHL." Oops.

And, yeah, I think I'll take Bossy's 1,126 points in 752 games over DeBlois' checking ability! Ugh, just thinking about this draft and writing about it here gives me a rash. Let's move on!

Like Beck, DeBlois made his NHL debut during the 1977-78 season. However, unlike Beck, he'd play in a Stanley Cup Final, as he did in 1979. DeBlois would later win the Stanley Cup in 1986 with the Montreal Canadiens.

After arriving in Denver, DeBlois would remain with the Rockies for the next two seasons. However, in July 1981, he was dealt to the Winnipeg Jets, where he served the franchise as team captain for two seasons.

After three seasons in the 'Peg, DeBlois traded one Canadian jersey for a Canadien jersey, playing for the Habs for two seasons.

Following his Stanley Cup victory, the Rangers, who were eliminated by DeBlois' Canadiens in the penultimate round of the 1986 Stanley Cup Playoffs, then brought the right-winger back into their fold, this time as a free agent.

DeBlois remained with the Rangers for the next three seasons in his second stint on Broadway, which lasted a little bit longer than his first one. Following the conclusion of the 1988-89 season ("Trader Phil's" last, but more on him to come), the now-successful journeyman returned to his home province, spending the next 84 games of his career with the Quebec Nordiques.

As the calendar flipped to 1991, DeBlois was now with another Canadian franchise, the Toronto Maple Leafs.

At the 1992 trade deadline, DeBlois was returned to the franchise he once captained, the Jets. He would spend the final eleven games of his career with the Jets - the final eleven games of a fantastic career.

Once retiring in 1992 at the age of 35, DeBlois, who played in seven games shy of 1,000, 993 in all, the two-time Ranger finished his career with a total of 525 points - which means he averaged a point every two games played.

Mike McEwen, the consolation-prize defenseman involved in this trade (especially since there was no way Shero was going to deal rearguard Ron Greschner), just like DeBlois, he, too, didn't last long in Colorado.

And also like DeBlois, the blue-liner from Hornepayne, Ontario, was also a Ferguson draft pick. McEwen was drafted a year prior to his teammate, as a third-round pick (42nd overall) of the 1976 NHL Amateur Draft.

And in one last comparison - like DeBlois - McEwen was also a key component of the Rangers' 1979 playoff run.

Now in Colorado, and like many other players from this time, McEwen clashed with Don Cherry. This would work out for the defenseman, as after a meeting of the minds, he was soon shipped off to the Islanders in 1981. He would then win three Stanley Cups with the Islanders, but since I'm a Rangers fan writing a Rangers' book - the less said about that the better!

Following his great run with New York's secondary hockey team, he bounced around in the mid-1980s, having short stints with the Kings, Capitals, and Red Wings.

After ping-ponging around the league, Rangers' General Manager, Craig Patrick (who, again, we'll soon get to), made McEwen a two-time Ranger in December 1985 (and again, more on that trade later).

However, McEwen's second stint in New York wouldn't be long, as during the same season, in March 1986, he was traded again, this time to the Hartford Whalers.

McEwen would remain with the green jersey for the rest of his NHL career, where he finished his 716 games-played career with the Whalers. He last played for the club in the 1987-88 season.

Following his three seasons in Hartford, he traveled overseas, playing in Switzerland for another three seasons.

He attempted an NHL comeback during the 1991-92 season with the New Haven Nighthawks (AHL), where he logged a 51-game season. However, no NHL team came calling. He then hung up his skates once and for all in 1992 at the age of 36.

Pat Hickey, a left-winger, the fourth and final regular NHLer involved in this trade, was the eldest player of the lot, with a birthday of May 15th, 1953.

Drafted in the second round (30th overall) by Emile Francis during the 1973 NHL Amateur Draft, the native of Brantford, Ontario, decided to play the first two seasons of his professional career in the WHA, where he did so with the Toronto Toros - a franchise that selected him 18th overall (also in the second round) of the 1973 WHA Amateur Draft.

After two seasons in the inferior professional league, Hickey made the jump to the NHL just in time for the tumultuous 1975-76 Rangers campaign.

However, Hickey, whose nickname was "Hitch," survived three tough seasons in New York, and like the other Rangers involved in this trade - became a featured player of the 1979 Stanley Cup Finalist Rangers.

Under Shero, Hickey played with the Swedish wonderkids - Anders Hedberg and Ulf Nilsson. (And may I remind you that both

Hedberg and Nilsson are prominently featured in my first book? I'm horrible, I know!)

Similar to DeBlois and McEwen - Hickey wouldn't last long in Colorado, and would also return to the Rangers.

In fact, Hickey barely had a cup of coffee with the Rockies. Following 24 games played in Denver, he was dealt off in another blockbuster trade where he and Wilf Paiement went to Toronto in exchange for Lanny McDonald and Joel Quenneville.

After parts of two seasons with the Leafs, Hickey returned to the Rangers in October 1981, after a trade made by Shero's successor, Craig Patrick.

However, just like others, this second stint wouldn't last as long as the first, after 53 games played with the Rangers during the 1981-82 season, he was back off to Canada, this time in Quebec with the Nordiques.

After finishing this season with seven games played with the *"fleur-de-lis,"* Hickey completed a full circle, as the general manager who drafted him into the NHL, Emile Francis, traded for him, this time in St. Louis during the summer of 1982.

"Hitch" would spend the final three seasons of his career in St. Louis, where he retired at the conclusion of the 1984-85 season.

In total, Hickey scored 404 points in 644 NHL games played. He also recorded 124 points during his 152 games played in the WHA.

Dean Turner, as mentioned earlier, was a career minor leaguer who, at the time of this trade, had only played in one NHL game with the Rangers.

Now, he would play in 31 games spanning two seasons in Colorado.

After moving on to Los Angeles during the 1982-83 season, he would play in three more games, games 33, 34, and 35 of his 35 games worth of an NHL career.

We're now at the point of this trade where we have to ask - *"who won?"*

This is a tough one. Beck meant so much to the Rangers for so many years - but after 25 games played during the 1985-86 season, the captain was done.

Beck would later come out of retirement, playing 52 games for the Kings during the 1989-90 season following his three-year sabbatical.

However, the shoulder injuries that forced him into his first retirement at age thirty (there was a separate issue with then Rangers Head Coach Ted Sator we'll get to later) meant that his comeback on the west coast was short-lived.

McEwen, Hickey, and DeBlois all had long careers, where all of them logged more NHL games than Beck's 615 games.

While Barry Beck was a great Ranger, a proud Ranger, and personified the word captain both during his playing days and after them (just look at his work with Mark Pavelich prior to the Olympian's passing) - this blockbuster trade was a slight loss - even if Colorado dumped everyone, and quickly at that, following this deal.

To be clear - no one can take away what Beck meant to the Rangers during his run. I am not disputing that.

At the same time, was Beck worth Hickey, McEwen, and DeBlois - three Rangers that the organization must have been high on since they eventually brought all three of these players back? I don't think so.

Plus, not only did the Rangers give up these three players, and two minor leaguers to boot - they also paid for the right to make this trade.

---

**DATE OF TRADE: March 11th, 1980**

**RANGERS ACQUIRE: Cam Connor and Third-Round Pick of the 1981 NHL Entry Draft (#50 - Peter Sundstrom)**

**EDMONTON OILERS ACQUIRE: Don Murdoch**

This trade is both a funny and a sad one.

I'm going to duck as I write this - Don Murdoch is covered in depth in my first book.

(And just like my first book, where I made a drinking game out of my frequent usage of the word "ironically" - I think we can now make a drinking game whenever I mention that I once wrote a book in the one that you're reading right now!)

D;hnjkijt34juLGR3i4j3j34lkj2lk43j4

lkjkljaljlajIslesSuckakjdajj3348343403kja

Sorry - I just played that drinking game myself! I even went back and took shots during all of my previous mentions of that title too! Okay, now, back to your regularly scheduled Rangers' trade book!

Without repeating everything I said in "The New York Rangers Rink of Honor and the Rafters of Madison Square Garden" (yep, take a swig), to sum up, Murdoch's career, not just as a Ranger but as an NHLer - it's a case of "what could have been."

Initially, a star on Broadway, the man known as "Murder," then at twenty years old, got caught up under the bright lights of New York City, where people pretending to be his friends routinely plied him with alcohol and drugs. He would then get caught smuggling drugs (cocaine) in 1977 while at the airport in Toronto, and that would be the beginning of the end, as a promising career went up in smoke - somewhat literally.

Back to Murdoch in a bit. Let's now get into Peter Sundstrom, and then into the funny part of this trade.

By the time centerman Peter Sundstrom was drafted, Fred Shero was already gone. (Then again, and as alleged by others, perhaps Shero had a drinking game going himself - as he may have been "gone" too.)

Sundstrom, from Skelleftea, Sweden, was a Craig Patrick draft pick, and a player who spent three seasons with the Rangers, which first began with the 1983-84 season.

Following the 1985-86 campaign, and following contract negotiations that didn't appease him, Sundstrom sat out of the 1986-87 season. A season later, he'd return to the NHL in a new jersey (not New Jersey, at least not yet, as you'll soon see) with the Washington Capitals.

After two seasons with the Capitals, Sundstrom was traded to New Jersey (and now wearing a new jersey too) in the summer of 1989, where he played in 21 games, his final 21 NHL games, with the Devils during the 1989-90 season.

Like many European players who don't pan out as full-time NHLers, Sundstrom returned to Sweden for the 1990-1991 season, where he played for the next five years. He retired in the summer of 1995.

It should be noted that Sundstrom's best seasons of his NHL career (338 games in all) came with the Rangers, where he posted back-to-back 44-point seasons (career highs) in New York during the 1983-84 and 1984-85 seasons.

At least the Rangers got some use out of Sundstrom, for as limited as it was.

The funny part of this trade was Cam Connor, the apple of both the NHL and WHA eye in 1974.

During the WHA and  NHL Amateur Drafts of 1974, the ruffian right-winger out of Winnipeg, Manitoba, was selected fourth overall by the Phoenix Road Runners, and fifth overall by the Montreal Canadiens.

Connor chose to play in the WHA rather than join the prestigious Canadiens.

In his *"View From the Penalty Box"* podcast, which debuted on August 29th, 2017 (I'm a day-one listener, by the way - I even have a t-shirt in support of the podcast), in his first episode, Connor talked about his decision to join the WHA, and said the decision was *"the biggest regret of my career."*

As Connor tells it, like many other players from his era, the WHA money was too good to turn down. In addition, in the WHA with the Road Runners, Connor would receive more playing time than he ever would with the Montreal Canadien dynasty teams from this era.

That said, Connor would have some good years in the WHA, where towards the end of his run there, and now with the Houston Aeros - he got to play with the legendary, iconic Gordie Howe.

However, despite four solid years in the WHA (and a litany of travel and rink issues, too) - Connor would never win the top prize of the league, the Avco Cup. Instead, he'd have to settle for a Stanley Cup!

Once the Houston Aeros folded in 1978, Connor connected with Scotty Bowman and continued his professional career in Montreal.

As he initially feared, it was tough to crack into the heralded Habs lineup, but he did suit up in eight playoff games during Montreal's 1979 Stanley Cup Playoff run. (You know who they beat in the Final already - so I won't remind you again!)

Following the Canadiens' 1979 Stanley Cup championship, the final Stanley Cup of the last Montreal dynasty, the league ruled that Connor didn't play in enough games to earn the right to have his name etched on the Cup. Once hearing that noise, Connor's teammates rallied behind him and demanded his name be included. The league acquiesced, and Connor was officially a Stanley Cup champion - and with a ring on his finger to prove it.

The childhood friend of Rowdy Roddy Piper (the famous wrestler repeatedly mentions Connor throughout his 2016 autobiography - a book which was published posthumously - and Connor, on his own podcast, talks about his days growing up and being a close friend of the "Hot Rod"), like Piper himself, was known for his fists and physical attributes.

Now for the previously teased funny part.

Murdoch had to go. As everyone around him said, including the Rangers as an organization - staying in New York would likely have killed him - whether it be an overdose or something else. So he had to be shipped out, not just for the Rangers but, more importantly - for Murdoch's well-being.

Shero, again, known as "The Fog," a nickname that many attributed to his penchant for the bottle, traded for Connor.

However, as the legend goes, and as Connor has even explained in detail on his own podcast - Shero thought he was trading for defenseman Colin Campbell, not the right-winger out of Winnipeg, Manitoba. It was up to Connor himself to tell his new boss about the error of his ways.

(And, yes, this is the same Colin Campbell who would later coach the Rangers for four seasons before becoming part of the league's office.)

Whatever "fog" Shero was in, it didn't matter. The trade with then Oilers' General Manager Glen Sather (a lot more on him later on, once we hit the year 2000), was upheld. Whether it was human error or the drink, Shero traded for the wrong guy.

Shero, not realizing what he did, wasn't too kind to Connor when his new player arrived in New York. In total, Connor played 28 games with the Rangers spanning three seasons. Outside of those 28 games, he primarily played in the AHL.

Following the 1982-83 season, Connor's last with the Rangers (and in the NHL too), he played one more season for the Tulsa Oilers (CHL). He retired in 1984.

Conversely, Murdoch, who had so much promise, played in only fifty games with the Oilers before moving on to Detroit.

What hurt Murdoch the most with the Oilers was that he was originally thought of as a player who could protect emerging superstar Wayne Gretzky. However, Jari Kurri soon came along, and that was the end of that.

"Murder" would play in 49 more NHL games with the Red Wings during the 1981-82 season. That would be it for his days as an NHLer, as he'd then continue his career in the minors, playing in the AHL, IHL, and CHL, before ultimately retiring in 1986.

This is a tough trade to grade. After all, Shero was gone by the time Sundstrom was drafted.

In addition, Murdoch had to go.

While who knows how Colin Campbell, Shero's original target, would've done with the Rangers - he did finish his NHL career with 636 games played. For comparison, Murdoch finished with 320 NHL games played and Connor finished with 89 NHL games played, in addition to his 274 games in the WHA.

As a final analysis, I think Shero has to receive the loss here.

After all, he didn't know who he was trading for. That alone should earn him the loss.

Plus, it wasn't Connor's fault that Shero may have been "foggy" here, even if he was forced to trade Murdoch - a Murdoch who never amounted to much once being dealt out of town.

**DATE OF TRADE: August 6th, 1980**

**RANGERS ACQUIRE: Gord Smith**

**WINNIPEG JETS ACQUIRE: Cash**

At the time of this trade, defenseman Gord Smith was 31 years old and a veteran of 299 games.

Ironically, Smith was a Francis draft pick, where the native of Perth, Ontario, was selected in the fifth round of the 1969 NHL Amateur Draft (59th overall).

During the 1979-80 season, Smith, who never played for the Rangers (the Washington Capitals snagged him during their 1974 expansion draft), played in thirteen games for the Jets. These contests would be the final thirteen NHL games of his career.

Once acquired by "The Fog," Smith finished his career in the AHL, where he last played in the 1982-1983 season for the Maine Mariners.

This trade, like many others from this time, was a loss - even if it was just a cash loss.

**DATE OF TRADE: November 11th, 1980**

**RANGERS ACQUIRE: Jeff Bandura and Jere Gillis**

**VANCOUVER CANUCKS ACQUIRE: Mario Marois and Jim Mayer**

Defenseman Jeff Bandura, the 22nd-overall draft pick of the 1977 NHL Amateur Draft (Canucks), never played for the franchise that drafted him - despite his status as a second-round draft pick.

In fact, he would only play in two NHL games his entire career, where he received both of these games during this 1980-81 season.

324

It was also during this season that the native of White Rock, British Columbia, spent most of his time with the New Haven Nighthawks (AHL) - which was also the last season of Bandura's AHL career.

Following this season, Bandura played for the lesser-known WIHL, where after 38 games played during the 1984-85 season, he retired.

Left-wing Jere Gillis was also a Canucks' 1977 NHL Amateur Draft pick, where Vancouver made him the fourth-overall pick of that year's draft. (And I feel like I have mentioned this 1977 NHL Amateur Draft often in this book, where - yep, just like the Rangers - the Canucks could have drafted Mike Bossy.)

Gillis made the jump right to the NHL, forgoing a stint in the WHA in the process, as he was the seventh-overall pick of the Cincinnati Stingers during their 1977 Amateur Draft.

Gillis had the best NHL seasons of his career in Vancouver, but it wouldn't last long. After three complete seasons and eleven games into his fourth season, he was moved to the Rangers in this trade.

The native of Bend, Oregon, would play in only 61 games with the Rangers over the course of the next two seasons.

He would later be traded on New Year's Eve-Eve (December 30th, 1981) to the Quebec Nordiques. He would play in only twelve games while as a Nordique.

Following his days in the French-speaking province, he'd bounce around between the NHL and AHL. After three games played with the Sabres during the 1982-83 season, he would then return to the Canucks before ultimately playing one more NHL game with the Flyers in the 1986-87 season.

Once finished in the NHL, and like so many others from this time, he, too, jumped over the pond, spending his European days in Italy and the United Kingdom.

In retirement, he'd later become a Scientologist - something that he's publicly touted on a few occasions.

Even wackier was Shero's decision to trade Mario Marios, a defenseman from Ancienne Lorette, Quebec.

Marios, another product of the 1977 NHL Amateur Draft (fourth round, 62nd overall, and as selected by the Rangers), finished his NHL career with 955 games played.

Starting his pro career with the Rangers in the 1977-78 season, he was also part of the 1979 Stanley Cup Finalist team, where he played in all eighteen playoff games.

Now in Vancouver, Marios would soon be traded again after representing the Canucks for only fifty games. On March 8th, 1981, he was dealt to the other side of the country, where he played for his home province of Quebec - with the Nordiques.

Ultimately, he would spend parts of six seasons with the Nordiques, where he was the team captain during his final three years with the club. He was then dealt to another Canadian franchise again, where this time he played for the Winnipeg Jets for parts of four seasons.

On December 6th, 1988, he was back in Quebec. However, his return wouldn't last as long as his initial stint, as, by the fall of 1990, he was now in St. Louis.

But wait, there's more.

By the time Thanksgiving of 1991 rolled around, Marois was back in Winnipeg, where after 31 games played during the 1991-92 season, he retired as an NHLer - and a successful one at that.

Right-wing Jim Mayer, from Capreol, Ontario, after four years at Michigan Tech, began his professional career during the 1976-77 season - in the WHA. He would play in the WHA for parts of three seasons, logging 74 games in all with the Calgary Cowboys, New England Whalers, and the Edmonton Oilers.

As Emile Francis' 239th-overall pick of the 1974 NHL Entry Draft, Mayer would join the Rangers for four games, the only games that he'd ever play in the NHL, during the 1979-80 season. After that,

326

he was back to the CHL and AHL, where he retired as Nighthawk following the 1981-82 season.

Mario Marois was not only the best player involved in this trade, he also played in more games, and his tenure was longer than anyone else involved in this transaction.

This was another loss for Shero, as "The Fog's" time in New York was now soon reaching its conclusion.

**DATE OF TRADE: November 18th, 1980**

**RANGERS ACQUIRE: Dale Lewis**

**CALGARY FLAMES ACQUIRE: Frank Beaton**

Dale Lewis, a left-winger out of Edmonton, Alberta, had previously played eight games (no points) with the Rangers during the disastrous 1975-76 season. He would never play in the NHL again, as instead, he spent time at both the CHL and AHL levels, where he would then retire after the 1980-81 season as a Nighthawk.

Frank Beaton, also a left-winger, but from Antigonish, Nova Scotia, had more professional success than Lewis, but not by much.

Having logged 153 WHA games prior to this trade, with the Cincinnati Stingers, Edmonton Oilers, and the Birmingham Bulls, Beaton only played in 25 NHL games, all with the Rangers, between his two games in the 1978-79 season and his twenty-three games in the 1979-80 season.

An undrafted player, Beaton would never play for the Flames. Instead, he finished out his career in the CHL, last playing for the Birmingham North Stars during the 1982-83 season.

In Shero's last trade as general manager, this trade was much ado about nothing.

Once the Shero era concluded, Sonny Werblin moved the team in a new direction. As a result of his Olympic success, "The Miracle on Ice," Craig Patrick (pictured right), the son of Lynn and the grandson of Lester, was hired. Come the 1981-82 season, Patrick's gold medal coach, Herb Brooks, was tasked to coach the Rangers.

Photo Credit: Public Domain via the Associated Press. Permission to print this picture was granted by AP.

## CRAIG PATRICK

Tenure as Rangers General Manager: November 21, 1980 – July 14, 1986

Not even three full seasons into his five-year deal, Fred Shero found himself in a "quit or be fired" situation. At the time, it was strongly suggested that Shero had off-ice issues and was disconnected from his team.

On November 21st, 1980, it was reported that Sonny Werblin had fired Shero, while Shero himself said that he had resigned from his positions. In either event, Shero was out, and Craig Patrick was in.

After the changes in management and behind the bench were made, Werblin told the media, *"we did not hire Fred to let him go, but he understood the situation and has been mature on where he stood.*

*His contract will be honored for the remaining 2 years. We accepted all of the requests by his agent."*

328

While the Patrick family had a long and storied history with the Rangers (grandfather Lester, father Lynn, and uncle Muzz), Craig Patrick, an eight-year veteran of the NHL himself, never played for the Rangers.

At the time of this transition in management, Shero's dismissal and Patrick's promotion didn't come off as a major surprise.

Patrick, then at only 34 years old, was named as the Rangers' Director of Operations on July 21st, 1980. While he wasn't the general manager just yet, in effect, he had the powers of one.

As you probably know, Patrick was initially hired due to his famous and life-changing success with "The Miracle on Ice" United States 1980 Olympic team, where he served the gold medal-winning team as its assistant general manager and assistant head coach.

When Werblin made his decision, Craig Patrick became the youngest general manager in franchise history. And like his predecessors before him, including his grandfather and uncle, he became the team's head coach. However, it was always known that Patrick, who coached the Rangers during the final sixty games of the 1980-81 season (and to the penultimate round of the 1981 Stanley Cup Playoffs), was always going to be a temporary fix behind the Rangers' bench.

When Patrick first replaced Shero, from day one, it was known that Patrick's friend, and his head coach of "The Miracle on Ice" team, Herb Brooks, would soon be hired.

Following the gold medal win, Brooks had previously turned down head coaching jobs from non-competitive clubs, including the Colorado Rockies and his hometown Minnesota North Stars. For the accomplished Brooks, he was biding his time for a job offer to come in from an NHL playoff contender.

Rather than sitting at home and waiting for an offer (while not desiring to sign a long-term deal with a non-contending NHL franchise), Brooks traveled overseas after agreeing to a one-year contract with the HC Davos of the Swiss League. His contract was set to expire in March 1981.

The Rangers' media, Werblin, and Patrick himself knew what was to come.

Werblin alluded to Brooks' eventual arrival at the time of Patrick's ascension when he said, *"I may have said at one time [July of 1980] that Craig Patrick would not coach the Rangers, but this is on an interim basis in a difficult situation."*

While Werblin played it coy, Patrick outright said that Brooks would be his man:

*"I would not be surprised if Herb wasn't the next coach of the Rangers. I have also talked with others in my dual role as operations director and will continue to do so.*

*"I go into this job with my mind open. I was prepared for something like this to happen, but we are continuing the search for a permanent coach. Under ideal conditions, we would know who that coach was and try to make my system compatible with his. Unfortunately, that is not possible now."*

In January 1981, and now in Switzerland, Brooks, like Shero, found himself in a "quit or be fired" situation - the end result of his team's poor record and the players themselves wanting a new coach due to Brooks' rough and infamous practices.

Come June 1st, 1981, Patrick officially hired Brooks to coach his team. Three days later, the two admitted that this hiring was predetermined once Patrick became general manager.

Aside from Patrick, Brooks coached the Rangers for most of Patrick's run as general manager. When Patrick fired Brooks on January 21st, 1985, Patrick returned to the bench for the remainder of the 1984-85 season.

Once hiring Ted Sator to coach the team for the 1985-86 season, in the Summer of 1986 - Patrick was fired, too. He'd later make his
330

NHL legacy with the Pittsburgh Penguins, where, due to his success in the Steel City, he joined his grandfather and father in the Hall of Fame as part of the Class of 2001.

As the general manager of the Rangers, Patrick is remembered for three things: "The Miracle on Ice" (not only did he bring Brooks into the fold, he signed/traded for several players from that team); a lack of playoff success against the hated Islanders; (the Isles beat the Rangers in the playoffs four years in a row, where following three of those Ranger losses, the Islanders went on to win the Stanley Cup) and for his acquisition of Mike Rogers.

Let's now take a look at Craig Patrick's Rangers - teams that always made the playoffs, but could never get past heated foes, including the Islanders and the Flyers.

Ironically, Rangers' fan favorite, Nick Fotiu, was involved in both the first and last trades that Patrick made.

Photo Credit: This signed picture is from my Rangers' memorabilia collection. The original photo was provided by the Rangers. The autograph was obtained by yours truly prior to a 2015 Stanley Cup Playoff game.

**DATE OF TRADE: January 15th, 1981**

**RANGERS ACQUIRE: Nick Fotiu**

**HARTFORD WHALERS ACQUIRE: Fifth-Round Pick of the 1981 NHL Entry Draft (#93 - Bill Maguire)**

Yep, you guessed it, the pride of Staten Island, NY, and the man who grew up rooting for the Rangers from Madison Square Garden's blue seats, Nick Fotiu, is heavily featured in "The New York Rangers Rink of Honor and the Rafters of Madison Square Garden."

Initially beginning his professional career in the WHA, where he played for two seasons with the New England Whalers (1974-75, 1975-76), the left-winger logged 110 games in the second league before joining the Rangers as an undrafted free agent before the start of the 1976-77 season.

Fotiu remained with the Rangers through the 1978-79 season. However, on June 13th, 1979, his original team, the New England Whalers of the WHA, now the Hartford Whalers of the NHL, drafted Fotiu with their second pick of the 1979 NHL Expansion Draft. Shero left Fotiu unprotected, and with his prior success with the Whalers, this was a no-brainer pick.

In Craig Patrick's first move as general manager of the Rangers, the grandson of the first general manager of franchise history brought the fan favorite back to New York. And all it cost him was a fifth-round pick.

Fotiu was welcomed back to the Rangers with open arms by both his teammates and the fan base alike. Defenseman Bill Maguire, the Whalers' eventual selection, never played in the NHL.

Instead, the southpaw out of Barrie, Ontario, remained in his native province, where he played for York University (Toronto) and earned his degree. Ten years later, Maguire served the York Lions as an assistant coach.

Fotiu's second stint with the Rangers ran for five seasons - two more seasons than his initial run for his home team.

He was later traded in March 1986 to the Flames, where he helped Calgary reach the Stanley Cup Final. He would remain in Calgary for one more season before moving on to the Flyers. Fotiu would play one more NHL game during the 1988-89 season, this time for the Oilers. He'd then finish his professional career in the AHL, where he played in 31 games for the New Haven Nighthawks during the 1989-90 season.

Now retired as an active player, Fotiu got into coaching, spending three seasons as the assistant coach of the Hartford Wolfpack during the early 2000s.

Fotiu, known for his penchant for pugilism and never shy to defend a teammate, the one-time kid from Staten Island to this day remains a featured member of the Rangers' alumni association.

This trade is as easy a win as it gets. Patrick got five seasons out of Fotiu. Maguire never entered an NHL locker room.

**DATE OF TRADE: March 10th, 1981**

**RANGERS ACQUIRE: John Hughes**

**EDMONTON OILERS ACQUIRE: Ray Markham**

Right-wing Ray Markham, from Windsor, Ontario, a Fred Shero third-round pick (43rd overall) of the 1978 NHL Amateur Draft, played in fourteen games during the 1979-80 season. He also played in seven games in the 1980 Stanley Cup Playoffs. These twenty-four games of NHL experience, all with the Rangers, would be the extent of his professional career.

Following this trade, Markham, whose career lasted six seasons, finished out at both the AHL and IHL levels.

After the 1983-84 season, he called it a day, where he last played for the Kalamazoo Wings (IHL).

John Hughes, a defenseman from Charlottetown, Prince Edward Island, had a much more successful professional career than Markham - but then again - that's not saying much!

Hughes played in only three games for the Rangers, all playoff games in the 1981 Stanley Cup Playoffs. The 1981-82 season following, he was demoted to the New Haven Nighthawks. He would play 76 games for the Hawks and retired once the season concluded.

Prior to this trade, Hughes spent five seasons in the WHA for five different teams (Roadrunners, Stingers, Aeros, Oilers, and Racers). During that time, he logged 372 games in the Avco Cup league.

Once the WHA folded, Hughes moved on to the NHL, spending the 1979-80 season with the Canucks.

A season later, Hughes was with the Oilers, where he only lasted for eighteen games before this transaction between the two teams that would go on to create history together.

While neither Markham nor Hughes did much after this trade, the Rangers' acquisition continued to play in the NHL - even if it was only for three playoff games. This trade is another win for Patrick, but obviously, nowhere as big as the Fotiu victory.

**DATE OF TRADE: September 8th, 1981**

**RANGERS ACQUIRE: Third-Round Pick of the 1983 NHL Entry Draft (#49 - Vesa Salo)**

**WINNIPEG JETS ACQUIRE: Doug Soetaert**

At the time of this trade, the Rangers were flooded with goaltenders. In fact, five different goaltenders found themselves in net for the Blueshirts during the 1981-82 season, including Steve Weeks (49 games), Eddie Mio (25 games), Steve Baker (6 games),

334

and two mini-generational franchise goalies - both John Davidson and John Vanbiesbrouck - who each played one game a piece.

It was hoped that JD would reclaim his form and be able to overcome his injuries. That never happened. "Beezer" received a spot start. He wouldn't take over the net until the 1983-84 season.

Goaltender Doug Soetaert, born in Edmonton, Alberta, was 26 years old at the time of this trade. He was considered expendable, where at the time of this trade, the Rangers traded him away for "future considerations." Future considerations developed into the form of Vesa Salo, a defenseman from Rauma, Finland, a player who never made it across the pond.

The then-eighteen-year-old Finn remained in his motherland, where he played hockey for nearly two decades, eighteen seasons in all. Outside of Finland, he briefly spent time in both Sweden and Germany.

In other words, this trade was already a loss, as Salo never had what it took - nor the desire - to play in the NHL. Unlike today, where you see more Europeans growing up with ambitions to play in the NHL - many players from this era solely grew up dreaming about playing for their home team.

While Salo was skating around in Europe, Soetaert, a Francis second-round pick of the 1975 NHL Amateur Draft (30th overall), was primarily a backup goalie in New York.

Starting his NHL career with the Rangers during the 1975-76 season, Soetaert played in ninety games for the Rangers over parts of six seasons.

Following the trade, the goaltender spent three seasons with the Jets. Playing in an era when many teams had high-powered offenses (hello, Edmonton Oilers), here were Soetaert's numbers in Winnipeg:

1981-82 season: a win-loss-tie record of 13-14-8, a goals-allowed average of 4.32, and a save percentage of .870.

1982-83 season: a win-loss-tie record of 19-19-6, a goals-allowed average of 4.12, and a save percentage of .869.

1983-84 season: a win-loss-tie record of 18-17-7, a goals-allowed average of 4.29, and a save percentage of .869.

Come the 1984-85 season, Soetaert was now in Montreal, where he later became the answer to a trivia question, and more importantly for him - won a Stanley Cup.

Here's the trivia question: what goaltender was pulled in favor of Patrick Roy, Roy's first-ever NHL game? The answer? Soetaert himself, during a game played on February 23, 1985.

A season later, Soetaert was backing up Roy, as #33 in Canadien red, white, and blue led the Habitants to the Stanley Cup - their first chalice victory since 1979.

(Soetaert was on the 1978-79 Rangers' roster, but he never played in the playoffs. He did play in seventeen regular season games. And of course, who did Montreal defeat in the penultimate round of the 1986 Stanley Cup Playoffs? Yep - the Blueshirts.)

Now with a ring on his finger, Soetaert returned to New York for the 1986-87 season. He was the first player that then general manager, Phil Esposito, ever signed as a free agent. Esposito gave Soetaert a three-year deal and told the press the following:

*"Doug's a winner, and it's my intent that his experience will rub off on the rest of the guys. My reason for getting him here is simple: Last season our backup situation, with just five wins without John Vanbiesbrouck, was not the best."*

Soetaert would play in thirteen games during the 1986-87 campaign, where he finished with a poor record of 2-7-2, a goals-allowed average of 5.16, and a save percentage of .842. The 31-

year-old retired at the end of the season, forgoing the final two years of his contract.

This trade is a loss on paper, but since the Rangers had five goalies at the time, this trade was understandable.

However, since there were a slew of players that all made it to the NHL, players who were drafted after Salo (including Rick Tocchet, Brian Bradley, Esa Tikkanen, Kevin Stevens, and others) - this move never panned out the way it could have.

**DATE OF TRADE: October 2nd, 1981**

**RANGERS ACQUIRE: Mike Rogers and Tenth-Round Pick of the 1982 NHL Entry Draft (#193 - Simo Saarinen)**

**HARTFORD WHALERS ACQUIRE: Chris Kotsopoulos, Gerry McDonald, and Doug Sulliman**

In Patrick's first multi-player deal, the general manager came out as a winner.

Chris Kotsopoulos, a big-boy bruising defenseman, who entered the NHL as an undrafted free agent, played 54 games for the Rangers in the 1980-81 season. Now in Hartford, he would remain there for the next four seasons.

In October 1985, the native of Scarborough, Ontario, was dealt to his native province, where he then played for the Leafs for four seasons.

The right-handed rearguard would play in two games for the Detroit Red Wings during the 1989-90 season. He retired upon the season's conclusion.

Kotsopoulos, a rare NHLer with a Greek surname, ultimately played in 479 NHL games. Despite playing 425 games elsewhere, today, "Kotsy" remains a regular participant at most Ranger alumni events. He also hosts a Rangers-themed podcast entitled "The Instigators."

337

Gerry McDonald, another right-handed defenseman that was never selected during an NHL Entry Draft, was an American boy out of Weymouth, Massachusetts.

During the 1980-81 season, he played for the New Haven Nighthawks but never played for the varsity club in New York.

Now in Hartford, he would play in only eight games between three NHL seasons. Five of those games took place during the 1983-84 season, mainly for Hartford's AHL affiliate, the Binghamton Whalers.

Following the season, he retired. In retirement, he opened an automobile retail business in Hartford, where he remains today as of this writing.

Doug Sulliman, a right-winger, was a first-round 1979 NHL Entry Draft pick of "The Fog," where the native of Glace Bay, Nova Scotia, was selected thirteenth overall. However, that draft pick was a mistake, considering that the Oilers selected Class of 2020 Hall of Famer Kevin Lowe eight spots later, at 21st overall. More on Lowe later.

Sulliman made his NHL debut with the Rangers, where he played in 31 games for the Rangers during the 1979-80 season. He would play in 32 more games as a Blueshirt in the season that followed. During these 62 games, he accumulated only 16 points. He'd go on to pick up 312 more in his next nine seasons in the NHL.

In the 1981-82 season, Sulliman's first in Hartford, he had the best season of his career behind a stat line of 29 goals, 40 assists, and 69 points - all career highs.

Sulliman would spend three seasons in Hartford and then moved on to the New Jersey Devils, where he spent the bulk of his career - four seasons in all - and where he was named the team's MVP during the 1986-87 season.

He was later put on waivers in October of 1988 when the Philadelphia Flyers claimed him. Sulliman would play two seasons with the Flyers, where after 28 games played during the 1989-90 season, he retired. Immediately after hanging up his skates, he rejoined the Devils, where he served the franchise as an assistant coach for three seasons.

Craig Patrick, who throughout his career (and not only with the Rangers), had a good eye for talent at the draft (especially European talent), struck out with the Helsinki, Finland native Simo Saarinen. To be fair, Saarinen was also a tenth-round pick.

The small-statured (5'9") defenseman played in eight games for the Rangers during the 1984-85 season. He'd then return to his mother country, where he spent the next ten years of his career. He retired after the 1995-96 season.

Center Mike Rogers (yep, featured in my first book), the big fish of the Whalers now going to Broadway, was a fifth-round draft pick (77th overall) of the NHL Vancouver Canucks, and a second-round draft pick of the WHA Edmonton Oilers in each league's 1974 Amateur Draft. The Calgarian Mike Rogers chose the WHA.

Rogers spent five seasons in the WHA, where midway through the 1975-76 season, he was moved to the New England Whalers.

All in all, Rogers totaled 396 games in the WHA, picking up 145 goals, 222 assists, and 367 points.

Once the WHA folded (or "merged," as WHA officials would say), at the start of the 1979-80 season, Rogers was no longer a WHA New England Whaler. He was now an NHL Hartford Whaler.

In his first season in the NHL, his "rookie" season, Rogers picked up 105 points. A season later, he'd pick up another 105 points. That's why the Rangers wanted him.

In his first season in New York, Rogers scored 38 goals and picked up 65 assists for a grand total of 103 points.

While Rogers never picked up 100+ points in one WHA season (his career high was 82 points during the 1976-77 season), he now had three straight 100+ point seasons in his first three in the NHL.

As a result, Rogers is part of an NHL trivia question.

*"Who are the only four players in NHL history to pick up 100+ points in their first three seasons?"*

Your answer? Mike Rogers, some guy named Wayne Gretzky, another no-name guy named Mario Lemieux, and that Peter Stastny fellow. Of the four, only Rogers isn't in the Hall of Fame - much to the chagrin of many.

Rogers ultimately spent four seasons with the Rangers. Nine games into his fifth season, the 1985-86 season, he was dealt to his first professional team, the Edmonton Oilers, now of the NHL, where Rogers played in eight more games.

Once retiring, Rogers, as mentioned, a native of Calgary, Alberta, then joined the Flames as their radio analyst, where he remained for a dozen years before hanging up the ear cans in 2013.

Rogers, who probably could have played a bit longer had he desired, in a 2020 interview for the Flames' alumni website, said the following about his early retirement:

*"Twelve years was enough. Ann [his wife] and I wanted to travel, and living in Calgary - you want to get away in the winter.*

*"The hockey travel grind had started to get to me a little bit, too. So a lot of factors entered into the decision. I sat down with my wife and said: "'Had a good run.' I'd never say a bad thing about those twelve years but they'd kind of taken a toll.*

*"I could've signed another contract after my last year in the NHL. But my stats weren't what they'd been. I knew I wasn't playing as well as I had and I didn't want to be one of those guys that just hung on for the sake of it."*

While he had good years in New York - Rogers never truly took to the city.

To this day, he appears at Carolina Hurricanes alumni events, as the Whalers relocated to Raleigh, North Carolina, at the start of the 1997-98 season, where they still remain today. He doesn't appear at Rangers' alumni events.

This trade was a win. Rogers was a big part of Rangers' success during the early 1980s, whereas if it weren't for the Islanders - ugh, enough said!

**DATE OF TRADE: October 16th, 1981**

**RANGERS ACQUIRE: Pat Hickey**

**TORONTO MAPLE LEAFS ACQUIRE: Fifth-Round Pick of the 1982 NHL Entry Draft (#99 - Sylvain Charland)**

Forward Sylvain Charland, from St-Hyacinthe, Quebec, never reached the NHL. Following four games played with the St. Catharines Saints (AHL), by 1983, he was out of hockey.

In return for this draft pick, and just like he did with Nicky Fotiu, Patrick brought Pat Hickey back to New York, as the general manager wanted players who had proven they could play in the Big Apple.

And as mentioned during the Barry Beck trade - Hickey's second stint with the Rangers wouldn't last long.

In just 53 games during the 1981-82 season, "Hitch" picked up 15 goals and 14 assists for a grand total of 29 points.

More on Hickey to come.

Since Charland never played in the NHL, and because Hickey not only played in 53 more games with the Rangers but was later flipped for assets - this was another win for Patrick.

**DATE OF TRADE: October 30th, 1981**

**RANGERS ACQUIRE: Tom Younghans**

**MINNESOTA NORTH STARS ACQUIRE: Cash**

Right-winger Tom Younghans was 28 years old at the time of this trade and had logged 382 games with the Minnesota North Stars in parts of six seasons with the franchise.

The native of St. Paul, Minnesota (where he also played college hockey for the state's university), came to the Rangers and played 47 games for the club, where the check liner recorded only eight points.

Not happy in New York, Younghans retired at the end of the 1981-82 season and moved back to Minnesota, where he became a salesman.

Without knowing how much Patrick paid for Younghans, this trade is a wash. It didn't hurt the Rangers, nor did it truly benefit them. In an attempt not to sound callous - he was pretty much a warm body for the Blueshirts.

**DATE OF TRADE: December 11th, 1981**

**RANGERS ACQUIRE: Eddie Mio**

**EDMONTON OILERS ACQUIRE: Lance Nethery**

The native of Toronto, Ontario, Lance Nethery, who was also a big-time college player at Cornell, and who, in retirement, had spent nearly forty years in Europe as both a coach and a player, was John Ferguson's eighth-round draft pick (131st overall) of the 1977 NHL Amateur Draft.

The center played in 33 games during the 1980-81 season for the Rangers and then played in five more games during the 1981-82 campaign.

Now in Edmonton, Nethery represented the Oilers for three more games. After fooling around in the minors, he made the jump overseas, where he later made connections that led to a long coaching and front-office career, spending the majority of his time in Germany.

Goaltender Eddie Mio, a late-round draft pick of both the 1974 NHL (124th overall) and WHA (138th overall) Amateur Drafts, took the WHA money, joining the Vancouver Blazers rather than hooking up with the Chicago Blackhawks. However, he'd never play in Vancouver.

Instead, starting with the 1977-78 season, the four-year standout of Colorado College began his professional career with the Indianapolis Racers. In the season that followed, he moved on to Edmonton, and once the Oilers became an NHL franchise during the 1979-80 season - he, too, became an NHLer.

With the orange and blue at the Rexall Arena, the native of Windsor, Ontario, played in 77 games.

In New York, Mio, who quickly became a fan favorite, played in 66 games for the Rangers, where Patrick soon involved him in another trade, a trade we'll soon get to.

As far as this trade, this was a win. Mio, despite his brief tenure in New York, was a fan favorite.

And in a "fun fact," Mio was also Wayne Gretzky's best man when "The Great One" married Janet Jones in July 1988 that dominated television screens in every Canadian home.

**DATE OF TRADE: December 30th, 1981**

**RANGERS ACQUIRE: Robbie Ftorek and Eighth-Round Pick of the 1982 NHL Entry Draft (#160 - Brian Glynn)**

**QUEBEC NORDIQUES ACQUIRE: Jere Gillis and Dean Talafous (Talafous refused to report to Quebec, and an NHL arbitrator substituted Pat Hickey on March 8th, 1982)**

This is a confusing, yet explainable trade.

The easy one to talk about here is Brian Glynn, a defenseman who played at the University of Minnesota-Duluth at the time of his draft. Once completing his college days in 1984, the native of Tonawanda, New York, never played hockey again.

Robbie Ftorek, who dabbled at both the center and left-wing positions, began his NHL career as an undrafted free agent during the 1972-73 season. The silver medal US Olympian (1972) (he'd later be inducted into the United States Hockey Hall of Fame in 1991, the WHA Hall of Fame in 2010, and the AHL Hall of Fame in 2020), started his career with the Red Wings. It would be short-lived.

The Wings, concerned about Ftorek's 5'9" and 153-pound frame, sent him to the AHL, where he then had immediate success. However, since he wasn't part of Detroit's plans, come the 1974-75 season, and like so many before him, the native of Needham, Massachusetts, jumped to the WHA.

After three years with the Phoenix Road Runners, and two more seasons with the Cincinnati Stingers, once the WHA folded he signed with a former WHA franchise, now an NHL franchise, the Quebec Nordiques. That's where he'd spend the next two full seasons of his career, and part of a third, prior to this trade.

Ftorek would finish his career in New York. He spent parts of four seasons in the Big Apple and played the final 48 games of his career with the Rangers during the 1984-85 season.

While never reaching the heights he attained in the WHA and in Quebec, Ftorek's best season with the Rangers' blue jersey on his back took place during the back half of the 1981-82 season when he scored eight goals and picked up 24 assists for a grand total of 32 points.

Ftorek, who also split time with the New Haven Nighthawks at the end of his career and is now an alumni of the club, he then coached the AHL team for three seasons. He'd later move on to the NHL head coaching ranks, where he was the bench boss of the Kings, Devils, and Bruins.

The 2002-2003 season would be his last season as an NHL coach. He then spent nearly the next twenty years of his life coaching at the OHL, AHL, and ECHL levels.

As mentioned earlier, Jere Gillis wasn't long for the Rangers, having played in 61 games in all.

Right-winger Dean Talafous, born in Duluth, Minnesota, was an American who wanted no part of the French-speaking province of Quebec.

Talafous, who played his college hockey at the University of Wisconsin, where he was also named MVP of the 1973 collegiate playoffs (Wisconsin won the tournament), began his NHL career during the 1974-75 season as a member of the Atlanta Flames.

The man from Minnesota wouldn't last long in Atlanta, as he helped orchestrate a trade to the North Stars during his rookie season. At the time of this trade, which took place on January 4th, 1975, he had only played in eighteen games for the Flames, where he finished with a paltry total of five points.

Talafous would remain with his home team throughout the 1977-78 season. At the end of the season, he signed a free-agent deal with the Rangers.

In three full seasons with the Rangers and 29 more games during the 1981-82 season prior to this trade, Talafous had earned himself a reputation of being reliable yet "shy" and "quiet." He was never boastful, even when pressed, including after his 100th NHL goal scored while as a Ranger that came in November of 1981.

Once traded to Quebec, Talafous said no way and opted to retire. He was only 28 years old and most likely had many seasons left in him. Rather than playing, he joined the collegiate coaching ranks.

When Talafous decided he'd rather retire than learn how to speak French, three months following the trade, an NHL arbitrator decided that Hickey had to go to Quebec as collateral to make this trade complete.

As mentioned earlier, Hickey accepted the assignment, played in seven games for the Nordiques, and then moved on, where he eventually finished his career in St. Louis.

In a final assessment, this trade is a wash, as Patrick never wanted to trade Hickey in the first place.

**DATE OF TRADE: February 2nd, 1982**

**RANGERS ACQUIRE: Rob McClanahan**

**HARTFORD WHALERS ACQUIRE: Tenth-Round Pick of the 1983 NHL Entry Draft (#193 - Reine Karlsson)**

Swedish forward Reine Karlsson never made the jump to America. Instead, he began his professional career during the 1982-83 season, playing for his hometown Sodertalje SK of the Swedish league. That's where he'd remain and retire after seven seasons at the end of the 1988-89 campaign.

Left-winger Rob McClanahan is known mainly for his role on the USA Olympic team, where he won the gold medal with the "Miracle on Ice" squad during the 1980 Olympics at Lake Placid.

The native of St. Paul, Minnesota, like so many at this time, including general manager Craig Patrick and head coach Herb Brooks, he was one of many from the "Miracle" team to receive a paycheck from the Rangers.

Following the gold medal win, McClanahan began his career with the Buffalo Sabres, where he lasted until October 5th, 1981. He was placed on waivers and soon became a Whaler.

McClanahan, a star on the USA team, but primarily a role player in the NHL, logged seventeen games in Hartford before traveling to New York.

346

The product of the University of Minnesota would finish his NHL career with the Rangers, where he played in 22 games at the end of this 1981-82 season, a complete 78-game season in the season that followed (including nine playoff games during the 1983 Stanley Cup Playoffs), and then in 41 more games during his final season, 1984-85.

Despite being a third and/or fourth liner, McClanahan had his best NHL seasons with the Rangers.

Since Karlsson never played in the NHL, this trade was an easy win for one of Patrick's favorite players.

**DATE OF TRADE: August 23rd, 1982**

**RANGERS ACQUIRE: Shawn Dineen**

**MINNESOTA NORTH STARS ACQUIRE: Dan McCarthy**

Dan McCarthy, a center from St. Mary's, Ontario, was Fred Shero's fifteenth-round pick (223rd overall) of the 1978 NHL Amateur Draft.

McCarthy, alumni of the OHA Sudbury Wolves, played in five games for the Rangers during the 1980-81 season. Despite scoring four goals in those five games, McCarthy would never play in the NHL again. Instead, he was a career minor leaguer, where he last played for the New Haven Nighthawks (AHL) in the 1985-86 season, logging 33 games in all.

Defenseman Shawn Dineen, a native of Detroit, Michigan, played in five less NHL games than Dineen, as he never made it to the show.

After graduating from the University of Denver in 1981, Dineen spent the next seven seasons of his career bouncing around in the IHL, CHL, and AHL. After fifteen games with the Phoenix Road Runners (IHL) during the 1989-90 season, he retired.

This trade was another wash, as neither player played in an NHL game following this trade.

**DATE OF TRADE: October 1st, 1982**

**RANGERS ACQUIRE: Kent-Erik Andersson**

**HARTFORD WHALERS ACQUIRE: Ed Hospodar**

At the time of this trade, Kent-Erik Andersson, a right-winger out of Orebro, Sweden, had spent five seasons with the Minnesota North Stars. On October 1st, 1982, and prior to joining the Rangers, the North Stars flipped him to the Whalers, and the Whalers then immediately flipped Andersson to New York.

As a Ranger, Andersson played in two seasons for the club, where he picked up 48 points during that time and finished his NHL career as a Blueshirt at the end of the 1983-84 season. He then returned to Sweden, rejoining his first professional club, Färjestad BK.

After winning the Swedish League championship in 1986, he was forced to retire due to an eye injury.

This trade was so peculiar because, at the time, Andersson was 31 years old. Ed "Boxcar" Hospodar, a defenseman, was only 23 years old.

Hospodar, the enforcer out of Bowling Green, Ohio, was Shero's second-round pick (34th overall) of the 1979 NHL Entry Draft. He also had the best three seasons of his career with the Rangers, which made this trade even odder.

The veteran of a career totaling 1,314 penalty minutes, Hospodar spent two seasons with the Whalers. After that, he spent a few seasons with the Flyers and North Stars. Then, he went to the Buffalo Sabres for the 1987-88 campaign, where he played 42 games for the club, the final 42 games of his 450-game NHL career. He retired at the end of the season.

While the Rangers had many Europeans at this time, including Anders Hedberg, this trade was a loss. It never made sense at the time, nor did it make much sense in the years that followed.

**DATE OF TRADE: January 4th, 1983**

**RANGERS ACQUIRE: Glen Hanlon and Vadav Nedomansky**

**ST. LOUIS BLUES ACQUIRE: Andre Dore**

Defenseman Andre Dore, the Rangers' fourth-round pick of the 1978 NHL Amateur Draft (60th overall), took a while to catch on in the NHL. Before the 1981-82 season, the native of Montreal, Quebec, had played in only nineteen games in three seasons.

At the start of the 1981-82 campaign, Dore was still playing for Ranger AHL affiliates, where he spent 23 games with the Springfield Indians. However, he would soon be recalled during this season, where he played 56 games for the Blueshirts. He also played in all ten Rangers' playoff games in the 1982 Stanley Cup Playoffs.

At the time of this trade, Dore was only 24 years old. He finished the 1982-83 season in St. Louis. Just like this trade, he'd be traded again during the 1983-84 season, where he was dealt to the Quebec Nordiques - a team from his home province.

Dore wouldn't last long in Quebec either, as the team waived him prior to the start of the 1984-85 season. Of course, the Rangers then claimed Dore, which made the rearguard a two-time Ranger. It was in New York where Dore began his career, where he would end his career too.

Just as he did at the start of his professional career, Dore would spend the 1984-85 season splitting time with both New Haven Nighthawks and the Rangers. After 25 games played in this season, Dore played out the remainder of the 1985-86 season with the Hershey Bears. He retired at the end of the campaign, where he logged 257 NHL games played in total.

While Dore didn't exactly take the league by storm, the Rangers gave up the promising young defenseman for two reasons; they wanted an established NHL goaltender to replace John Davidson, and they had been chasing Vaclav Nedomansky for fifteen years.

Vaclav Nedomansky, a center from then-communist Hodonin, Czechoslovakia, was first approached by Emile Francis and the Rangers all the way back in 1967. At the time, Nedomansky was one of the biggest stars of the soon-to-be Czech Republic (1993) and was sought after by many North American hockey teams.

Despite numerous offers, including "The Cat's," Nedomansky remained home. It would take five more years from the time of Francis's initial offer for Nedomansky to defect from Czechoslovakia when he did so in 1974, leaving his country for good and heading to Toronto - via the always neutral Switzerland.

However, Nedomansky didn't join the Leafs. Instead, he signed with the Toronto Toros of the WHA.

The southpaw, after two seasons with the Toros, played two more seasons in the WHA, where he last played for the Birmingham Bulls during the 1977-78 season. However, he would play in only twelve games for the Bulls this season before jumping to the NHL, where he first began his NHL career with the Detroit Red Wings.

After five seasons with the Wings, Nedomansky was now approaching the age of 39. The 1982-83 campaign would turn out to be his final NHL season.

Following 22 games with St. Louis, he played 35 games for the Rangers during the 1982-83 season, amassing twelve goals and eight assists. He retired as a veteran of 252 WHA games and 421 more in the NHL.

Furthermore, Nedomansky, the first Czechoslovakian player to defect to North America, also played in 388 CSSR games (the Czech equivalent of the NHL).

Nedomansky, who was inducted into the Hockey Hall of Fame in 2019 (also featured in a slew of European Hockey Hall of Fames), wouldn't be allowed to return to his native country until the fall of the Iron Curtain (1990) due to his monumental defection.

While Nedomansky was a great player, he was at the end of the line when the Rangers acquired him. Goaltender Glen Hanlon was the centerpiece of this trade for the Blueshirts.

Hanlon, out of Brandon, Manitoba, began his NHL career during the 1977-78 season with the Vancouver Canucks. Mainly a backup, Hanlon spent parts of five seasons with the Canucks. Prior to the 1982 NHL Trade Deadline, he was traded to St. Louis.

Now with the Blues, and before this trade, Hanlon played in only sixteen games for St. Louis. Due to JD never being able to make a comeback as many had hoped, Hanlon would spend the next four seasons with the Rangers, where he last played for the club during the 1985-86 season.

By that time (1985-86), John Vanbiesbrouck had emerged from the Rangers' rotating goalie pack and claimed the number-one spot.

Hanlon was serviceable with the Rangers, with his best season taking place during the 1983-84 season, where he finished with a win/loss/tie record of 28-14-4 - his only winning record as a Ranger. In every other season, he finished with a losing win/loss/tie record, including a 5-12-1 record in his last season in the Big Apple.

He'd later be traded by Phil Esposito to the Detroit Red Wings in a trade that was a rare win for Espo (more on that to come).

Now in Detroit, Hanlon played with the spoked wheel for a respectable five seasons. Hanlon finished his career as a Red Wing and retired after the 1990-91 season.

In retirement, Hanlon, as he still does to this day, got into coaching, where he's coached all over the world for the last thirty-plus years.

Hanlon also has the unique distinction of giving up the first goal of Wayne Gretzky's career, as "The Great One" beat Hanlon for the first of his 894 career goals during a game between the Oilers and

Canucks on October 14, 1979. In later years, Hanlon, on #99, would jokingly say, *"I created a monster!"*

Ironically, Hanlon would also be around for another "Great's First," this time in "The Great Eight" Alex Ovechkin, as Hanlon coached the future Hall of Famer in his first game in Washington.

This trade was a win for Patrick. Dore would soon be back, and while Nedomansky would have been better had he defected fifteen years prior - Hanlon served his role well with the Rangers and for a good amount of time to boot.

**DATE OF TRADE: June 13th, 1983**

**RANGERS ACQUIRE: Mike Blaisdell, Willie Huber, and Mark Osborne**

**DETROIT RED WINGS ACQUIRE: Ron Duguay, Eddie Johnstone, and Eddie Mio**

In his biggest trade yet, involving six players, Patrick was urged to make this transaction on behalf of his head coach at the time, Herb Brooks. Unfortunately, while Brooks was a fan of this deal, Ranger fans and the Ranger players going to Detroit were not.

Ron Duguay was the centerpiece (literally, too, as he was a center). Once a quiet kid out of Sudbury, Ontario, the former number ten in Rangers' blue had become immersed in the New York City nightlife scene, routinely spotted with the likes of Andy Warhol, Farrah Fawcett, and Cher.

While never falling into the wrong crowd that teammate Don Murdoch did, Duguay's name was often featured in the "Page Six" column of the New York Post for his after-hour exploits, whether it was Studio 54 or elsewhere. Brooks thought that Duguay was more worried about enjoying New York than playing hockey for the Rangers - the genesis of this trade.

At the time of the trade, Duguay told the New York Times the following:

*"I wasn't shocked because there's been so much talk about it, but I was very disappointed. I'm very disappointed because I love New York and I hate to leave there. I've got businesses there, like the restaurant, and I was planning other things. It'll hurt, but it's my work, it's what I get paid to do, so I'll have to live with it.*

*"'I don't want to say anything bad about Detroit. It really doesn't matter what team it was - just being traded from New York is what hurts."*

Duguay also expressed that he felt Brooks had *"got his way."*

Duguay has stayed consistent from the time of these comments, as nearly forty years later, on his *"Up in the Blue Seats"* podcast (ironically hosted by the New York Post, the same newspaper that helped facilitate this trade with all of their *"Page Six"* coverage of him), he has echoed the same sentiment today as he did back in 1983.

While Duguay has said that, over time, perhaps Brooks was right in his assessment of him, he still hates that he didn't get to play with the Rangers his entire career. Statistically, Duguay had the best individual seasons of his career in Detroit, including an 80-point season in his first year with a red jersey on his back, followed by a career high 89-point season with the Wings during the 1984-85 campaign.

After six seasons with the Rangers, Duguay played in parts of three seasons with the Wings. He was later dealt to Pittsburgh prior to the NHL Trade Deadline of 1986. With the Penguins, Duguay played in 53 games before returning to New York on January 21st, 1987, as his buddy and former teammate, Phil Esposito, now in the big chair, brought him back to the Rangers.

Duguay's second stint with the Rangers wasn't long. Thirteen months later, on February 23rd, 1988, Esposito made another trade involving Duguay, when he sent his pal to Los Angeles. This worked out for Duguay, as once in Los Angeles, he got to play with Wayne Gretzky.

Duguay would play in seventy games for the Kings during the 1988-89 season, his last NHL season.

Following his final NHL game, Duguay dabbled in the minor leagues, playing mainly for the San Diego Gulls. He then moved on to another beach locale, where he last played for the Jacksonville Barracudas. He also coached the club to a league championship in 2004.

Eddie Johnstone, like Ron Duguay, was profiled heavily in my first book, where I listed both men in "The New York Rangers Rink of Honor." And just like Duguay, Johnstone was also a career Ranger at this point in time, having made his NHL debut during the 1975-76 season.

And yep, just like Duguay, Johnstone wasn't a fan of this trade either, but he also acknowledged that this was the nature of the business.

Johnstone, a right-winger, drafted in the sixth round (104th overall) by Emile Francis during the 1974 NHL Amateur Draft, the native of Brandon, Manitoba, wasn't long for Detroit either.

Following a 46-game stint with the Wings during the 1983-84 season, Johnstone was then demoted to the AHL during the 1984-85 campaign. He would play in three more NHL games with the Wings in the 1985-86 season and six more games in the 1986-87 campaign.

At the end of the 1986-87 season, and mainly an AHLer at this point, Johnstone retired from hockey at the age of 33.

Goaltender Eddie Mio, as discussed earlier, wasn't with the Rangers for long, but during his short time in New York, he won over the hearts of the fans.

Right after the trade, Patrick implied that Mio was disposable (without saying the word verbatim) when the general manager mentioned that he was happy with Glen Hanlon and Steve Weeks.

But, more importantly, Patrick praised a nineteen-year-old goaltender named John Vanbiesbrouck.

Mio, like Duguay and Johnstone, didn't last long in Detroit. Similar to Johnstone, Mio split time between the Red Wings and their AHL affiliate, the Adirondack Red Wings.

All in all, Mio played 49 games with the Wings, where he retired following the 1985-86 season.

Coming to the Rangers was left-winger Mark Osborne - the only Red Wing involved in this trade that didn't ask for a trade, as both Willie Huber and Mike Blaisdell did.

Osborne, a native of Toronto, Ontario, was the Wings' third-round pick (46th overall) of the 1980 NHL Entry Draft. He had an impressive rookie season in 1981-82, backed by 26 goals and 41 assists for a total of 67 points. These 41 assists and 67 points would be his career highs until the 1989-90 season, when he scored 23 goals, picked up 50 assists, and finished with 73 points. (His 26 goals from his rookie season would remain his career-best.)

Osborne spent parts of four seasons with the Rangers before being moved in 1987 to his hometown Toronto Maple Leafs - a trade made by Phil Esposito.

Osborne (who would later finish his career with the Rangers during the lockout-impacted 1994-95 season), posted respectable numbers with the Rangers, but his most productive seasons didn't come with the Original Six Rangers. Instead, he played his best hockey with two other Original Six teams - the Red Wings and Maple Leafs.

We'll get more into Osborne once we hit the date of March 5th, 1987.

The 6'5" and 225-pound German-born Willie Huber, the hulking defenseman, was Detroit's first-round (9th overall) pick of the 1978 NHL Amateur Draft. (Huber was born in Straßkirchen, Germany, but his family moved to Hamilton, Ontario as an infant.)

Despite his massive frame, Huber wasn't a stay-at-home defenseman as perhaps you'd imagine/expect. Instead, he was a gifted offensive defenseman, where he served the Wings as their power-play quarterback - which was also impressive, considering that at the time of his NHL debut, Huber was the biggest/largest player in NHL history. (Since then, many NHLers have increased in height and weight.)

At the time of this trade, Huber was one of the best D-men in the league, averaging over fourteen goals and forty points a season with a bad Detroit team.

Being tired of losing, with a contract dispute with the Wings at the time, following the trade, Huber told the New York Times:

*"It's so frustrating being on a losing team. If Reed Larson or I didn't score, it seemed we'd lose. Management was always on us to do more, but you can't do it by yourself, it's a team game. I'm grateful to be going to New York."*

Despite spending parts of the next five seasons with the Rangers (like many during the "Trader Phil" era, Esposito would later trade Huber too), Huber could never post the same numbers nor find the same success in New York as he had in Detroit.

Huber, who Patrick couldn't wait to pair on his blue line with Barry Beck, suffered back-to-back injuries. During the 1983-84 season, his first in New York, Huber tore ligaments in his left knee. Then, a season later, he tore ligaments in his right knee.

After these two injuries, Huber was never the same player, as the once explosive and mobile defenseman had now lost a step.

We'll get more into Huber once we get to November 4th, 1987.

Somehow, right-winger Mike Blaisdell, born in Moose Jaw, Saskatchewan, grew up rooting for the Rangers and Canadiens. Born on January 18th, 1960, at least Blaisdell saw one of his favorite teams win the Stanley Cup. It's just a shame that it wasn't the Rangers!

Blaisdell, like Huber, was also tired of losing in Detroit. Once arriving in New York, Blaisdell told the New York Times:

*"I'm really happy to get out of there. I'd like to play in a playoff game, too. I've never done that."*

Little did Blaisdell know at the time, not only would he never play in a playoff game with the Rangers - he'd rarely play at the NHL level with the Blueshirts either.

Blaisdell ended up playing in 48 games with the Rangers across two seasons. The rest of the time, the eleventh-overall pick of the 1980 NHL Entry Draft (Detroit) spent time diddling around with the Rangers' minor-league affiliates, even going down to play at the low CHL level for the Tulsa Oilers.

After being waived before the start of the 1985-86 season, Blaisdell ended up in Pittsburgh, playing 76 games over the next two seasons.

With the Penguins, and just as he did in New York - mainly spent time in the minors.

In July 1987, Blaisdell moved on to the Leafs, where again, he spent the bulk of his days at the minor-league level.

After nine games with the Leafs during the 1988-89 season, Blaisdell, who couldn't crack it at the NHL level, jumped the pond and spent the next decade playing hockey primarily in the United Kingdom, aka Hockeytown! (And, yes, I'm joking about the Union Jack country being a hockey town!)

In retirement, Blaisdell remained in England, where he then coached various British teams for the next decade and beyond, last during the 2005-06 season.

When assessing this trade, Ron Duguay went on to have the best career of the lot. Plus, he had impressive back-to-back seasons in Detroit once there. Of course, perhaps the new location, with no longer having the New York nightlife distraction, contributed to that.

Johnstone and Mio never did much afterward, despite their status as Blueshirt fan favorites. Ditto Blaisdell in New York.

Willie Huber had the most upside, but injuries robbed him of his prime years.

Mark Osborne was able to hang around in the league and was a serviceable role player, but he never matched the numbers Duguay posted.

This trade was a loss for Patrick, although this could have been a different story if Huber had not had his bouts with injuries. However, he did, and that's why this trade is considered a loss - although not as devastating as some make it out to be, due to how beloved Duguay, Mio, and Johnstone were.

**DATE OF TRADE: October 5th, 1983**

**RANGERS ACQUIRE: Dave Barr**

**BOSTON BRUINS ACQUIRE: Dave Silk**

Right-winger Dave Silk, as mentioned earlier in this book, had the best seasons of his career in New York. Silk, who played in two games with the Rangers after the 1980 Olympic gold medal win during the 1979-80 season, played in two complete seasons with the Blueshirts, and sixteen more games in the 1982-83 season.

In his last season with the Rangers, the 1982-83 campaign, Silk was relegated to the minor-league levels, playing in both the AHL and the CHL.

Silk, a native of Massachusetts, born on January 1st, 1958, in the town of Scituate, now joined his home-state Boston Bruins due to this trade.

358

Silk's time with the Bruins wouldn't be long.

Following 35 games played during the 1983-84 season in Boston, he played in 29 more games during the season afterward. He was waived in December 1984.

Now in Detroit, Silk played in twelve games with the Red Wings. A season later, the 1985-86 season, Silk was now in Winnipeg with the Jets, where he played the final 32 games of his NHL career, 249 in all, before moving on to Germany.

The American gold medalist would spend five seasons in Germany, where he retired after the 1990-91 season, having last played in Berlin.

And not a "fun fact" here: did you know that Silk was the cousin of Rangers' agitator and nemesis Mike Milbury? Now you know!

Dave Barr, also a right-winger, was born in Toronto, Ontario. Barr, who would get into coaching following his thirteen seasons (614 NHL games played) as a player, spent only six games with the Rangers before being dealt to St. Louis.

As a journeyman, both as a player and as a hockey lifer, due to his work as a coach, Barr has carved out a life-long career in the game that he loves. More on his post-Ranger days to come shortly - as he was soon traded again by Patrick.

As far as this particular trade goes, it's pretty much a wash. Not that Barr would truly "bite the Rangers in the ass" in the years to come, but from the time of this trade, Barr would go on to have much more success than Silk did. The Rangers just weren't part of it.

**DATE OF TRADE: January 20th, 1984**

**RANGERS ACQUIRE: Ninth-Round Pick of the 1984 NHL Entry Draft (#189 - Heinz Ehlers)**

**EDMONTON OILERS ACQUIRE: Rick Chartraw**

Rick Chartraw, born in Caracas, Venezuela, but as an American who grew up in Erie, Pennsylvania (his father was working/living in Venezuela at the time of his birth), Chartraw was Montreal's first-round pick (10th overall) of the 1974 NHL Amateur Draft.

With the Canadiens, the defenseman (who later converted to a right-winger during the latter stages of his career) won four Stanley Cups as a member of the last Montreal dynasty teams (late 1970s).

Prior to the 1981 NHL Trade Deadline, Chartraw was traded to Los Angeles. Two years later, and after being waived by the Kings - on January 13th, 1983, the Rangers claimed him.

Chartraw, approaching thirty years old at the time of this trade to Edmonton, had played in four games with the Rangers during the 1983-84 season.

The Oilers, looking to bolster their ranks for a Stanley Cup run, saw value in the four-time champion. In turn, Chartraw played in 24 more regular season games for the orange and blue during the 1983-84 season. He'd then play in one more game in the 1984 Stanley Cup Playoffs, his last - and now as a member of the 1984 Stanley Cup champs.

The now five-time Stanley Cup champion, a veteran of 420 career NHL games (thirty with the Rangers), then retired after adding a ring to his thumb.

Heinz Ehlers, born in Aalborg, Denmark, was a left-winger selected by the Rangers in the NHL Draft that followed this trade. He never made the jump to North America. Instead, he spent the next seventeen seasons playing in both the Swedish and Danish leagues.

Craig Patrick and the Rangers took a shot here, dealing off a soon-to-be retiring veteran for a potential young player. It didn't work. This happens often. This trade is a wash.

---

**DATE OF TRADE: March 5th, 1984**

**RANGERS ACQUIRE: Larry Patey and Bob Brooke**

**ST. LOUIS BLUES ACQUIRE: Dave Barr, Third-Round Pick in the 1984 NHL Entry Draft (#56 - Alan Perry), and Cash**

Southpaw center Larry Patey, out of Toronto, Ontario, was originally selected in the ninth round of the 1973 NHL Amateur Draft (130th overall) by the California Seals. He spent parts of three seasons with the woeful club before moving on to St. Louis in November 1975.

Patey would then spend parts of nine seasons with the Blues. Then, at the age of 31, Patey joined the Rangers for the 1984 Stanley Cup Playoffs, where he played in four of the five Rangers' first-round series games against the Islanders - a series loss for the Blueshirts.

In the following season, 1984-85, Patey played seven more NHL games for the Rangers, his last seven of a 717-game NHL career.

Now with the AHL Nighthawks, Patey retired after the 1984-85 season, where he logged sixteen regular season games for the Rangers in total.

The right-handed center out of Acton, Massachusetts, Bob Brooke was like many Rangers from this era - acquired by Patrick and later dealt by Phil Esposito.

Initially drafted in the fourth round of the 1980 NHL Entry Draft (75th overall) by the Blues, Brooke never suited up for the Blue note. Instead, he made his NHL debut with the Blueshirts during the 1983-84 season, playing in nine games following this trade.

A graduate from Yale University, Brooke was a regular for the Rangers during the 1984-85 and 1985-86 seasons before being sent to the Minnesota North Stars in November of 1986. More on that trade to come.

Brooke wound up playing in the NHL for seven seasons, where his best season took place as a Ranger. In this season, 1985-86, Brooke scored 24 goals and racked up 20 assists for a total of 44 points. All of these numbers were his career highs.

As mentioned earlier, Barr had played only six games for the Rangers - six of his 614 NHL games. He had some good seasons in St. Louis, but he would also bounce around the league, playing for the Bruins, Whalers, Red Wings, Devils, and Stars.

Alan Perry, a goaltender out of Providence, Rhode Island, never made it to the NHL. Following the 1984 NHL Entry Draft, the netminder spent the next decade of his life bouncing around the minors, where he played at the OHL, AHL, CHL, and IHL levels. In other words, sending this draft pick to St. Louis didn't hurt Patrick here - although there were eventual NHLers drafted after Perry.

Fun Fact: Another goaltender was drafted five spots before Perry in this same 1984 NHL Draft, as the Montreal Canadiens selected some guy named Patrick Roy.

This trade was a tiny win for Patrick. Patey joined the team for a playoff run. It cost the general manager a pick and some cash. Barr and Brooke, born a month apart at the end of 1960, had solid careers. Plus, Brooke did his best work on Broadway too.

**DATE OF TRADE: May 23rd, 1984**

**RANGERS ACQUIRE: Future Considerations**

**DETROIT RED WINGS ACQUIRE: Rob McClanahan**

This trade was much ado about nothing, as McClanahan never played for the Red Wings, which is why the Rangers never received any "future considerations" in return.

At the time, McClanahan was disappointed in his lack of playing time, and he actually requested this trade. He'd fare no better in Detroit, as he didn't make the team.

After trying to hook up with Vancouver, where an NHL roster spot wasn't afforded to him either, rather than playing in the minors, one of the heroes of the "Miracle on Ice" team decided to call it a career.

Patrick tried to help a player out that he'd forever be associated with, but this trade meant nothing at the end of the day.

**DATE OF TRADE: September 5th, 1984**

**RANGERS ACQUIRE: Future Considerations (Third-Round Pick of the 1986 NHL Entry Draft) (#53 - Shaun Clouston)**

**HARTFORD WHALERS ACQUIRE: Steve Weeks**

This was a trade out of necessity for Patrick. After all, as Patrick explained at the time, the Rangers had two excellent goaltenders in the minors, with both goalies soon-to-be NHL ready, in Ron Scott and John Vanbiesbrouck - a tandem who just came off winning the 1984 CHL championship (Tulsa Oilers).

And as you should be aware, that John Vanbiesbrouck guy worked out.

In a true numbers game in every aspect (amount of goaltenders a team could carry/play, and age, as Steve Weeks was 26 years old at the time), Weeks was sent to Hartford. If he played well, the Rangers would get a nice draft pick in return. Weeks did okay in Hartford and served as the Whalers' backup goalie for parts of four seasons.

Fun Fact: The general manager of the Hartford Whalers at the time? Old friend, Emile Francis, who had just finished his first full season with the Rangers' rival. ("The Cat" would remain with the Whalers until the end of the 1988-89 season.)

Following his time with the Whalers, Weeks spent parts of four seasons in Vancouver. The native of Scarborough, Ontario, would then return to New York during the 1991-92 season - with the Islanders.

Weeks wouldn't stay with the inferior New York hockey club for long, as after 23 games played, he was sent 3,000 miles away to Los Angeles. He finished the 1991-92 season with the Kings.

In the offseason that followed, the Washington Capitals signed the now-struggling goalie, but would soon trade him to the Ottawa Senators prior to the start of the 1992-93 season.

Nearing the age of 35 and his best days long behind him, Weeks couldn't reclaim his magic with the Senators. After seven games with the Senators, where he had an awful goals-allowed average of 7.23 and an even worse save percentage of .792, Weeks called it a career on February 20th, 1993.

Craig Patrick was fired by the Rangers on July 14th, 1986. A week later, on July 21st, the NHL held its annual entry draft. In other words - Patrick wasn't around to make this pick.

Phil Esposito, who took over for Patrick, was new to the job at the time of the draft. While his selection of center Shaun Clouston from Viking, Alberta (hell of a city name!), didn't pan out, the former #77 of the Rangers is the GM on record of the Rangers' first-round pick (9th overall) of that 1986 NHL Entry Draft - Brian Leetch. As you may have gathered - Leetch did pretty well for himself.

This trade was a win, as it opened up the path for John Vanbiesbrouck to claim the starter's job in New York. After all, in the season following this trade, "Beezer" won the Vezina Trophy and also brought the Rangers to the penultimate round of the 1986 Stanley Cup Playoffs.

**DATE OF TRADE: November 27th, 1984**

**RANGERS ACQUIRE: Cash**

**EDMONTON OILERS ACQUIRE: Mark Morrison**

Center Mark Morrison, from Delta, British Columbia, was initially drafted by the Rangers in the third round of the 1981 NHL Entry Draft (51st overall). He played nine games for the Blueshirts in the

1981-82 season. He would play in one more game, his last NHL game, in the 1983-84 season.

Now under the Edmonton umbrella, Morrison was sent to the AHL. He would play eleven games for the Nova Scotia Oilers during the 1984-85 season. These would be his last eleven games in North America.

Starting with the 1985-86 season, Morrison went to Europe, where he played hockey in Italy. Come the 1993-94 season (a great season for the Rangers - as you may have heard), Morrison relocated to England, where he spent the next twelve seasons playing for the Fife Flyers of the BHL. He retired after the 2004-05 season.

Whatever money Patrick got for Morrison here was gravy. This was another microscopic victory for Patrick.

**DATE OF TRADE: December 6th, 1984**

**RANGERS ACQUIRE: Steve Patrick and Jim Wiemer**

**BUFFALO SABRES ACQUIRE: Dave Maloney and Chris Renaud**

This trade was centered around Dave Maloney, the former captain of the Rangers, and yep, you guessed it - another featured member of my "New York Rangers Rink of Honor."

The Rangers' first-round pick (14th overall) of the 1974 NHL Amateur Draft, the defenseman had spent a decade of his life with the Rangers, where he played across parts of eleven consecutive seasons and where he also amassed 605 games with the Blueshirts.

Only 28 years old at the time of this trade, Maloney was critical of both Rangers' head coach Herb Brooks and Craig Patrick, as the defenseman-turned-forward was unhappy with the team's roster and style of play. Ironically, just a little over a month later, from the time of this trade - Patrick fired Brooks on January 21st, 1985.

While Dave Maloney was a great Ranger and most certainly an emotional player, he was often criticized for his emotions and was known for his crying.

Maloney's penchant for the waterworks was even brought up immediately following this trade, as he said the following to the hockey media:

*"I'm not embarrassed when it's time to cry. I bet people are saying he probably cried for a half-hour today and I did. Maybe my emotions rubbed people the wrong way."*

Craig Patrick tried to brush off Maloney's crying when the general manager said the following after the trade:

*"I've always respected his emotions. This is the kind of trade we would have made if things were going well."*

The legendary Scotty Bowman, now in Buffalo as both the team's head coach and general manager, when asked about Maloney's tears, responded to the hockey media with:

*"That's just the type we're looking for, someone with emotion, with the intangibles. I'm convinced a change of scenery will help him."*

The change of scenery didn't help Maloney.

After 52 games with the Sabres, the still relatively young Dave Maloney retired at the end of the 1984-85 season. He would soon get into the field of finance before returning to hockey in a variety of announcing and broadcasting roles - which he still maintains to this day for his favorite hockey team, the New York Rangers.

Had this trade never happened, Maloney, the kid out of Kitchener, Ontario, most likely would've extended his career. However, he was in the wrong part of New York and opted to move on with his life instead.

Chris Renaud, another defenseman out of Ontario (Windsor), never made it to the NHL.

An undrafted free agent from Colgate University, Renaud, after two seasons with the Tulsa Oilers (CHL), was now a New Haven Nighthawk (AHL) at the time of this trade. Now with the Sabres' organization, Renaud remained at the AHL level, playing in 52 games for the Rochester Americans.

At the end of the 1984-85 season, Renaud, just 25 years old, retired from professional hockey.

With Maloney and Renaud retiring in the spring of 1985, this trade was already a win for the Rangers and Patrick - even if Maloney was a big fan favorite.

Southpaw defenseman Jim Wiemer, from Sudbury, Ontario, was the Sabres' fourth-round pick of the 1980 NHL Entry Draft when he was selected 83rd overall. After getting his feet wet at the AHL level for two seasons, Wiemer first became a full-time NHLer during the 1983-84 season.

However, following that season, Wiemer's career was split between the NHL and AHL.

With the Rangers, Wiemer played in 29 games in all, during both the 1984-85 and 1985-86 seasons. He'd later be traded to Edmonton by "Trader Phil." With the Oilers, Wiemer would receive a Stanley Cup ring in 1988 - although his name is not engraved onto the Stanley Cup due to the NHL's engraving requirements.

Following his days in Alberta, Wiemer later played for the Kings and Bruins, where in Boston, he had some of the better days of his career that spanned eleven seasons that saw the defenseman play in 325 NHL games.

Despite Philadelphia, the city known for its "brotherly love" not being involved in this transaction - this trade had many sibling connections.

While Dave Maloney was now split from brother Don with the Rangers, Steve Patrick, from Winnipeg, Manitoba, and the only forward involved in this trade (right-wing), was now united with his brother James in New York.

And if that wasn't enough, when Chris Renaud was sent to Rochester, he was united with his brother Mark. So that's right, three sets of brothers were impacted by this one trade.

Steve Patrick, who was the Sabres' first-round pick of the 1980 NHL Entry Draft (20th overall) was caught in a right-wing logjam in Buffalo. At the time, Bowman's team had eight right-wingers on the roster. Despite Patrick's young age and status as a first-round pick - it was Patrick who was considered to be the most expendable.

Patrick, who spent parts of five seasons with the Sabres at the time of this trade, would finish out the 1984-85 season with the Rangers, and then would be involved in another Craig Patrick (no relation) trade in the season that followed.

After 27 games played with the Quebec Nordiques during the 1985-86 season, and like everyone else involved in this trade - Patrick retired young, at the age of 25, and 250 NHL games under his belt.

For what it's worth, Steve Patrick's 43 games with the Rangers during the 1984-85 season were the best of his career, where he posted career highs in goals (11), assists (18), and points (29).

While it was tough for some Ranger fans to say goodbye to Maloney, this trade was a win for Craig Patrick, as Steve Patrick had the most success with his new club. Wiemer also did better than Renaud, which also helps Patrick's case.

At this time, it should be mentioned that while signing free agents and firing & hiring coaches in between, Craig Patrick wouldn't make another trade for over a year.

While Patrick never made a true "blockbuster" deal, starting with our next trade, the general manager, in what would be his final season with the Rangers (1985-86), made a flurry of moves in an attempt to improve his club and earn a contract extension. (Patrick's contract was due to expire on July 30th, 1986, but as the season moved along, it was known that the Rangers were getting sweet on ex-Ranger, and the team's broadcaster at the time, Phil Esposito.)

---

**DATE OF TRADE: December 9th, 1985**

**RANGERS ACQUIRE: Roland Melanson**

**MINNESOTA NORTH STARS ACQUIRE Second-Round Pick of the 1986 NHL Entry Draft (#30 - Neil Wilkinson) and Fourth-Round Pick of the 1987 NHL Entry Draft (#73 - John Weisbrod)**

After being idle for over a year, Patrick returned to the trade market, where he made the first three-way trade of his career.

Rollie Melanson, the Islanders' third-round selection of the 1979 NHL Entry Draft (59th overall), served as Billy Smith's backup for two Stanley Cup championships (1982 and 1983).

Now in Minnesota, the reliable and serviceable backup goaltender from Moncton, New Brunswick, was dealt to the Rangers, where Patrick sent two draft picks in return. Next, Patrick flipped Melanson to Los Angeles for two more pieces, which we'll soon discuss.

Lou Nanne, general manager of the Minnesota North Stars at the time of this trade (he's also the grandfather of one-time Ranger Vinni Lettieri), drafted Neil Wilkinson and John Weisbrod.

Wilkinson, a right-handed defenseman from Selkirk, Manitoba, spent two seasons with the North Stars. He then became a journeyman, where he also logged time for the Sharks, Blackhawks, Jets, and Penguins.

The 1998-99 season would be his last NHL season, where as a Penguin, he finished his career with 460 games played. The man known as "Big Daddy," a nickname in honor of his bruising brand of hockey, would attempt a comeback in 2003, where he then played at the ECHL level, but it was short-lived.

John Weisbrod, a center out of Syosset, New York, who played four years at Harvard University, never played professional hockey.

Melanson had the most success of all three players involved here, but he was just a piece for Patrick to move in his next deal.

---

**DATE OF TRADE: December 9th, 1985**

**RANGERS ACQUIRE: Brian MacLellan and the Fourth-Round Pick of the 1987 NHL Entry Draft (#69 - Mike Sullivan)**

**LOS ANGELES KINGS ACQUIRE: Grant Ledyard and Roland Melanson**

After his brief stint in Minnesota, Melanson moved on to Los Angeles, where he had good seasons, including in the 1986-87 and 1987-88 campaigns - where he received the most playing time of his career.

By the time he was thirty, the three-time Stanley Cup champ (Islanders - ugh) was now with the Devils, where he played only one game for the red-and-black attack, as he played for New Jersey's AHL team that season, the Utica Devils.

The 1991-92 season would be Melanson's last in the NHL, where he played nine games for the Montreal Canadiens.

Since the Rangers were already set in the net with Vanbiesbrouck and Mike Richter soon to come - moving on from Melanson was no big deal.

Defenseman Grant Ledyard, a native of Winnipeg, Manitoba, was the apple of the eye of Kings' General Manager Rogie Vachon, as at the time, Los Angeles had injuries on their blue line.

Ledyard, who began his NHL career with the Rangers as an undrafted free agent during the 1984-85 season, had spent his entire career in New York prior to this trade. Once traded, Ledyard told the *Los Angeles Times* the following:

*"I didn't expect anything like this. I'm still shocked and it's going to take me a while to get over this. I've got a lot of Ranger blood in me."*

Ledyard had played 69 games with the Rangers. When he retired at the end of the 2001-02 season - he had totaled a whopping 1,028 NHL games in his career.

Despite his seventeen seasons in the NHL, where aside from the Rangers and the Kings, the journeyman also played for the Capitals, Sabres, Stars, Canucks, Bruins, Senators, and Lightning - he never won the Stanley Cup.

Mike Sullivan, yes, the same Mike Sullivan who would later go on to serve the Rangers not only as an assistant head coach during the John Tortorella era but would go on to win two Stanley Cups (2016 and 2017) as the bench boss of the Pittsburgh Penguins, was a Phil Esposito draft pick.

While Sullivan would later receive a Rangers' paycheck as an assistant head coach, the native of Marshfield, Massachusetts, declined the Rangers' offer to play for the club after being drafted. Instead, he played for four years at Boston University.

Once graduating in 1990, the southpaw center began his eleven-season career as a player with the San Jose Sharks, with his first NHL game taking place during the 1991-92 season.

In January 1994, Sullivan was waived by the Sharks. The Calgary Flames claimed him, and Sullivan would remain in Alberta until the end of the 1996-97 season.

After a one-and-done 1997-98 season with his hometown Boston Bruins, Sullivan headed out west, playing the final four seasons of his career with the Phoenix Coyotes. Once the 2001-02 season was complete, Sullivan retired and began a coaching career that still lasts today, where he first served as an assistant head coach for his beloved black-and-gold B's.

While you can't blame Esposito (and definitely not Patrick) for Sullivan's decision to make his education his number one priority, none of Sullivan's 709 NHL games were played as a Ranger.

Brian MacLellan, a left-winger out of Guelph, Ontario, is the same MacLellan who would later win the Stanley Cup in 2018 as the general manager of the Washington Capitals.

At the time of this trade, MacLellan, a Bowling Green State University graduate who had signed with the Kings as an undrafted free agent for the 1982-83 season, had been struggling. However, he was high on Craig Patrick's list, although he wouldn't be so high on Phil Esposito's list.

Following the trade, MacLellan said to the *Los Angeles Times*:

*"I've got mixed emotions. I'm excited to be going to New York, but I'll miss L.A. I've built up a lot of friendships. I didn't really expect it. I know that my name has been mentioned around the league as being traded, but I still didn't expect it. I guess it's part of the job."*

Patrick, in a better mood than MacLellan, told *Newsday*:

*"We've been interested in him (MacLellan) for a long time. We tried a number of things, but none seemed to work. Acquiring Melanson gave us some flexibility to move a goaltender and something else. We feel he (MacLellan) can add an awful lot to our hockey club. We feel very fortunate that things fell into place."*

MacLellan would play in 51 games for the Rangers during the 1985-86 season, where he scored 11 goals and added 21 assists for a grand total of 32 points. He also played all sixteen of the Rangers' playoff games in the 1986 Stanley Cup Playoffs.

Esposito, now in the big chair, promptly traded MacLellan to Minnesota in the offseason that followed. In the 1986-87 season, MacLellan nearly tripled his goal production from his time with the Rangers, scoring 32 goals. He also fell one-point shy of doubling his point total, picking up 63 points.

After three solid seasons with the North Stars, MacLellan then played three more seasons with the Calgary Flames. After 23 games with the Detroit Red Wings during the 1991-92 season, the man of 606 NHL games called it a career.

It's tough to say if this trade was a win or loss, or at least in regards to Craig Patrick since he was fired following this 1985-86 season.

This trade did feel desperate at the time, as Patrick was trying to give his team a jolt. MacLellan did work out, and the team lost to that year's Stanley Cup champs in the semifinal round of the 1986 playoffs.

Despite all of the moving parts here, this trade is a wash for Patrick, but with an asterisk for Esposito and the Rangers - who take the loss overall.

After all, no one involved with this trade would ever play for the Rangers after the Spring of 1986, while Ledyard, Sullivan, MacLellan, Melanson, and Wilkinson all enjoyed lengthy careers elsewhere.

**DATE OF TRADE: December 19th, 1985**

**RANGERS ACQUIRE: Larry Melnyk and Todd Strueby**

**EDMONTON OILERS ACQUIRE: Mike Rogers**

Mike Rogers, as discussed not only in "The New York Rangers Rink of Honor and the Rafters of Madison Square Garden" but in this book, was 31 years old at the time of this trade and on his last legs.

Beginning his career with the Oilers (WHA) during the 1974-75 season, Rogers skated in eight more games for Edmonton (NHL).

He retired at the end of the season -which also tells you that Patrick didn't lose this trade.

Todd Strueby, a left-handed center out of Lanigan, Saskatchewan, was the Oilers' second-round pick (29th overall) of the 1981 NHL Entry Draft. In parts of three seasons prior to this trade, Strueby had only played in five games for Edmonton - the only five games of his NHL career.

Strueby never came to New York, as instead, he remained at the IHL level, where he played for the Muskegon Lumberjacks. He would later try his hand overseas, where he saw limited action in Germany. By the 1991-92 season, he was back in America, where he returned to the IHL and retired after one season with the Salt Lake Golden Eagles.

Larry Melnyk, a defenseman from Winnipeg, Manitoba, who began his career with the Boston Bruins, was a two-time Stanley Cup champion (1984 and 1985) with the Edmonton Oilers at the time of this trade.

Melnyk, who was added to help the Rangers' playoff chances, played all sixteen games for the Blueshirts during the 1986 Stanley Cup Playoffs. He then played one complete season with the Rangers during the 1986-87 season. Just fourteen games into the 1987-88 season, Esposito, as he would always do in his tenure, flipped the Patrick import to Vancouver, where Melnyk spent the final three seasons of his career.

With solid production and contributions on behalf of Melnyk for the Rangers, this trade is considered an easy win.

**DATE OF TRADE: December 26th, 1985**

**RANGERS ACQUIRE: Mike McEwen**

**DETROIT RED WINGS ACQUIRE: Steve Richmond**

As mentioned earlier, Fred Shero had previously traded Mike McEwen to Colorado, as the defenseman was one of the moving parts in the big Barry Beck trade, which took place in November 1979.

McEwen wouldn't last long in his second go-around in New York, as Patrick would soon involve the native of Hornepayne, Ontario, in another trade less than three months after this one.

In fact, McEwen played in only sixteen games for the Rangers during this 1985-86 season, where he scored two goals and picked up five assists.

Steve Richmond, another defenseman, was a native of Chicago, Illinois, and joined the Rangers as an undrafted free agent in 1982.

A graduate of the University of Michigan, the Wolverine split his Ranger days with the varsity and junior varsity clubs, the New Haven Nighthawks, and the Tulsa Oilers.

All in all, Richmond played 77 games for the Rangers.

In Detroit, just like in New York, Richmond continued to split time between the AHL and NHL, finishing the 1985-86 season playing in 29 games. A season later, he was back on the east coast, this time with the New Jersey Devils, where he played in 44 games for the Rangers' Hudson River rivals during the 1986-87 season - a career high.

Still toiling in the minors, Richmond would play in nine games for the Los Angeles Kings during the 1988-89 season - his last season in the NHL.

This trade is pretty much even, although McEwen was most certainly the better player between the two.

**DATE OF TRADE: February 6th, 1986**

**RANGERS ACQUIRE: Wilf Paiement**

**QUEBEC NORDIQUES ACQUIRE: Steve Patrick**

Steve Patrick, as mentioned earlier, was involved in the Dave Maloney/brother trade from just two years and two months prior. He played the final 27 games of his career with the Nordiques during the 1985-86 season.

Wilf Paiement, the first-round pick (second overall) of the 1974 NHL Amateur Draft was selected by the Kansas City Scouts. When the Scouts became the Colorado Rockies prior to the start of the 1976-77 season, he was one of several players to play in the franchise's first game in their new city. (He wouldn't make it a hat trick when Colorado relocated to New Jersey prior to the start of the 1982-83 season.)

At the time of this trade, the native of Earlton, Ontario, was thirty years old, where the right-winger had also spent parts of three seasons with the Toronto Maple Leafs before being dealt to Quebec in March of 1982.

In his peak years, around the 1980-81 season, Paiement set career highs in goals (40), assists (57), and points (97) - all with the Leafs. Before this trade, he had seven goals and 12 assists in 44 games during the 1985-86 season.

Paiement, who finished his career with 946 games played, logged only eight games with the Rangers, where he scored one goal and added six assists. However, like others at this time, he was added for the 1986 Stanley Cup Playoff run, where he, too, played all sixteen games, picking up five goals and five assists during the postseason.

Phil Esposito waived Paiement after the 1986 playoffs. Paiement would then have a bounce-back season with the Sabres. He played the final 23 games of his thirteen-year career with the Pittsburgh Penguins and retired after the 1987-88 season.

This trade was a win for Craig Patrick, as he added veteran help for the playoffs, while Steve Patrick finished out his career just a few weeks later.

**DATE OF TRADE: March 11th, 1986**

**RANGERS ACQUIRE: Bob Crawford**

**HARTFORD WHALERS ACQUIRE: Mike McEwen**

For the last time as general manager, Craig Patrick involved Mike McEwen in another trade, this time sending the defenseman to Hartford.

McEwen, after ten games played at the end of the 1985-86 season, then played 48 more games for the Whalers in the season that followed. After nine games played during the 1987-88 season, he finished his days in the NHL as a veteran of 716 NHL contests.

Right-winger Bob Crawford, originally selected by the St. Louis Blues in the fourth round (65th overall) during the 1979 NHL Entry Draft, he was then waived by the Blues in October 1983. The Whalers claimed him, and in turn, the native of Belleville, Ontario, had the best seasons of his career in Hartford.

The 1983-84 season, Crawford's best, saw him score 36 goals and 25 assists, good for 61 points overall - all career highs.

Now with the Rangers, he played eleven regular season games and seven more contests in the 1986 Stanley Cup Playoffs.

After only three games played during the 1986-87 season, he would soon be involved in one of the worst trades in New York Rangers history, and perhaps even the second-worst trade of all time, depending on who you talk to and how you think. We'll get to that soon enough.

Patrick made a hockey trade here as he looked to help his forwards out at the expense of an aging defenseman. However, this one-for-one deal didn't work out, so it's a minimal loss at worst.

**DATE OF TRADE: March 11th, 1986**

**RANGERS ACQUIRE: Future Considerations (Sixth-Round Pick of the 1987 NHL Entry Draft)**

**CALGARY FLAMES ACQUIRE: Nick Fotiu**

In Craig Patrick's final trade as general manager, he finished his tenure as it began - with a trade of fan-favorite Nick Fotiu.

At the start of Patrick's run as the man who called the shots, he brought Fotiu back to New York. However, at this point, Fotiu had been battling injuries, as he tore a ligament in his left knee and hadn't played since November 8th, 1985.

Of course, because it's the Rangers way, once in Calgary, Fotiu recovered and helped the Calgary Flames reach the Stanley Cup Final in 1986, where he played eleven postseason games.

Fotiu would remain in Calgary in the season that followed. After 23 games with the Flyers in the 1987-88 season, he would play in one more NHL game, this time for the Oilers during the 1988-89 season. All in all, he played 646 NHL games and 110 WHA games.

For a cherry on top, the Rangers never received Calgary's sixth-round pick of the 1987 NHL Entry Draft, as this trade was more of Patrick unloading a player that he thought was at the end. (Fotiu had to pass a physical, which he later did.)

This trade was a loss, especially since Fotiu was able to play in the 1986 Stanley Cup Playoffs. While he was never a true scorer, who knows if he would've been able to help the Rangers topple Montreal in their five-game semifinal loss to the Habs? (Okay, probably not.)

Up next - a whirlwind known as "The Trader Phil" era - which we'll cover in Volume II. Also covered in Volume II? "The Big Deal Neil" era - and the Rangers 1994 Stanley Cup victory.

And a quick author's note here - the name of Phil Esposito, between my first book and this book, has given me carpal tunnel syndrome!

Make sure to check out the other volumes of this title by visiting BlueCollarBlueShirts.com or Amazon.com! We still have a ways to go! Plus, don't you want to read my "acknowledgments" section during the final volume of this deep look at Rangers' history?

Your favorite author with three of my favorite people (and sometimes proofreaders), my nieces Chelsea, Erin, and Cayleigh! Now that they are starting to read, whenever I publish a book, they immediately flip to the end to see a picture of themselves. This is a tradition I plan on continuing! Hi guys! Don't have a poopster party without me!

# SHAMELESS PLUGS SEGMENT!

You can find my other books (and the three other volumes of this title) on Amazon.com:

— "The New York Rangers Rink of Honor and the Rafters of Madison Square Garden"

— "One Game at a Time - a Season to Remember" - Volume 1 - "Dawn of a New Day"

— "One Game at a Time - a Season to Remember" - Volume 2 - "The Rise of Czar Igor"

— "One Game at a Time - a Season to Remember" - Volume 3 - "The Tree of Trouba"

— "One Game at a Time - a Season to Remember" - Volume 4 - "The Playoffs"

— "Tricks of the Trade – A Century-Long Journey Through Every Trade Made In New York Rangers' History" Volumes I, II, III, and IV.

Make sure to check out all four volumes of "Tricks of the Trade – A Century-Long Journey Through Every Trade Made In New York Rangers' History." Now on sale at BlueCollarBlueShirts.com and Amazon.com.

## Volume 1

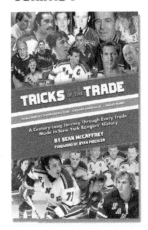

## Volume 2

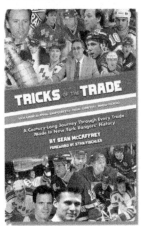

## Volume 3

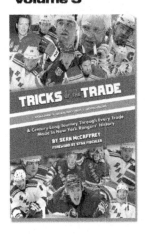

## Volume 4

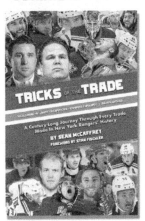

Made in the USA
Coppell, TX
29 October 2022

85409136R00225